LAW, LEGISLATION AND LIBERTY

Volume 2

THE MIRAGE OF SOCIAL JUSTICE

By the same author

The Constitution of Liberty
Prices and Production
Profits, Interest and Investment
The Road to Serfdom
Studies in Philosophy, Politics and Economics

Law, Legislation and Liberty
Volume 1   Rules and Order
Volume 2   The Mirage of Social Justice
Volume 3   The Political Order of a Free Society (*forthcoming*)

LAW, LEGISLATION AND LIBERTY

*A new statement of the liberal princip es
of justice and political economy*

Volume 2

THE MIRAGE OF SOCIAL JUSTICE

Friedrich A. Hayek

The University of Chicago Press
Chicago and London

The University of Chicago Press, Chicago 60637
The University of Chicago Press, Ltd., London

© 1976 by F. A. Hayek
All rights reserved. Published 1976
Phoenix Edition 1978
Printed in the United States of America

82 81 80 79 78   98765432

ISBN: 0-226-32083-9
LCN: 73-82488

In a free society the state does not administer the affairs of men. It administers justice among men who conduct their own affairs.

(Walter Lippmann, *An Inquiry into the Principles of a Good Society* (Boston, 1937), p. 267)

CONTENTS

CONTENTS

PREFACE

Several circumstances have contributed to delay the publication
of the second volume of this work beyond the short time I thought
I would need to get a completed draft ready for the printers. The
chief one was my dissatisfaction with the original version of the
central chapter dealing with the subject which gives this volume
its subtitle. I had devoted to this subject an enormous chapter in
which I had tried to show for a large number of instances that
what was claimed as demanded by 'social justice' could not be
justice because the underlying consideration (one could hardly call
it a principle) was not capable of general application. The point
I was then mainly anxious to demonstrate was that people would
never be able to agree on what 'social justice' required, and that
any attempt to determine remunerations according to what it was
thought was demanded by justice would make the market unworkable. I have now become convinced, however, that the people
who habitually employ the phrase simply do not know themselves
what they mean by it and just use it as an assertion that a claim is
justified without giving a reason for it.

In my earlier efforts to criticize the concept I had all the time
the feeling that I was hitting into a void and I finally attempted,
what in such cases one ought to do in the first instance, to construct as good a case in support of the ideal of 'social justice' as was
in my power. It was only then that I perceived that the Emperor
had no clothes on, that is, that the term 'social justice' was entirely
empty and meaningless. As the boy in Hans Christian Andersen's
story, I 'could not see anything, because there was nothing to be
seen.' The more I tried to give it a definite meaning the more it
fell apart—the intuitive feeling of indignation which we undeniably
often experience in particular instances proved incapable of being
justified by a general rule such as the conception of justice demands. But to demonstrate that a universally used expression
which to many people embodies a quasi-religious belief has no

content whatever and serves merely to insinuate that we ought to consent to a demand of some particular group, is much more difficult than to show that a conception is wrong.

In these circumstances I could not content myself to show that particular attempts to achieve 'social justice' would not work, but had to explain that the phrase meant nothing at all, and that to employ it was either thoughtless or fraudulent. It is not pleasant to have to argue against a superstition which is held most strongly by men and women who are often regarded as the best in our society, and against a belief that has become almost the new religion of our time (and in which many of the ministers of old religion have found their refuge), and which has become the recognized mark of the good man. But the present universality of that belief proves no more the reality of its object than did the universal belief in witches or the philosopher's stone. Nor does the long history of the conception of distributive justice understood as an attribute of individual conduct (and now often treated as synonymous with 'social justice') prove that it has any relevance to the positions arising from the market process. I believe indeed that the greatest service I can still render to my fellow men would be if it were in my power to make them ashamed of ever again using that hollow incantation. I felt it my duty at least to try and free them of that incubus which today makes fine sentiments the instruments for the destruction of all values of a free civilization—and to try this at the risk of gravely offending many the strength of whose moral feelings I respect.

The present version of the central chapter of this volume has in consequence of this history in some respects a slightly different character from the rest of the volume which in all essentials was completed six or seven years earlier. There was, on the one hand, nothing I could positively demonstrate but my task was to put the burden of proof squarely on those who employ the term. On the other hand, in re-writing that chapter I no longer had that easy access to adequate library facilities which I had when I prepared the first draft of this volume. I have in consequence not been able in that chapter systematically to take account of the more recent literature on the topics I discussed as I had endeavoured to do in the rest of this volume. In one instance the feeling that I ought to justify my position *vis-à-vis* a major recent work has also contributed to delay the completion of this volume. But after careful consideration I have come to the conclusion that what I might have to say about John Rawls' *A Theory of Justice* (1972) would not assist in the pursuit of my immediate object because the differences between us seemed more verbal than substantial. Though the first impression of readers may be different, Rawls' statement which I quote later in this volume (p. 100) seems to me to show that we agree on what is to me the essential point. Indeed, as I indicate in a note to that passage, it appears to me that Rawls has been widely misunderstood on this central issue.

Although an almost complete draft of volume 3 of this work is in existence, I hardly dare again to express the hope that it will appear fairly soon. I rather hope that when I turn to that old manuscript I shall find that my ideas have substantially advanced in the interval. But I shall do my best to bring the volume concluding this series out as soon as the advance of old age permits.

CORRIGENDA TO VOLUME I

p. 6, line 8 from foot: for 'analyses' read 'analysis'

p. 13, line 15 from top: for 'whom' read 'which'

p. 24, line 18: for 'phrases' read 'phases'

p. 35, line 13 of quotation: for 'the society' read 'human society'

p. 53, line 2 from foot: for 'general, use' read 'general use,'

p. 60, line 3 from foot: for 'seventeen' read 'seventeenth'

p. 77, line 11 from foot: for 'justiry' read 'justify'

p. 81: delete line 20 except last word

p. 96, line 2: delete 'not'

p. 102, line 5: for 'expectation' read 'expectations'

p. 106, last line: for 'concrete' read 'correct'

p. 127, line 3 from foot: for *'theses'* read *'theseis'*

p. 130, line 5 from foot: for 'than of' read 'than that of'

p. 133, line 14 from top: for 'action' read 'actions'

p. 144, line 5, for 'political' read 'politician'

SEVEN

GENERAL WELFARE AND PARTICULAR PURPOSES

It is evident, that if men were to regulate their conduct . . . , by the view of a peculiar *interest*, either public or private, they would involve themselves in endless confusion, and would render all government, in a great measure, ineffectual. The private interest of every one is different; and though the public interest in itself be always one and the same, yet it becomes the source of great dissentions, by reason of the different opinions of particular persons concerning it. . . . Were we to follow the same advantage, in assigning particular possessions to particular persons, we should disappoint our end, and perpetuate the confusion, which that rule is intended to prevent. We must, therefore, proceed by general rules, and regulate ourselves by general interests, in modifying the law of nature concerning the stability of possessions.

David Hume*

In a free society the general good consists principally in the facilitation of the pursuit of unknown individual purposes

It is one of the axioms of the tradition of freedom that coercion of individuals is permissible only where it is necessary in the service of the general welfare or the public good. Yet though it is clear that the stress on the general or common or public character[1] of the legitimate objects of governmental power is directed against its use in the service of particular interests, the vagueness of the different terms which have been employed has made it possible to declare almost any interest a general interest and to make large numbers serve purposes in which they are not in the least interested. The common welfare or the public good has to the present time remained a concept most recalcitrant to any precise definition and therefore capable of being given almost any content suggested by the interests of the ruling group.[2]

The chief reason for this has probably been that it seemed natural to assume that the public interest must in some sense be a sum of all the private interests,[3] and that the problem of aggregating all those private interests seemed insoluble. The fact, however, is that in a Great Society in which the individuals are to be free to use their own knowledge for their own purposes, the general welfare at which a government ought to aim cannot consist of the sum of particular satisfactions of the several individuals for the simple reason that neither those nor all the circumstances determining them can be known to government or anybody else. Even in the modern welfare societies the great majority and the most important of the daily needs of the great masses are met as a result of processes whose particulars government does not and cannot know. The most important of the public goods for which government is required is thus not the direct satisfaction of any particular needs, but the securing of conditions in which the individuals and smaller groups will have favourable opportunities of mutually providing for their respective needs.

That the prime public concern must be directed not towards particular known needs but towards the conditions for the preservation of a spontaneous order which enables the individuals to provide for their needs in manners not known to authority was well understood through most of history. For those ancient authors whose ideas chiefly provide the foundations of the modern ideal of freedom, the Stoics and Cicero, public utility and justice were the same. And on the frequent occasions when *utilitas publica* was invoked during the Middle Ages, what was generally meant was simply the preservation of peace and justice. Even to seventeenth century writers like James Harrington the 'public interest . . . was no other than the common right and justice excluding all partiality or private interest' and therefore identical with 'the empire of laws and not of men'.[4]

Our concern at this stage is solely whether those rules of individual conduct which serve the general welfare can aim at some aggregate of known particular results or merely at creating conditions likely to improve the chances of all in the pursuit of their aims. Apart from the fact that the particular aims pursued by the different individuals must be mostly unknown to those who lay down or enforce the rules, it is also not part of the general interest that every private desire be met. The order of the Great Society does rest and must rest on constant undesigned frustrations of some efforts—efforts which ought not to have been made but in free men can be discouraged only by failure. The interest of some individuals will always be that some changes in the structure of society made necessary by changes in circumstances to which in the general interest that structure ought to adapt itself, should not be allowed to take place. In the process of exploration in which each individual examines the facts known to him for their suitability for his own uses, the necessity of abandoning false leads is as important as the adoption of more successful means when they become generally known. Nor can the choice of the appropriate set of rules be guided by balancing for each of the alternative set of rules considered the particular predictable favourable effects against the particular predictable unfavourable effects, and then selecting the set of rules for which the positive net result is greatest; for most of the effects on particular persons of adopting one set of rules rather than another are not predictable. It will not be the interests of particular people but kinds of interests which we shall alone be able to balance against each other; and the classification for this purpose of interests into different kinds possessing different degrees of importance will not be based on the importance of these interests to those directly concerned, but will be made according to the importance to the successful pursuit of certain kinds of interests for the preservation of the overall order.

Moreover, while agreement is not possible on most of the particular ends which will not be known except to those who pursue them (and would be even less possible if the ultimate effects of the decision on particular interests were known), agreement on means can to a great extent be achieved precisely because it is not known which particular ends they will serve. Among the members of a Great Society who mostly do not know each other, there will exist no agreement on the relative importance of their respective ends. There would exist not harmony but open conflict of interests if agreement were necessary as to which particular interests should be given preference over others. What makes agreement and peace in such a society possible is that the individuals are not required to agree on ends but only on means which are capable of serving a great variety of purposes and which each hopes will assist him in the pursuit of his own purposes. Indeed, the possibility of extending an order of peace, beyond the small group which could agree on particular ends, to the members of the Great Society who could not agree on them, is due to the discovery of a method of collaboration which requires agreement only on means and not on ends.

It was the discovery that an order definable only by certain abstract characteristic would assist in the pursuit of a great multiplicity of different ends which persuaded people pursuing wholly different ends to agree on certain multi-purpose instruments which were likely to assist everybody. Such agreement became possible not only in spite of but also because of the fact that the particular results it would produce could not be foreseen. It is only because we cannot predict the actual result of the adaptation of a particular rule, that we can assume it to increase everyone's chances equally. That it is thus ignorance of the future outcome which makes possible agreement on rules which serve as common means for a variety of purposes is recognized by the practice in many instances of deliberately making the outcome unpredictable in order to make agreement on the procedure possible: whenever we agree on drawing lots we deliberately substitute equal chances for the different parties for the certainty as to which of them will benefit from the outcome.[5] Mothers who could never agree whose desperately ill child the doctor should attend first, will readily agree before the event that it would be in the interest of all if he attend the children in some regular order which increased his efficiency. When in agreeing on such a rule, we say that 'it is better for all of us if . . .' we mean not that we are certain that it will in the end benefit all of us, but that, on the basis of our present knowledge, it gives us all a better chance, though some will certainly in the end be worse off than they would have been if a different rule had been adopted.

The rules of conduct which prevail in a Great Society are thus not designed to produce particular foreseen benefits for particular people, but are multi-purpose instruments developed as adaptations to certain *kinds* of environment because they help to deal with certain *kinds* of situations. And this adaptation to a kind of environment takes place through a process very different from that in which we might decide on a procedure designed to achieve particular foreseen results. It is based not on anticipation of particular needs, but on the past experience that certain kinds of situations are likely to occur with various degrees of probability. And the result of such past experience gained through trial and error is preserved not as a recollection of particular events, or as explicit knowledge of the kind of situation likely to occur, but as a sense of the importance of observing certain rules. The reason why one rule rather than another was adopted and passed on will be that the group that had adopted it did in fact prove the more efficient, not that its members foresaw the effects the adoption of the rule would have. What would be preserved would be only the effects of past experiences on the selection of rules, not the experiences themselves.

Just as a man, setting out on a walking tour, will take his pocket knife with him, not for a particular foreseen use but in order to be equipped for various possible contingencies, or to be able to cope with kinds of situations likely to occur, so the rules of conduct developed by a group are not means for known particular purposes but adaptations to kinds of situations which past experience has shown to recur in the kind of world we live in. Like the knowledge that induces one to take his pocket knife with him the knowledge embodied in the rules is knowledge of certain general features of the environment, not knowledge of particular facts. In other words, appropriate rules of conduct are not derived from explicit knowledge of the concrete events we will encounter; rather, they are an adaptation to our environment, an adaptation which consists of rules we have developed and for the observance of which we will usually not be able to give adequate reasons. In so far as such rules have prevailed because the group that had adopted them was more successful, nobody need ever have known why that group was successful and why in consequence its rules became generally adopted. In fact, the reason why these were adopted in the first instance, and the reason why they have proved to make this group strong, may be quite different. And although we can endeavour to find out what function a particular rule performs within a given system of rules, and to judge how well it has performed that function, and may as a result try to improve it, we can do so always only against the background of the whole system of other rules which together determine the order of action in that society. But we can never rationally reconstruct in the same manner the whole system of rules, because we lack the knowledge of all the experiences that entered into its formation. The whole system of rules can therefore never be reduced to a purposive construction for known purposes, but must remain to us the inherited system of values guiding that society.

In this sense the general welfare which the rules of individual conduct serve consists of what we have already seen to be the purpose of the rules of law, namely that abstract order of the whole which does not aim at the achievement of known particular results but is preserved as a means for assisting in the pursuit of a great variety of individual purposes.

The general interest and collective goods

Though the maintenance of a spontaneous order of society is the prime condition of the general welfare of its members, and the significance of these rules of just conduct with which we are chiefly concerned, we must, before we further examine these relations between rules of individual conduct and welfare, briefly consider another element of the general welfare which must be distinguished from the one in which we shall be mainly interested. There are many kinds of services which men desire but which, because if they are provided they cannot be confined to those prepared to pay for them, can be supplied only if the means are raised by compulsion. Once an apparatus for coercion exists, and particularly if this apparatus is given the monopoly of coercion, it is obvious that it will also be entrusted with supplying the means for the provision of such 'collective goods', as the economists call those services which can be rendered only to all the members of various groups.

But though the existence of an apparatus capable of providing for such collective needs is clearly in the general interest, this does not mean that it is in the interest of society as a whole that all collective interests should be satisfied. A collective interest will become a general interest only in so far as all find that the satisfaction of collective interests of particular groups on the basis of some principle of reciprocity will mean for them a gain in excess of the burden they will have to bear. Though the desire for a particular collective good will be a common desire of those who benefit from it, it will rarely be general for the whole of the society which determines the law, and it becomes a general interest only in so far as the mutual and reciprocal advantages of the individuals balance. But as soon as government is expected to satisfy such particular collective, though not truly general, interests, the danger arises that this method will be used in the service of particular interests. It is often erroneously suggested that all collective interests are general interests of the society; but in many instances the satisfaction of collective interests of certain groups may be decidedly contrary to the general interests of society.

The whole history of the development of popular institutions is a history of continuous struggle to prevent particular groups from abusing the governmental apparatus for the benefit of the collective interest of these groups. This struggle has certainly not ended with the present tendency to define as the general interest anything that a majority formed by a coalition of organized interests decides upon.

That this service-part of governmental activities which aims at the needs of particular groups has in modern times achieved such prominence is a result of the fact that it is with such particular aimed services that politicians and civil servants are mainly concerned, and that it is through providing them that the former can earn the support of their constituents. It is a sad fact that a service aimed at the truly general welfare will gain little credit because nobody feels that he specially benefits by it, and few even know how it will affect them. For the elected representative a specific gift in his hands is much more interesting and a more effective key to power than any benefits he can procure indiscriminately for all.

The provision of collective goods for particular groups is, however, frequently not in the general interest of society. A restriction of output, or some other limitation, will often be a collective good to all members of a particular trade, but it will certainly not be in the general interest that this collective good be provided.

While the comprehensive spontaneous order which the law serves is a precondition for the success of most private activity, the services which the government can render beyond the enforcement of rules of just conduct are not only supplementary or subsidiary[6] to the basic needs which the spontaneous order provides for. They are services which will grow in volume as wealth and the density of population increase, but they are services which must be fitted into that more comprehensive order of private efforts which government neither does nor can determine, and which ought to be rendered under the restrictions of the same rules of law to which the private efforts are subject.

Government, in administering a pool of material resources entrusted to it for the purpose of providing collective goods, is of course itself under the obligation to act justly in doing so, and cannot limit itself to ensuring that the individuals do not act unjustly. In the case of services aimed at particular groups, the justification for financing them through taxation is that only thus can we make those who benefit pay for what they receive; similarly justice clearly requires that what each group receives out of the common pool should be roughly proportional to what it is made to contribute. A majority is here evidently under an obligation to be just; and if we entrust decisions of this kind to democratic or majority government, we do so because we hope that such government is more likely to serve the public interest in this sense. But it would obviously be a perversion of that ideal if we were to define the general interest as whatever the majority desires.

So far as it is possible within the framework of this book, where for reasons of space most of the problems of public finance must be left out, we shall later have to consider the relations between what are usually described as the private and the public sector of the economy (in volume 3). Here we shall consider further only those aspects of general welfare which the rules of just individual conduct serve. We return thus to the question of the aim, not of the rules of organization of government (the public law), but of those rules of individual conduct which are required for the formation of spontaneous order.

Rules and ignorance

To proceed with this task we must recall once more the fundamental fact stressed at the beginning of this study: the impossibility for anyone of knowing all the particular facts on which the overall order of the activities in a Great Society is based. It is one of the curiosities of intellectual history that, in the discussions of rules of conduct, this crucial fact has been so little considered although it alone makes the significance of these rules intelligible. Rules are a device for coping with our constitutional ignorance. There would be no need for rules among omniscient people who were in agreement on the relative importance of all the different ends. Any examination of the moral or legal order which leaves this fact out of account misses the central problem.

The function of rules of conduct as a means for overcoming the obstacle presented by our ignorance of the particular facts which must determine the overall order is best shown by examining the relation between two expressions which we have regularly employed together to describe the conditions of freedom. We have described these conditions as a state in which the individuals are allowed to use their own knowledge for their own purposes.[7] The utilization of factual knowledge widely dispersed among millions of individuals is clearly possible only if these individuals can decide on their actions on the basis of whatever knowledge they possess. What still needs to be shown is that they can do so only if they are also allowed to decide for which purposes they will use their knowledge.

For in an uncertain world the individuals must mostly aim not at some ultimate ends but at procuring means which they think will help them to satisfy those ultimate ends; and their selection of the immediate ends which are merely means for their ultimate ends, but which are all that they can definitely decide upon at a particular moment, will be determined by the opportunities known to them. The immediate purpose of a man's efforts will most often be to procure means to be used for unknown future needs—in an advanced society most frequently that generalized means, money, which will serve for the procurement of most of his particular ends. What he will need in order to choose successfully from among the opportunities known to him are signals in the form of known prices he can get for the alternative services or goods he can produce. Given this information, he will be able to use his knowledge of the circumstances of his environment to select his immediate aim, or the role from which he can hope for the best results. It will be through this choice of immediate aims, for him merely a generalized means for achieving his ultimate ends, that the individual will use his particular knowledge of facts in the service of the needs of his fellows; and it is thus due to the freedom of choosing the ends of one's activities that the utilization of the knowledge dispersed through society is achieved.

Such utilization of dispersed knowledge is thus also made possible by the fact that the opportunities for the different individuals are different. It is because the circumstances in which the different individuals find themselves at a given moment are different, and because many of these particular circumstances are known only to them, that there arises the opportunity for the utilization of so much diverse knowledge—a function which the spontaneous order of the market performs. The idea that government can determine the opportunities for all, and especially that it can ensure that they are the same for all, is therefore in conflict with the whole *rationale* of a free society.

That at any given moment the position of each individual in society is the result of a past process of tentative exploration, in the course of which he or his ancestors have with varying fortunes pushed into every nook and corner of their (physical and social) environment, and that in consequence opportunities which any change in conditions creates are likely to be acted upon by someone, is the basis of that utilization of widely dispersed factual knowledge on which the affluence and adaptability of a Great Society rests. But it is at the same time the cause of undesigned and unavoidable inequalities of opportunity which the decisions of one generation create for their descendants. That parents in their choice of a place to live or of their occupation usually consider the effects their decisions will have on the prospects of their children is an important factor in the adaptation of the use of human resources to foreseeable future developments. But so long as the individual is free to make such decisions, these considerations will be taken into account only if the risk is borne not only by those who decide but also by their descendants. If they were assured that wherever they moved or whatever occupations they chose, government would have to guarantee that the chances for their children would be the same, and that these children would be sure of the same facilities whatever their parents decided, an important factor would be left out of account in those decisions which in the general interest ought to guide them.

That the opportunities of the different members of a large and widely distributed population, resulting from circumstances which from the point of view of the present must appear as accidental, will of necessity be different, is thus inevitably connected with the effectiveness of that discovery procedure, which the market order constitutes. We need merely to consider the effects that would be produced if government succeeded in making equal the substantive chances of all in order to see that it would thereby deprive the whole system of its rationale. To succeed therein, government would have to do more than merely ensure that the conditions affecting the positions of the individuals were the same for all which necessarily depend on its actions. It would have to control effectively all the external conditions influencing the success of an individual's efforts. And, conversely, freedom of choice would lose all importance if somebody had power to determine, and therefore would know, the opportunities of the different individuals. In order to make the chances of different individuals substantively equal, it would be necessary to compensate for those differences in individual circumstances which government cannot directly control. As in some games which are played for the pleasure of the game and not for the result, government would have to handicap the different individuals so as to compensate for individual advantages or disadvantages. But the result would be to make it not worthwhile for the individual to act in accordance with what is the rationale of the whole system, that is, to take advantage of those peculiar opportunities which chance has thrown in his way but not in that of others.

Once we see that, in the absence of a unified body of knowledge of all the particulars to be taken into account, the overall order depends on the use of knowledge possessed by the individuals and used for their purposes, it becomes clear that the role of government in that process cannot be to determine particular results for particular individuals or groups, but only to provide certain generic conditions whose effects on the several individuals will be unpredictable. It can enhance the chances that the efforts of unknown individuals towards equally unknown aims will be successful by enforcing the observance of such abstract rules of conduct as in the light of past experience appear to be most conducive to the formation of a spontaneous order.

The significance of abstract rules as guides in a world in which most of the particulars are unknown

We are in general little aware of the degree to which we are guided in most of our plans for action by the knowledge not of concrete particular facts but by knowledge of what kinds of conduct are 'appropriate' in certain kinds of circumstances—not because they are means to a particular desired result, but because they are a restriction on what we may do without upsetting an order on whose existence we all count in deciding on our actions. The extent to which all that is truly social is of necessity general and abstract in a Great Society, and as such will limit but not fully determine our decisions, is easily overlooked. We are accustomed to think of the familiar and well-known as the concrete and tangible, and it requires some effort to appreciate that what we have in common with our fellows is not so much a knowledge of the same particulars as a knowledge of some general and often very abstract features of a kind of environment.

That this is so is most vividly brought home to us only on rare occasions such as when we visit a part of our native country which we had not known before. Though we have never before seen the people who live in that part, their *manner* of speech, and their *type* of physiognomy, their *style* of building and their *ways* of cultivating the land, their *modes of conduct* and their moral and aesthetic *values* will be familiar to us. We will usually not be able to define what it is that we recognize, and since we recognize it 'intuitively' we will be rarely aware that what we thus recognize are abstract features of the objects or events. In one sense it is of course obvious that what can be common to the views and opinions of men who are members of a Great Society must be general and abstract. Only in the small 'face-to-face-society', in which every member knows every other, will it be mainly particular things. But the greater the society the greater the likelihood that the knowledge which its members will have in common will be abstract features of things or actions; and in the Great or Open Society the common element in the thinking of all will be almost entirely abstract. It is not attachment to particular things but attachment to the abstract rules prevailing in that society which will guide its members in their actions and will be the distinguishing attribute of its peculiar civilization. What we call the *tradition* or the national *character* of a people, and even the characteristic man-made features of the landscape of a country, are not particulars but manifestations of rules governing both the actions and the perceptions[8] of the people. Even where such traditions come to be represented by concrete symbols—a historical site, a national flag, a symbolic shrine, or the person of a monarch or leader—these symbols 'stand for' general conceptions which can be stated only as abstract rules defining what is and what is not done in that society.

What makes men members of the same civilization and enables them to live and work together in peace is that in the pursuit of their individual ends the particular monetary impulses which impel their efforts towards concrete results are guided and restrained by the same abstract rules. If emotion or impulse tells them what they want, the conventional rules tell them how they will be able and be allowed to achieve it. The action, or the act of will, is always a particular, concrete, and individual event, while the common rules which guide it are social, general, and abstract. Though individual men will have similar desires in the sense that they aim at similar objects, the objects in themselves will in general be different particulars. What reconciles the individuals and knits them into a common and enduring pattern of a society is that to these different particular situations they respond in accordance with the same abstract rules.

Will and opinion, ends and values, commands and rules, and other terminological issues

As the range of persons extends among whom some agreement is necessary to prevent conflict, there will necessarily be less and less agreement on the particular ends to be achieved; agreement will increasingly be possible only on certain abstract aspects of the kind of society in which they wish to live. This is a consequence of the fact that the more extensive society becomes, the fewer will be the particular facts known to (or the particular interests shared by) all members of that society. People living in the great urban centres and reading metropolitan newspapers often have the illusion that the facts of the world which they currently learn are largely the same as those that become known to most of their fellow-citizens; but for the greater part of the population of the world, or even of the different sections of a big country, it is probably true that there are very few common elements in the assortment of particular concrete events which become known to them. And what is true of the particular facts known to them is equally true of the particular aims of their activities and of their desires.

But though for this reason there can exist little agreement between them on concrete and particular acts, there may still exist, if they belong to the same culture or tradition, a far-reaching similarity in their *opinions*—an agreement which concerns not particular concrete events but certain abstract features of social life which may prevail at different places and at different times. But to bring this out clearly is made difficult by the vagueness of the expressions at our disposal.

Ordinary language in this field is so imprecise with respect to some of the key terms that it seems necessary to adopt certain conventions in our use of them. Though I believe that the sense in which I shall use them is close to their central meaning, they are certainly not always used in this sense and have a somewhat blurred range of connotations some of which we must exclude. We shall consider the main terms in question in pairs, of which the first will always be used here to refer to a particular or unique event, while the second will describe general or abstract features.

The first of these pairs of terms to be so distinguished, and perhaps the most important, or at least the one which through disregard of the distinction has caused the greatest confusion in political theory, is *will* and *opinion*. [9] We shall call *will* only the aiming at a particular concrete result which, together with the known particular circumstances of the moment, will suffice to determine a particular action. In contrast, we shall call *opinion* the view about the desirability or undesirability of different forms of actions, or actions of certain kinds, which leads to the approval or disapproval of the conduct of particular persons according as they do or do not conform to that view. Such opinions, referring only to the manner of acting, would therefore not be sufficient fully to determine a particular action except in combination with concrete ends. An act of will determines what shall be done at a particular moment, while an opinion will tell us merely what rules to observe when the occasion arises. The distinction is related to that between a particular *impulse* evoking action and a mere *disposition* to act in a certain manner. Aiming at a particular result, the will ceases when the 'end' is achieved, while an opinion, constituting a lasting disposition,[10] will guide many particular acts of will. And while a will always aims at a purpose, we would rightly suspect the genuineness of an opinion if we knew that it was determined by a purpose.

We shall similarly distinguish between particular *ends*, i.e. particular expected effects which motivate particular actions, and *values*, which term we shall understand to refer to generic classes of events, defined by certain attributes and generally regarded as desirable. By 'desirable' in this connection we thus mean more than that a particular action is in fact desired by somebody on a particular occasion; it is used to describe a lasting attitude of one or more persons towards a *kind* of event. We shall accordingly say that, e.g., the law or the rules of just conduct serve not (concrete or particular) ends but (abstract and generic) values, namely the preservation of a kind of order.

There exists a close relationship between the distinction within each of these pairs of terms and the distinction which we have discussed earlier between a *command* and a *rule*. A command regularly aims at a particular result or particular foreseen results, and together with the particular circumstances known to him who issues or receives the command will determine a particular action. By contrast, a rule refers to an unknown number of future instances and to the acts of an unknown number of persons, and merely states certain attributes which any such action ought to possess.

Finally, the observance of rules, or the holding of common values, may secure, as we have seen, that a pattern or order of actions will emerge which will possess certain abstract attributes; but it will not be sufficient to determine the particular manifestation of the pattern or any one particular event or result.

It may be useful, before leaving these terminological questions, to mention here briefly a few other terms which are currently employed in connection with the problems we are considering. There is in the first instance the widely used description of a *free* society as *pluralistic*. This, of course, is intended to express that it is governed by a multiplicity of individual ends which are not ordered in a particular hierarchy binding on the members.

The multiplicity of independent ends implies also a multiplicity of independent centres of decision, and different types of society are accordingly sometimes distinguished as monocentric and polycentric.[11] This distinction coincides with the distinction we have introduced earlier between an organization (*taxis*) and a spontaneous order (*kosmos*), but seems to stress only one particular aspect of the differences between the two kinds of order.

Finally, I understand that Professor Michael Oakeshott, in his oral teaching, has long used the terms *teleocratic* (and *teleocracy*) and *nomocratic* (and *nomocracy*) to bring out the same distinction. A teleocratic order, in which the same hierarchy of ends is binding on all members, is necessarily a made order or organization, while a nomocratic society will form a spontaneous order. We shall occasionally make use of these terms when we want to stress the end-governed character of the organization or the rule-governed character of the spontaneous order.

Abstract rules operate as ultimate values because they serve unknown particular ends

Rules of just conduct assist the settlement of disputes about particulars in so far as agreement exists about the rule applicable to the case in hand, even though there may exist no agreement about the importance of the particular aims pursued by the disputing parties. When in a dispute a rule is pointed out which has invariably been observed in past instances that had some abstract features in common with the present issue, the only recourse open to the other party is to point to another rule, also recognized as valid as soon as stated and equally applicable to the present instance, which would require a modification of the conclusions derived from the first rule. Only if we can discover such another rule, or can show that our opponent would himself not accept the first rule in all instances to which it applies, can we demonstrate that a decision based only on the first rule would be wrong. Our whole conception of justice rests on the belief that different views about particulars are capable of being settled by the discovery of rules that, once they are stated, command general assent. If it were not for the fact that we often can discover that we do agree on general principles which are applicable, even though we at first disagree on the merits of the particular case, the very idea of justice would lose its meaning.

The applicable rules define the features which are relevant for the decision as to whether an act was just or unjust. All features of the particular case must be disregarded which cannot be brought under a rule that once it is stated is accepted as defining just conduct. The important point here is not that the rule has been explicitly stated before, but that when articulated it is accepted as corresponding to general usage. The first formulation of what has already guided the sense of justice and, when first stated, is recognized as expressing what men have long felt, is as much a discovery as any discovery of science—even though, like the latter, it will often be only a better approximation to what it aims at than anything that had been stated before.

It is of little significance for our present purpose whether such general rules came to govern opinion because the advantages to be gained from observing them were recognized, or because groups who happened to accept rules which made them more efficient came to prevail over others obeying less effective rules. A more important point is that the rules which have been adopted because of their beneficial effects in the majority of cases will have these beneficial effects only if they are applied to all cases to which they refer, irrespective of whether it is known, or even true, that they will have a beneficial effect in the particular case. As David Hume put it in his classical exposition of the rationale of rules of justice:[12]

> a single act of justice is frequently contrary to *public interest*; and were it to stand alone, without being followed by other acts, may, in itself, be very prejudicial to society . . . Nor is every single act of justice, considered apart, more conducive to private interest, than to public; . . . But however single acts of justice may be contrary, either to public or private interest, it is certain, that the whole plan or scheme is highly conducive, or indeed absolutely requisite, both to the support of society, and to the well-being of every individual.

The resolution of this apparent paradox is, of course, that the enforcement of those abstract rules serves the preservation of an equally abstract order whose particular manifestations are largely unpredictable, and that this order will be preserved only if it is generally expected that those rules will be enforced in all cases, irrespective of the particular consequences some may foresee. This means that, though these rules ultimately serve particular (though mostly unknown) ends, they will do so only if they are treated not as means but as ultimate values, indeed as the only values common to all and distinct from the particular ends of the individuals. This is what is meant by the principle that the ends do not justify the means, and by such adages as *fiat justitia, pereat mundus* (let justice prevail even if the world perish). Only if applied universally, without regard to particular effects, will they serve the permanent preservation of the abstract order, a timeless purpose which will continue to assist the individuals in the pursuit of their temporary and still unknown aims. Those rules which are common values serve the maintenance of an order of whose existence those who apply them are often not even aware. And however much we may often dislike the unforeseeable consequences of applying the rules in a particular case, we can usually not see even all the immediate consequences, and still less the more remote effects that will be produced if the rule were not expected to be applied in all future instances.

The rules of just conduct are thus not concerned with the protection of particular interests, and all pursuit of particular interests must be subject to them. This applies as much to the tasks of government in its capacity as administrator of common means destined for the satisfaction of particular purpose, as to the actions of private persons. And this is the reason why government, when it is concerned with the temporary and particular, should be under a law which is concerned with the permanent and general; and why those whose task it is to formulate rules of just conduct should not be concerned with the temporary and particular ends of government.

The constructivist fallacy of utilitarianism

The constructivist interpretation of rules of conduct is generally known as 'utilitarianism'. In a wider sense the term is, however, also applied to any critical examination of such rules and of institutions with respect to the function they perform in the structure of society. In this wide sense every one who does not regard all existing values as unquestionable but is prepared to ask why they should be held would have to be described as a utilitarian. Thus Aristotle, Thomas Aquinas,[13] and David Hume,[14] would have to be described as utilitarians, and the present discussion of the function of rules of conduct might also be so called. No doubt utilitarianism owes much of its appeal to sensible people to the fact that thus interpreted it includes all rational examination of the appropriateness of existing rules.

Since the late eighteenth century 'utilitarianism' has, however, been used in moral and legal theory in a narrower sense, and that is how we shall here employ the term. This special meaning is partly the result of a gradual change of meaning of the term utility itself. Originally 'utility', as the term 'usefulness' still clearly does, expressed an attribute of *means*—the attribute of being capable of potential uses. That something was useful indicated it was capable of uses in situations likely to occur, and the degree of usefulness depended on the likelihood of the occurrence of those situations in which the thing might prove helpful and the importance of the needs it was likely to satisfy.

It was only comparatively late that the term utility denoting an attribute of means came to be used to describe a supposedly common attribute of the different ends which they served. Since the means were seen in some measure to reflect the importance of the ends, utility came to mean some such common attribute of the ends as the pleasure or satisfaction which were connected with them. Though it had in earlier times been fully understood that most of our efforts must be directed to providing means for unforeseen particular purposes, the rationalist desire explicitly to derive the usefulness of means from known ultimate ends led to the attribution to these ends of a measurable common attribute for which either the term pleasure or the term utility was employed.

The distinction which it is necessary to make for our purposes is one between the usefulness of something for known particular ends and its usefulness for various kinds of needs expected to occur in a kind of environment or in kinds of likely situations. Only in the former instance would the usefulness of an object or practice be derived from the importance of particular foreseen future uses, and would constitute a reflection of the importance of particular ends. In the latter instance the property of usefulness would be judged on the basis of past experience as an instrumental property not depending on particular known ends but as a means of dealing with a variety of situations likely to occur.

The strict utilitarianism of Jeremy Bentham and his school[15] undertakes to judge the appropriateness of conduct by an explicit calculation of the balance of the pleasure and the pain that it will cause. Its inadequacy was long concealed by the utilitarians relying in the defence of their position on two different and irreconcilable contentions which have only recently been clearly distinguished,[16] neither of which by itself provides an adequate account of the determination of moral or legal rules. Of these two positions between which the utilitarians constantly shifted the first is incapable of accounting for the existence of *rules* and therefore for the phenomena which we normally describe as morals and law, while the other is bound to assume the existence of rules not accountable for by utilitarian considerations and thus must abandon the claim that the whole system of moral rules can be derived from their known utility.

Bentham's conception of a calculus of pleasure and pain by which the greatest happiness of the greatest number is to be determined presupposes that all the particular individual effects of any one action can be known by the acting person. Pursued to its logical conclusion it leads to a particularistic or 'act' utilitarianism which dispenses with rules altogether and judges each individual action according to the utility of its known effects. Bentham, it is true, safeguarded himself against such an interpretation by a constant recourse to such statements as that every action (now interpreted as any action of a certain *kind*) should have the *tendency* to produce *on the whole* a maximum balance of pleasure. But at least some of his followers clearly saw that the logic of the argument demanded that each individual action should be decided upon in the light of a full knowledge of its particular consequences. Thus we find Henry Sidgwick maintained that 'we have in each case to compare all the pleasures and pains that can be foreseen as probable results of the different alternatives of conduct, and adopt the alternative which seems likely to lead to the greatest happiness of the whole';[17] and G. E. Moore that 'it must always be the duty of every agent to do that one among all actions which he *can* do on any given occasion, whose *total consequences* will have the greatest intrinsic value.'[18]

The alternative interpretation as a generic or, as it is now usually called, 'rule' utilitarianism was expressed most clearly by William Paley when he demanded that a *kind* of action, to be morally approved, 'must be expedient on the whole, at the long run, in all its effects collateral and remote, as well as in those which are immediate and direct; as it is obvious, that, in computing consequences, it makes no difference in what way or what distance they ensue'.[19]

The extensive discussion of recent years of the respective merits of particularistic ('act-') and generic ('rule-') utilitarianism has made it clear that only the former can claim to be consistent in basing the approval or disapproval of actions exclusively on their foreseen effects of 'utility', but that at the same time, in order to do so, it must proceed on a factual assumption of omniscience which is never satisfied in real life and which, if it were ever true, would make the existence of those bodies of rules which we call morals and law not only superfluous but unaccountable and contrary to the assumption; while, on the other hand, no system of generic or rule utilitarianism could treat all rules as fully determined by utilities known to the acting person, because the effects of any rule will depend not only on its being always observed but also on the other rules observed by the acting persons and on the rules being followed by all the other members of the society. To judge the utility of any one rule would therefore always presuppose that some other rules were taken as given and generally observed and not determined by any known utility, so that among the determinants of the utility of any one rule there would always be other rules which could not be justified by their utility. Rule-utilitarianism consistently pursued could therefore never give an adequate justification of the whole system of rules and must always include determinants other than the known utility of particular rules.

The trouble with the whole utilitarian approach is that, as a theory professing to account for a phenomenon which consists of a body of rules, it completely eliminates the factor which makes rules necessary, namely our ignorance. It has indeed always amazed me how serious and intelligent men, as the utilitarians undoubtedly were, could have failed to take seriously this crucial fact of our necessary ignorance of most of the particular facts, and could have proposed a theory which presupposes a knowledge of the particular effects of our individual actions when in fact the whole existence of the phenomenon they set out to explain, namely of a system of rules of conduct, was due to the impossibility of such knowledge. It would seem that they never grasped the significance of rules as an adaptation to this inescapable ignorance of most of the particular circumstances which determine the effects of our actions, and thus disregarded the whole rationale of the phenomenon of rule-guided action.[20]

Man has developed rules of conduct not because he knows but because he does not know what all the consequences of a particular action will be. And the most characteristic feature of morals and law as we know them is therefore that they consist of rules to be obeyed irrespective of the known effects of the particular action. How we should wish men to behave who were omniscient and could foresee all the consequences of their actions is without interest to us. Indeed there would be no need for rules if men knew everything—and strict act-utilitarianism of course must lead to the rejection of all rules.

Like all general purpose tools, rules serve because they have become adapted to the solution of recurring problem situations and thereby help to make the members of the society in which they prevail more effective in the pursuit of their aims. Like a knife or a hammer they have been shaped not with a particular purpose in view but because in this form rather than in some other form they have proved serviceable in a great variety of situations. They have not been constructed to meet foreseen particular needs but have been selected in a process of evolution. The knowledge which has given them their shape is not knowledge of particular future effects but knowledge of the recurrence of certain problem situations or tasks, of intermediate results regularly to be achieved in the service of a great variety of ultimate aims; and much of this knowledge exists not as an awareness of an enumerable list of situations for which one has to be prepared, or of the importance of the kind of problems to be solved, or of the probability that they will arise, but as a propensity to act in certain types of situations in a certain manner.

Most rules of conduct are thus not derived by an intellectual process from the knowledge of the facts of the environment, but constitute the only adaptation of man to these facts which we have achieved, a 'knowledge' of them of which we are not aware and which does not appear in our conceptual thought, but which manifests itself in the rules which we obey in our actions. Neither the groups who first practised these rules, nor those who imitated them, need ever have known why their conduct was more successful than that of others, or helped the group to persist.

It must be stressed that the importance we attach to the observation of particular rules does not simply reflect the importance of particular ends which may depend on their observance; the importance attached to a rule is rather a compound result of two distinct factors which we shall rarely be able to assess separately: the importance of particular effects and the frequency of their occurrence. Just as in biological evolution it may matter less for the preservation of the species if no provision is made to avoid certain lethal but rare effects than if a frequently occurring kind of event doing only slight damage to the individual is avoided, so the rules of conduct that have emerged from the process of social evolution may often be adequate to prevent frequent causes of minor disturbances of the social order but not rare causes of its total disruption.

The only 'utility' which can be said to have determined the rules of conduct is thus not a utility known to the acting persons, or to any one person, but only a hypostatized 'utility' to society as a whole. The consistent utilitarian is therefore frequently driven to interpret the products of evolution anthropomorphically as the product of design and to postulate a personified society as the author of these rules. Though this is rarely admitted as naively as by a recent author who explicitly maintained that to the utilitarian society must appear 'as a sort of single great person',[21] such anthropomorphism is characteristic of all constructivist conceptions of which utilitarianism is but a particular form. This basic error of utilitarianism has been most concisely expressed by Hastings Rashdall in the contention that 'all moral judgements are ultimately judgements as to the value of ends.'[22] This is precisely what they are not; if agreement on particular ends were really the ground for moral judgments, moral rules as we know them would be unnecessary.[23]

The essence of all rules of conduct is that they label *kinds* of actions, not in terms of their largely unknown effects in particular instances, but in terms of their probable effect which need not be foreseeable by the individuals. It is not because of those effects of our actions which we knowingly bring about, but because of the effects our actions have on the continuous maintenance of an order of actions, that particular rules have come to be regarded as important. Like the order which they serve, but at one further remove, they assist only indirectly the satisfaction of particular needs by helping to avoid kinds of conflicts which past experience has shown to occur in the normal pursuit of a great variety of aims. They serve not to make any particular plan of action successful, but to reconcile many different plans of actions. It is the interpretation of rules of conduct as part of a plan of action of 'society' towards the achievement of some single set of ends which gives all utilitarian theories their anthropomorphic character.

Utilitarianism, to succeed in its aims, would have to attempt a sort of reductionism which traces all rules to the deliberate choice of means for known ends. As such it is about as likely to be successful as an attempt to account for the particular features of a language by tracing the effects of successive efforts at communication through a few thousand generations. Rules of conduct as well as rules of speech are the product not of direct adaptation to particular known facts, but of a cumulative process in which at any moment the chief factor is the existence of a factual order determined by already established rules. It will always be within such an order, functioning more or less adequately, that new rules will develop; and it will at every stage be only as part of such a working system that the expediency of any one rule can be judged. Rules in this sense have a function within an operating system but not a purpose—a function which cannot be derived from known particular effects on particular needs, but only from an understanding of the whole structure. But in fact nobody has yet achieved such a full understanding or succeeded in reconstructing an altogether new system of moral or legal rules from the knowledge of the needs and the effects of known means. [24]

Like most tools, rules are not part of a plan of action but rather equipment for certain unknown contingencies. Indeed, a great part of all our activities is also guided not by a knowledge of the particular ultimate needs which they serve, but by a desire to accumulate a stock of tools and of knowledge, or to manoeuvre for positions, in short to accumulate 'capital' in the widest sense of the term, which we think will come in useful in the kind of world in which we live. And this sort of activity seems indeed to become more prevalent the more intelligent we become. We adapt more and more, not to the particular circumstances, but so as to increase our adaptability to kinds of çircumstances which may occur. The horizon of our sight consists mostly of means, not of particular ultimate ends.

We may of course aim at the 'greatest happiness of the greatest number' if we do not delude ourselves that we can determine the sum of this happiness by some calculation, or that there is a known aggregate of results at any one time. What the rules, and the order they serve, can do is no more than to increase the opportunities for unknown people. If we do the best we can to increase the opportunities for any unknown person picked at random, we will achieve the most we can, but certainly not because we have any idea of the sum of utility of pleasure which we have produced.

*All valid criticism or improvement of rules of conduct must proceed
within a given system of such rules*

Since any established system of rules of conduct will be based on
experiences which we only partly know, and will serve an order of
action in a manner which we only partly understand, we cannot
hope to improve it by reconstructing anew the whole of it. If we
are to make full use of all the experience which has been transmitted
only in the form of traditional rules, all criticism and efforts at
improvement of particular rules must proceed within a framework
of given values which for the purpose in hand must be accepted as
not requiring justification. We shall call 'immanent criticism' this
sort of criticism that moves within a given system of rules and
judges particular rules in terms of their consistency or compatibility
with all other recognized rules in inducing the formation of a
certain kind of order of actions. This is the only basis for a critical
examination of moral or legal rules once we recognize the irreduci-
bility of the whole existing system of such rules to known specific
effects that it will produce.

The consistency or compatibility of the different rules which
make up a system is not primarily logical consistency. Consistency
in this connection means that the rules serve the same abstract
order of actions and prevent conflict between persons obeying these
rules in the kind of circumstances to which they have been adapted.
Whether any two or more rules are consistent or not will therefore
depend in part on the factual conditions of the environment; and
the same rules may therefore be sufficient to prevent conflict in one
kind of environment but not in another. On the other hand, rules
which are logically inconsistent in the sense that they may lead in
any given situation to requirements or prohibitions of acts of any
one person which are mutually contradictory, may yet be made
compatible if they stand in a relation of superiority or inferiority to
each other, so that the system of rules itself determines which of
the rules is to 'overrule' the other.

All real moral problems are created by conflicts of rules, and
most frequently are problems caused by uncertainty about the
relative importance of different rules. No system of rules of conduct
is complete in the sense that it gives an unambiguous answer to all
moral questions; and the most frequent cause of uncertainty is
probably that the order of rank of the different rules belonging to a
system is only vaguely determined. It is through the constant

necessity of dealing with such questions to which the established system of rules gives no definite answer that the whole system evolves and gradually becomes more determinate, or better adapted to the kind of circumstances in which the society exists.

When we say that all criticism of rules must be immanent criticism, we mean that the test by which we can judge the appropriateness of a particular rule will always be some other rule which for the purpose in hand we regard as unquestioned. The great body of rules which in this sense is tacitly accepted determines the aim which the rules being questioned must also support; and this aim, as we have seen, is not any particular event but the maintenance or restoration of an order of actions which the rules tend to bring about more or less successfully. The ultimate test is thus not consistency of the rules but compatibility of the actions of different persons which they permit or require.

It may at first seem puzzling that something that is the product of tradition should be capable of both being the object and the standard of criticism. But we do not maintain that all tradition as such is sacred and exempt from criticism, but merely that the basis of criticism of any one product of tradition must always be other products of tradition which we either cannot or do not want to question; in other words, that particular aspects of a culture can be critically examined only within the context of that culture. We can never reduce a system of rules or all values as a whole to a purposive construction, but must always stop with our criticism at something that has no better ground for existence than that it is the accepted basis of the particular tradition. Thus we can always examine a part of the whole only in terms of that whole which we cannot entirely reconstruct and the greater part of which we must accept unexamined. As it might also be expressed: we can always only tinker with parts of a given whole but never entirely redesign it.[25]

This is so mainly because the system of rules into which the rules guiding the action of any one person must be fitted does not merely comprise all the rules governing his actions but also the rules which govern the actions of the other members of the society. There is little significance in being able to show that if everybody adopted some proposed new rule a better overall result would follow, so long as it is not in one's power to bring this about. But one may well adopt a rule which within the existing system of rules leads to less disappointment of expectations than the established rules, and thus by introducing a new rule increase the likelihood that the expectations of others will not be disappointed. This apparently paradoxical result, that a change of the rules introduced by one may lead to less disappointment of expectations on the part of others, and may in consequence ultimately prevail, is closely connected with the fact that the expectations which guide us refer less to the actions which other persons will take than to the effects of these actions, and that the rules on which we count are mostly not rules prescribing particular actions but rules restraining actions —not positive but negative rules. It may well be customary in a particular society to allow the run-off of water or other substances from one's land to damage the land of one's neighbour, and such carelessness may therefore be tolerated although it will again and again upset somebody's expectations. If then anyone, out of consideration for his neighbour, adopts the new rule of preventing such damaging run-off, he will, by acting differently from the common practice, reduce the frequency of disappointments of the expectations on which people base their plans; and such a new rule adopted by one may come to be generally accepted because it fits better into the established system of rules than the practice which had so far prevailed.

The necessity of immanent criticism thus derives in a great measure from the circumstance that the effects of any person's action will depend on the various rules which govern the actions of his fellows. The 'consequences of one's actions' are not simply a physical fact independent of the rules prevailing in a given society, but depend very largely on the rules which the other members of society obey; and even where it is possible for one to discover a new rule which, if generally adopted, might be more beneficial for all, the rules which the others in fact follow must be among the data from which he will have to derive his belief in the more beneficial character of the new rule which he proposes. This may well mean that the rule one ought to follow in a given society and in particular circumstances in order to produce the best consequences, may not be the best rule in another society where the system of generally adopted rules is different. This circumstance greatly restricts the extent to which the private moral judgment of any individual can produce an improvement over the established system of rules; it also accounts for the fact that, if he moves in different kinds of societies, different rules may on different occasions be obligatory for the same individual.

The much discussed question of 'moral relativity' is thus clearly connected with the fact that all moral (and legal) rules serve an existing factual order which no individual has the power to change fundamentally; because such change would require changes in the rules which other members of the society obey, in part unconsciously or out of sheer habit, and which, if a viable society of a different type were to be created, would have to be replaced by other rules which nobody has the power to make effective. There can, therefore, be no absolute system of morals independent of the kind of social order in which a person lives, and the obligation incumbent upon us, to follow certain rules derives from the benefits we owe to the order in which we live.

It would seem to me, for instance, to be clearly morally wrong to revive an already unconscious old Eskimo who, at the beginning of their winter migration,[26] in accordance with the morals of his people and with his approval, had been left behind by his group to die—and to be right only if I regarded it as right, and in my power, to transfer him into a wholly different society in which I was able and willing to provide for his survival.

That our moral obligations derive from our benefiting from an order which rests on certain rules is simply the reverse of the fact that it is the observance of common rules which integrates the individuals into the order which we call a society, and that such a society can persist only if some sort of pressure exists to make the members conform to such rules. There are, undoubtedly, many forms of tribal or closed societies which rest on very different systems of rules. All that we are here maintaining is that we know only of one kind of such systems of rules, undoubtedly still very imperfect and capable of much improvement, which makes the kind of open or 'humanistic' society possible where each individual counts as an individual and not only as a member of a particular group, and where therefore universal rules of conduct can exist which are equally applicable to all responsible human beings. It is only if we accept such a universal order as an aim, that is, if we want to continue on the path which since the ancient Stoics and Christianity has been characteristic of Western civilization, that we can defend this moral system as superior to others—and at the same time endeavour to improve it further by continued immanent criticism.

'Generalization' and the test of universalizability

Closely connected with the test of internal consistency as a means of developing a system of rules of conduct are the questions commonly discussed under the headings of generalization or universalization. In fact, used as a test of the appropriateness of a rule, the possibility of its generalization or universalization amounts to a test of consistency or compatibility with the rest of the accepted system of rules or values. But before we show why this must be so it is necessary to consider briefly the meaning in which the conception of generalization is properly used in this connection. It is usually interpreted[27] as referring to the question of what would be the consequences if everybody did a certain thing. But most actions, except the most ordinary ones, would become obnoxious if everybody performed them. The necessity of generally forbidding or enjoining a certain *kind* of action, like rules in general, follows from our ignorance of what the consequences of a kind of action have in particular instances. To consider the simplest and most typical case: we frequently know that a certain kind of action will often be harmful, but neither we (or the legislator) nor the acting person will know whether that will be so in any particular instance. When therefore we try to define the kind of action which we wish to be avoided, we will as a rule only succeed in so defining it that it includes most of the instances in which it will have harmful effects, but also many in which it will not. The only way to prevent the harmful effects will then be to prohibit this class of action generally, irrespective of whether in fact it will have a harmful effect on a particular given occasion; and the problem will be whether we should generally prohibit this kind of action or accept the harm that will follow from it in a certain number of instances.

If we now turn to the more interesting question of what is meant when it is asked whether such a generalization is 'possible' or whether something 'can' be made a general rule, it is evident that the 'possibility' referred to is not a physical possibility or impossibility, nor the practical possibility of generally enforcing obedience to such a rule. The appropriate interpretation is suggested by the manner in which Immanuel Kant approached the problem, namely by asking whether we can 'want' or 'will' that such a rule be generally applied. Here the obstacle to generalization which is contemplated is evidently itself a moral one and this must mean a conflict with some other rule or value which we are not prepared to sacrifice. In other words, the test of 'universalizability' applied to any one rule will amount to a test of compatibility with the whole system of accepted rules—a test which, as we have seen, may either lead to a clear 'yes' or 'no' answer or may show that, if the system of rules is to give definite guidance, some of the rules will have to be modified, or so arranged into a hierarchy of greater or lesser importance (or superiority and inferiority), that in case of conflict we know which is to prevail and which is to give.

To perform their functions rules must be applied through the long run

The facts that rules are a device for coping with our ignorance of the effects of particular actions, and that the importance we attach to these rules is based both on the magnitude of the possible harm that they serve to prevent and the degree of probability that will be inflicted if they are disregarded, show that such rules will perform their function only if they are adhered to for long periods. This follows from the circumstance that the rules of conduct contribute to the formation of an order by being obeyed by the individuals and by being used by them for their purposes, mostly unknown to those who may have laid down the rules or are entitled to alter them. Where, as is the case with law, some of the rules of conduct are deliberately laid down by authority, they will thus perform their function only if they become the basis of the planning of the individuals. The maintenance of a spontaneous order through the enforcement of rules of conduct must therefore always aim at results in the long run, in contrast to the rules of organization serving known particular purposes which must essentially aim at predictable short run results. Hence the conspicuous difference in outlook between the administrator, necessarily concerned with particular known effects, and the judge or law-giver, who ought to be concerned with the maintenance of an abstract order in disregard of the particular foreseen results. A concentration on particular results necessarily leads to a short run view, since only in the short run will the particular results be foreseeable, and raises in consequence conflicts between particular interests that can be decided only by an authoritative decision in favour of one or the other. Predominant concern with the visible short run effects thus progressively leads to a dirigist organization of the whole society. Indeed, what will certainly be dead in the long run if we concentrate on immediate results is freedom. A nomocratic society must confine coercion wholly to the enforcement of rules serving a long run order.

The idea that a structure whose surveyable parts are not

comprehended as meaningful, or show no recognizable design, and where we do *not* know why particular things happen, should be a more effective foundation for the successful pursuit of our ends than a deliberately constructed organization, and that it may even be to our advantage that changes occur for which nobody knows the reason (because they register facts which as a whole are not known to anybody), is so contrary to the ideas of constructivist rationalism which have governed European thought since the seventeenth century, that it will become generally accepted only with the spreading of an evolutionary or critical rationalism that is aware not only of the powers but also of the limits of reason, and recognizes that this reason itself is a product of social evolution. The demand for that kind of pellucid order which would satisfy the standards of the constructivists, on the other hand, must lead to a destruction of an order much more comprehensive than any we can deliberately construct. Freedom means that in some measure we entrust our fate to forces which we do not control; and this seems intolerable to those constructivists who believe that man can master his fate—as if civilization and reason itself were of his making.

EIGHT

THE QUEST FOR JUSTICE

Every single legal rule may be thought of as one of the bulwarks
or boundaries erected by society in order that its members shall
not collide with each other in their actions.

P. Vinogradoff*

Justice is an attribute of human conduct

We have chosen the term 'rules of just conduct' to describe those
end-independent rules which serve the formation of a spontaneous
order, in contrast to the end-dependent rules of organization. The
former are the *nomos* which is at the basis of a 'private law society'[1]
and makes an Open Society possible; the latter, so far as they are
law, are the public law which determines the organization of
government. We did not contend, however, that all rules of just
conduct which may in fact be obeyed should be regarded as law,
nor that every single rule which forms part of a system of rules of
just conduct is by itself a rule defining just conduct. We have still
to examine the vexing question of the relation between justice and
law. This question has been confused as much by the belief that
all that can be decided by legislative decision must be a question
of justice, as by the belief that it is the will of the legislature which
determines what is just. We shall first consider some often disregarded limitations of the applicability of the term justice.

Strictly speaking, only human conduct can be called just or unjust. If we apply the terms to a state of affairs, they have meaning
only in so far as we hold someone responsible for bringing it about
or allowing it to come about. A bare fact, or a state of affairs which
nobody can change, may be good or bad, but not just or unjust.[2]
To apply the term 'just' to circumstances other than human
actions or the rules governing them is a category mistake. Only if
we mean to blame a personal creator does it make sense to describe
it as unjust that somebody has been born with a physical defect, or

been stricken with a disease, or has suffered the loss of a loved one. Nature can be neither just nor unjust. Though our inveterate habit of interpreting the physical world animistically or anthropo-morphically often leads us to such a misuse of words, and makes us seek a responsible agent for all that concerns us, unless we believe that somebody could and should have arranged things differently, it is meaningless to describe a factual situation as just or unjust.

But if nothing that is not subject to human control can be just (or moral), the desire to make something capable of being just is not necessarily a valid argument for our making it subject to human control; because to do so may itself be unjust or immoral, at least when the actions of another human being are concerned.

In certain circumstances it may be a legal or moral duty to bring about a certain state of affairs which then can often be described as just. That in such instances the term 'just' refers in fact to the actions and not to the results becomes clear when we consider that it can apply only to such consequences of a person's actions as it has been in his power to determine. It presupposes not only that those whose duty it is thought to be to bring about that state can actually do so, but that the means by which they can do so are also just or moral.

The rules by which men try to define kinds of actions as just or unjust may be correct or incorrect; and it is established usage to describe as unjust a rule which describes as just a kind of action which is unjust. But though this is a usage that is so general that it must be accepted as legitimate, it is not without danger. What we really mean when we say, e.g., that a rule which we all thought to be just proves to be unjust when applied to a particular case, is that it is a wrong rule which does not adequately define what we regard as just, or that the verbal formulation of the rule does not ade-quately express the rule which guides our judgment.

Evidently, not only the actions of individuals but also the con-certed actions of many individuals, or the actions of organizations, may be just or unjust. Government is such an organization, but society is not. And, though the order of society will be affected by actions of government, so long as it remains a spontaneous order, the particular results of the social process cannot be just or unjust. This means that the justice or injustice of the demands which government makes on the individual must be decided in the light of rules of just conduct and not by the particular results which will follow from their application to an individual case. Government certainly ought to be just in all it does; and the pressure of public opinion is likely to drive it to extend any discernible principles on which it acts to their possible limits, whether it intends to do so or not. But how far its duty in justice extends must depend on its power to affect the position of the different individuals in accordance with uniform rules.

Only those aspects of the order of human actions which can be determined by rules of just conduct do therefore raise problems of justice. To speak of justice always implies that some person or persons ought, or ought not, to have performed some action; and this 'ought' in turn presupposes the recognition of rules which define a set of circumstances wherein a certain kind of conduct is prohibited or required. We know by now that the 'existence' of a recognized rule does not in this context necessarily mean that the rule has been stated in words. It requires only that a rule can be found which distinguishes between different kinds of conduct on lines which people in fact recognize as just or unjust.

Rules of just conduct refer to such actions of individuals as affect others. In a spontaneous order the position of each individual is the resultant of the actions of many other individuals, and nobody has the responsibility or the power to assure that these separate actions of many will produce a particular result for a certain person. Though his position may be affected by the conduct of some other person or of the concerted actions of several, it will rarely be dependent on them alone. There can, therefore, in a spontaneous order, be no rules which will determine what anyone's position ought to be. Rules of individual conduct, as we have seen, determine only certain abstract properties of the resulting order, but not its particular, concrete content.

It is, of course, tempting to call 'just' a state of affairs that comes about because all contributing to it behave justly (or not unjustly); but this is misleading where, as in the case of a spontaneous order, the resulting state was not the intended aim of the individual actions. Since only situations which have been created by human will can be called just or unjust, the particulars of a spontaneous order cannot be just or unjust: if it is not the intended or foreseen result of somebody's action that A should have much and B little, this cannot be called just or unjust. We shall see that what is called 'social' or 'distributive' justice is indeed meaningless within a spontaneous order and has meaning only within an organization.

Justice and the law

We are not contending that all rules of just conduct which are in fact observed in a society are law, nor that all that is commonly called law consists of rules of just conduct. Our contention is rather that the law which consists of rules of just conduct has a very special standing which not only makes it desirable that it have a distinct name (such as *nomos*), but also makes it exceedingly important that it be clearly distinguished from other commands called law, so that in developing this sort of law its characteristic properties are clearly seen. The reason for this is that, if we want to preserve a free society, only that part of the law which consists of rules of just conduct (i.e. essentially the private and criminal law) must be binding for, and be enforced on, the private citizen— whatever else may also be law binding those who are members of the organization of government. We shall see that the loss of the belief in a law which serves justice and not particular interests (or particular ends of government) is largely responsible for the progressive undermining of individual freedom.

We need not dwell here on the much discussed question of what is required for a recognized rule of just conduct to be entitled to the name of law. Though most people would hesitate to give this name to a rule of just conduct which, though usually obeyed, was in no way enforced, it seems difficult to deny it to rules which are enforced by a largely effective though unorganized social pressure, or the exclusion of the breaker of a rule from the group.[3] There is evidently a gradual transition from such a state to what we regard as a mature legal system in which deliberately created organizations are charged with the enforcement and modification of this primary law. The rules governing these organizations are of course part of the public law and, like government itself, are superimposed upon the primary rules, for the purpose of making these more effective.

But if, in contrast to the public law, the private and criminal law aims at establishing and enforcing rules of just conduct, this does not mean that every one of the separate rules in which they are stated, taken by itself, is a rule of just conduct, but only that the system as a whole[4] serves to determine such rules. All rules of just conduct must refer to certain states of affairs; and it is often more convenient to define by separate rules these states of affairs to which particular rules of conduct refer than to repeat these definitions in every rule which refers to such a state. The individual domains which the rules of just conduct protect will have to be referred to again and again, and the manner in which such domains are acquired, transferred, lost, and delimited will usefully be stated once and for all in rules whose function will be solely to serve as points of reference for rules of just conduct. All the rules which state the conditions under which property can be acquired and transferred, valid contracts or wills made, or other 'rights' or 'powers' acquired and lost, serve merely to define the conditions on which the law will grant the protection of enforceable rules of just conduct. Their aim is to make the relevant states of affairs recognizable, and to ensure that the parties will understand each other in entering obligations. If a form is omitted which the law prescribes for a transaction, this does not mean that a rule of just conduct has been infringed, but that the protection of certain rules of just conduct will not be granted which would have been granted had the form been observed. Such states as 'ownership' have no significance except through the rules of conduct which refer to them; leave out those rules of just conduct which refer to ownership, and nothing remains of it.

Rules of just conduct are generally prohibitions of unjust conduct

We have seen earlier (chapter 5) how from the process of gradual extension of rules of just conduct to circles of persons who neither share, nor are aware of, the same particular ends, a type of rule has developed which is usually described as 'abstract'. This term is appropriate, however, only if it is not used in the strict sense in which it is employed in logic. A rule applying only to persons whose finger-prints show a particular pattern, definable by an algebraic formula, would in the sense in which this term is used in logic certainly be an abstract rule. But since experience has taught us that every individual is uniquely identified by his finger-prints, such a rule would in fact apply only to an ascertainable individual. What is meant by the term abstract is expressed in a classical juridical formula that states that the rule must apply to an unknown number of future instances.[5] Here legal theory has found it necessary explicitly to acknowledge our inevitable ignorance of the particular circumstances which we wish those to use who learn of them.

We have already indicated earlier that such reference to an unknown number of future instances is closely connected with certain other properties of those rules which have passed through the process of generalization, namely that these rules are almost all negative in the sense that they prohibit rather than enjoin particular kinds of actions, [6] that they do so in order to protect ascertainable domains within which each individual is free to act as he chooses, [7] and that the possession of this character by a particular rule can be ascertained by applying to it a test of generalization or universalization. We shall try to show that these are all necessary characteristics of those rules of just conduct which form the foundation of a spontaneous order, but do not apply to those rules of organization which make up the public law. [8]

That practically all rules of just conduct are negative in the sense that they normally impose no positive duties on any one, unless he has incurred such duties by his own actions, is a feature that has again and again, as though it were a new discovery, been pointed out, but scarcely ever systematically investigated. [9] It applies to most rules of conduct but not without exception. Some parts of family law impose duties which do not result from a deliberate action (such as duties of children towards parents) but from a position in which the individual has been placed by circumstances beyond his control. And there are a few other rather exceptional instances in which a person is deemed by the rules of just conduct to have been placed by circumstances in a particular close community with some other persons and in consequence to incur a specific duty towards them. It is significant that the English common law appears to know only one such case, namely the case of assistance in danger on the high seas. [10] Modern legislation tends to go further and in some countries has imposed positive duties of action to preserve life where this is in the power of a particular person. [11] It may be that in the future there will be further developments in this direction; but they will probably remain limited because of the great difficulty of specifying by a general rule on whom such a duty rests. At present, at any rate, rules of just conduct which require positive action remain rare exceptions, confined to instances where accident has temporarily placed persons in a close community with others. We shall not go far wrong if for our purposes we treat all rules of just conduct as negative in character.

That they had to become so is a necessary effect of the process of extension of rules beyond the community which can share, or even know of, the same purposes. [12] Rules which are end-independent, in the sense that they are not confined to those following particular designated purposes, can also never fully determine a particular action but only limit the range of permitted kinds of action and leave the decision on the particular action to be taken by the actor in the light of his ends. We have seen already that this leads to the confinement of rules to prohibitions of actions towards others which are likely to harm them, and that this can be achieved only by rules which define a domain of the individuals (or organized groups) with which others are not allowed to interfere.

We have also seen that rules of conduct cannot simply prohibit all actions that cause harm to others. To buy or not to buy from, and to serve or not to serve, a particular person, is an essential part of our freedom; but if we decide not to buy from one or not to serve another, this may cause great harm if those affected have counted on our custom or our services; and in disposing of what is ours, a tree in our garden, or the façade of our house, we may deprive our neighbour of what to him has great sentimental value. Rules of just conduct cannot protect all interests, not even all interests which to somebody are of great importance, but only what are called 'legitimate' expectations, that is expectations which the rules define and which the rules of law may sometimes have created in the first instance.[13]

The chief function of rules of just conduct is thus to tell each what he can count upon, what material objects or services he can use for his purposes, and what is the range of actions open to him. They cannot, if they are to secure to all the same freedom of decision, give similar assurance of what others will do, unless these others have voluntarily and for their own purposes consented to act in a particular manner.

The rules of just conduct thus delimit protected domains not by directly assigning particular things to particular persons, but by making it possible to derive from ascertainable facts to whom particular things belong. Though this ought to have been made clear for all time by David Hume and Immanuel Kant,[14] whole books have been based on the erroneous assumption that 'the law confers on each person a wholly unique set of liberties with regard to the use of material goods and imposes on each person a unique set of restrictions with regard thereto. . . . In regard to acts which involve the use of those things I own, the law favours me above everyone else.'[15] Such an interpretation misses completely the aim of abstract rules of just conduct.

What rules of just conduct in fact do is to say under what

conditions this or that action will be within the range of the permissible; but they leave it to the individuals under these rules to create their own protected domain. Or, in legal terms, the rules do not confer rights on particular persons, but lay down the conditions under which such rights can be acquired. What will be the domain of each will depend partly on his actions and partly on facts beyond his control. The rules serve merely to enable each to deduce from facts which he can ascertain the boundaries of the protected domain which he and others have succeeded in cutting out for themselves.[16]

Since the consequences of applying rules of just conduct will always depend on factual circumstances which are not determined by these rules, we cannot measure the justice of the application of a rule by the result it will produce in a particular case. In this respect what has been correctly said of John Locke's view on the justice of competition, namely that 'it is the way in which competition is carried on, not its result, that counts',[17] is generally true of the liberal conception of justice, and of what justice can achieve in a spontaneous order. That it is possible for one through a single just transaction to gain much and for another through an equally just transaction to lose all,[18] in no way disproves the justice of these transactions. Justice is not concerned with those unintended consequences of a spontaneous order which have not been deliberately brought about by anybody.[19]

The rules of just conduct thus merely serve to prevent conflict and to facilitate co-operation by eliminating some sources of uncertainty. But since they aim at enabling each individual to act according to his own plans and decisions, they cannot wholly eliminate uncertainty. They can create certainty only to the extent that they protect means against the interference by others, and thus enable the individual to treat those means as being at his disposal. But they cannot assure him success in the use of these means, neither in so far as it depends only on material facts, nor in so far as it depends on the actions of others which he expects. They can, for instance, not assure him that he will be able at the expected price to sell what he has to offer or to buy what he wants.

Not only the rules of just conduct, but also the test of their justice, are negative

As in the extension of rules from the end-connected tribal society (or teleocracy) to the rule-connected open society (or nomocracy) these rules must progressively shed their dependence on concrete ends, and by passing this test become gradually abstract and negative, so the legislator who undertakes to lay down rules for a Great Society must subject to the test of universalization what he wants to apply to such a society. The conception of justice as we understand it, that is, the principle of treating all under the same rules, did only gradually emerge in the course of this process; it then became the guide in the progressive approach to an Open Society of free individuals equal before the law. To judge actions by rules, not by particular results, is the step which has made the Open Society possible. It is the device man has tumbled upon to overcome the ignorance of every individual of most of the particular facts which must determine the concrete order of a Great Society.

Justice is thus emphatically not a balancing of particular interests at stake in a concrete case, or even of the interests of determinable classes of persons, nor does it aim at bringing about a particular state of affairs which is regarded as just. It is not concerned with the results that a particular action will in fact bring about. The observation of a rule of just conduct will often have unintended consequences which, if they were deliberately brought about, would be regarded as unjust. And the preservation of a spontaneous order often requires changes which would be unjust if they were determined by human will.

It should perhaps be pointed out here that in a society of omniscient persons there would be no room for a conception of justice: every action would have to be judged as a means of bringing about known effects, and omniscience would presumably include knowledge of the relative importance of the different effects. Like all abstractions, justice is an adaptation to our ignorance—to our permanent ignorance of particular facts which no scientific advance can wholly remove. It is as much because we lack the knowledge of a common hierarchy of the importance of the particular ends of different individuals as because we lack the knowledge of particular facts, that the order of the Great Society must be brought about by the observance of abstract and end-independent rules.

The test which the rules of just conduct have passed in the process of their evolution to become general (and usually negative) is itself a negative test which makes necessary a gradual reformulation of these rules so as to eliminate all references to particular facts or effects that cannot be known to those who are to obey the rules. Only those rules can pass this test which are end-independent and refer only to facts which those who are to obey them can know or readily ascertain.

Rules of just conduct are thus determined not by 'will' or 'interest', or any similar aim at particular results, but develop through a persistent effort (Ulpian's 'constans et perpetua voluntas') [20] to bring consistency into a system of rules inherited by each generation. The legislator who wishes deliberately to fit into the existing system new rules of the same sort as those that have made possible the Open Society, must subject these rules to such a negative test. Operating upon and within such a system, and faced with the task of improving the function of an existing order of actions, he will generally have little choice which rule to lay down.

The persistent application of the negative test of universalizability, or the necessity of commitment to the universal application of the rules laid down, and the endeavour to modify and supplement the existing rules so as to eliminate all conflict between them (or with yet unarticulated but generally acceptable principles of justice), may in the course of time bring about a complete transformation of the whole system. But while the negative test will assist us in selecting from, or modifying, a given body of rules, it will never provide us with a positive reason for the whole. It is irrelevant (and, of course, normally unknown) from which initial system of rules this evolution started; and it is quite possible that one kind of system of such rules is so much more effective than all others in producing a comprehensive order for a Great Society that, as a result of the advantages derived from all changes in the direction towards it, there may occur in systems with very different beginnings a process corresponding to what biologists call 'convergent evolution'. 'The necessities of human society' [21] may bring about an independent emergence, at many different times and places, of the same sort of system, such as that based on private property and contract. It would indeed seem that wherever a Great Society has arisen, it has been made possible by a system of rules of just conduct which included what David Hume called 'the three fundamental laws of nature, *that of stability of possession, of its transference by consent*, and *of the performance of promises*', [22] or, as a modern author sums up the essential content of all contemporary systems of private law, 'freedom of contract, the inviolability of property, and the duty to compensate another for damage due to his fault.' [23]

Those who are entrusted with the task of articulating, interpreting, and developing the existing body of rules of just conduct will thus always have to find answers to definite problems, and not to impose their unfettered will. They may originally have been chosen because they were believed to be most likely to formulate rules that would satisfy the general sense of justice and fit into the whole system of existing rules. Though the naive constructivist interpretation of the origin of social institutions tends to assume that the rules of law must be the product of somebody's will, this is in fact contrary to actual development and just as mythical as the origin of society from a social contract. Those who were trusted to formulate the rules were not given unlimited power to invent whatever rules they thought fit. They were chosen because they had shown skill in finding formulations which satisfied the rest and which proved workable. It is true that their success often placed them in a position which enabled them to keep the trust when they no longer deserved it, or to preserve their power without the trust. This does not alter the fact that they derived their authority from their presumed capacity to put into effect what was required by an accepted kind of order, and to discover what would be regarded as just. In short, theirs was an authority derived from their presumed capacity to find justice, not to create it.

The task of developing a system of law is thus an intellectual task of great difficulty which cannot be performed without taking certain rules as given and moving within the system determined by them. It is a task which can be performed more or less successfully, but which will not normally leave those entrusted with it free to follow their own will. It is more like the search for truth than to the construction of some new edifice. In the effort to disentangle and reconcile a complex of unarticulated rules and to transform it into a system of explicit rules, conflicts among what are accepted values will often be encountered. It will occasionally be necessary to reject some accepted rules in the light of more general principles. The guiding principle will always be that justice, i.e. the generally applicable rule, must prevail over the particular (though perhaps also generally felt) desire.

Though our sense of justice will generally provide the starting point, what it tells us about the particular case is not an infallible or ultimate test. It may be and can be proved to be wrong. Though the justification of our subjective feeling that some rule is just must be that we are prepared to commit ourselves to apply it universally, this does not exclude the possibility that we may later discover cases to which, if we had not committed ourselves, we should wish not to apply the rule, and where we discover that what we had thought to be quite just is in fact not so; in which event we may be forced to alter the rule for the future. Such a demonstration of a conflict between the intuitive feeling of justice and rules we wish also to preserve may often force us to review our opinion.

We shall later have to consider further the changes in the recognized rules which will be necessary for the preservation of the overall order if the rules of just conduct are to be the same for all. We shall then see that often effects which seem unjust to us may still be just in the sense that they are necessary consequences of the just actions of all concerned. In the abstract order in which we live and to which we owe most of the advantages of civilization, it must thus in the last resort be our intellect and not intuitive perception of what is good which must guide us. Our present moral views undoubtedly still contain layers or strata deriving from earlier phases of the evolution of human societies—the small horde to the organized tribe, the still larger groups of clans and the other successive steps towards the Great Society. And though some of the rules or opinions emerging in later stages may actually presuppose the continued acceptance of earlier ones, other new elements may be in conflict with some of those of earlier origins which still persist.

The significance of the negative character of the test of injustice

The fact that, though we have no positive criteria of justice, we do have negative criteria which show us what is unjust, is very important in several respects. It means, in the first instance, that, though the striving to eliminate the unjust will not be a sufficient foundation for building up a wholly new system of law, it can be an adequate guide for developing an existing body of law with the aim of making it more just. In such an effort towards the development of a body of rules, most of which are accepted by the members of society, there will therefore also exist an 'objective' (in the sense of being inter-personally valid, but not of universal—because it will be valid only for those other members of the society who accept most of its other rules) test of what is unjust. Such a test of injustice may be sufficient to tell us in what direction we must develop an established system of law, though it would be insufficient to enable us to construct a wholly new system of law.

It should be mentioned here that it was solely in the sense of such a negative test, to be applied in the development of an established system of law, that in his philosophy of law Immanuel Kant employed the principle of the categorical imperative. This has often been overlooked because in his theory of morals he used the principle as if it were an adequate premise from which the whole system of moral rules could be deductively derived. So far as his philosophy of law is concerned, Kant was fully aware that the categorical imperative provided only a necessary but not a sufficient condition of justice, or only what we have called a negative test which enables us progressively to eliminate what is unjust, namely the test of universalizability. He also saw more clearly than most later philosophers of law that as a result of passing this test, 'juridical laws [must] abstract altogether from our ends, they are essentially negative and limiting principles which merely restrict our exercise of freedom.'[24]

It is significant that there exists a close parallel between this treatment of rules of justice as prohibitions and as subject to a negative test and the modern development in the philosophy of science, especially by Karl Popper,[25] which treats the laws of nature as prohibitions and regards as their test the failure of persistent efforts of falsification, a test which, in the last resort, also proves to be a test of internal consistency of the whole system. The positions in the two fields are analogous also in that we can always only endeavour to approach truth, or justice, by persistently eliminating the false or unjust, but can never be sure that we have achieved final truth or justice.

Indeed it would seem that as little as we can believe what we will, or hold to be true what we will, can we regard as just what we will. Though our desire that something should be regarded as just may long overrule our reason, there are necessities of thought against which such desire is powerless. While I may possibly convince myself by spurious reasoning that something I would wish to be just was really just, whether it is so clearly is not a matter of will but of reason. It will not merely be the contrary view of others which will prevent me from regarding as just what is in fact not so, nor some strong sentiment which the particular question at issue arouses in me, but the necessity of consistency without which thought would become impossible. This will drive me to test my belief in the justice of the particular act by the compatibility of the rule by which I judge it with all the other rules in which I also believe.

The contrary belief, that objective criteria of justice must be positive criteria, has historically been of great influence. Classical liberalism depended on a belief in objective justice. Legal positivism, however, did succeed in demonstrating that there are no positive criteria of justice; and it drew from this the false conclusion that there could be no objective criteria of justice whatsoever. Indeed legal positivism is largely the product of such a despair of finding any objective criteria of justice.[26] From the seeming impossibility of doing so it concluded that all questions of justice were solely a matter of will, or interests, or emotions. If this were true, the whole basis of classical liberalism would collapse.[27]

The positivist conclusion was, however, reached only through the tacit but erroneous assumption that objective criteria of justice must be positive criteria, i.e. premises from which the whole system of rules of just conduct could be logically deduced. But if we do not insist that the test of justice must enable us to build up a whole system of new rules of just conduct, but are content persistently to apply the negative test of injustice to the parts of an inherited system, the greater part of whose rules are universally accepted, we may accept the contention of positivism that there are no positive criteria of justice; yet we can still maintain that the further development of the rules of just conduct is not a matter of arbitrary will but of inner necessity, and that solutions to open problems of justice are discovered, not arbitrarily decreed. The fact that there are no positive criteria of justice does not leave unfettered will as the only alternative. We may still be bound by justice to develop the existing system in a particular way, and be able to demonstrate that we must alter particular rules in a certain way to eliminate injustice.

Legal positivism has become one of the main forces which have destroyed classical liberalism because the latter presupposes a conception of justice which is independent of the expediency for achieving particular results. Legal positivism, like the other forms of constructivists pragmatism of a William James[28] or John Dewey[29] or Vilfredo Pareto,[30] are therefore profoundly antiliberal in the original meaning of the word, though their views have become the foundations of that pseudo-liberalism which in the course of the last generation has arrogated the name.

The ideology of legal positivism

Since there exists some uncertainty about the precise meaning of the term 'legal positivism', and as the term is currently used in several different senses,[31] it will be useful to start the examination of this doctrine with a discussion of the original meaning of the term 'positive law'. We shall see that the suggestion contained in this term that only deliberately made law is real law still provides the essential core of the positivist doctrine on which all its other assertions depend.

As we have seen earlier,[32] the use of the term 'positive' with respect to law derives from the Latin rendering as *positus* (that is 'set down') or *positivus* of the Greek expression *thesei* which described that which was deliberate creation of a human will, in contrast to what had not been so invented but had arisen *physei*, by nature. We find this stress on the deliberate creation of all law by human will clearly at the beginning of the modern history of legal positivism, in Thomas Hobbes' 'non veritas sed auctoritas facit legem'[33] and his definition of law as 'the command of him that have the legislative power'.[34] It has rarely been expressed more crudely than by Jeremy Bentham, who maintained that 'the whole body of law . . . is distinguished into two branches—the arrangements of one of which are arrangements which have really been made— made by hands universally acknowledged as duly authorized, and competent to the making of such arrangements. . . . This branch of law may stand distinguished . . . by the name of *real* law, really existing law, legislator-made law; under the English Government it stands already distinguished by the name of *statute* law. . . . The arrangements supposed to be made by the other branch . . . may stand distinguished by the appellation of unreal, not really existing, imaginary, fictitious, spurious, judge-made law. Under the English Government the division is actually distinguished by the unexpressive, uncharacteristic, and inappropriate names of *common* law and *unwritten* law.'[35] It is from Bentham that John Austin derived his conception of 'all law being laid down by an intelligent being' and that 'there can be no law without a legislative act.'[36] This central contention of positivism is equally essential to its most highly developed modern form, the version of Hans Kelsen, which maintains that 'norms prescribing human behaviour can emanate only from human will, not from human reason.'[37]

So far as this is intended to assert that the *content* of all rules of law has been deliberately made by an act of will it is simply a naive expression of the constructivist fallacy and as such factually false. There is, however, a fundamental ambiguity in the contention that the legislator 'determines' what is to be the law, an ambiguity which assists the positivists to escape some conclusions which would too evidently show the fictitious character of their basic assumption.[38] The contention that the legislator determines what is to be law may mean merely that he instructs the agents which enforce the law how they have to proceed in order to find what the law is. In a mature legal system, where there is a single organization which has the monopoly of enforcing the law, the head of this organization, (and that is today the legislator) must clearly give such instructions to the agencies of the organization which he has set up. But this does not necessarily imply that the legislator determines the *content* of that law, or need even know what that content is. The legislator may instruct the courts to maintain the common law and have little idea what the content of that law is. He may instruct the courts to enforce customary rules, native law, or the observation of good faith or equity—all instances where the content of the law that is to be enforced is certainly not created by the legislator. It is an abuse of words to assert that in such instances the law expresses the will of the legislator. If the legislator merely tells the courts how to proceed in order to find out what the law is, this by itself tells us nothing about how the content of this law is determined. Positivists, however, seem to believe that when they have established that the former is true in all mature legal systems, they have shown that it is the will of the legislator which determines the content of the law. From this conclusion follow almost all the characteristic tenets of positivism.

It is evident that so far as legal rules of just conduct, and particularly the private law, are concerned, the assertion of legal positivism that their content is always an expression of the will of the legislator is simply false. This, of course, has been shown again and again by the historians of private law and especially of the common law.[39] It is necessarily true only of those rules of organization which constitute the public law; and it is significant that nearly all the leading modern legal positivists have been public lawyers and in addition usually socialists—organization men, that is, who can think of order only as organization, and on whom the whole demonstration of the eighteenth century thinkers that rules of just conduct can lead to the formation of a spontaneous order seems to have been lost.

Positivism has for this reason tried to obliterate the distinction between rules of just conduct and the rules of organization, and has insisted that all that is currently termed law is of the same character, and, particularly, that the conception of justice has nothing to do with determining what the law is. From the insight that there are no positive criteria of justice they erroneously conclude that there can be no objective test of justice whatever (and, in addition, think of justice not as a matter of just conduct but as a problem of distributive justice); and that, as Gustav Radbruch revealingly expressed it, 'if nobody can ascertain what is just, somebody must determine what shall be legal.'[40]

After demonstrating without difficulty that the part of law in which they are chiefly interested, namely the law of the organization of government or the public law, has nothing to do with justice, they proceed to assert that this must be true of all that is commonly called law, including the law which serves the maintenance of a spontaneous order. Here they completely disregard the fact that the rules which are required to maintain an operating spontaneous order and the rules which govern an organization have altogether different functions. The existence of a private law appears to them, however, rather as an anomaly which is bound to disappear. To Radbruch it is explicitly a 'temporarily reserved and constantly diminishing sphere of free initiative within the all-comprehensive public law';[41] and to Hans Kelsen 'all genuine laws' are conditional orders to officials to apply sanctions.[42] Under the influence of the positivists we are in fact approaching such a state: theirs is becoming a sort of self-fulfilling prophecy.

The positivist insistence that all that as a result of a particular historical development is today *called* 'law' must have the same character, leads to the claim that the theorist must give the word a single definition which covers all the instances to which the word 'law' is applied, and that all that satisfies this definition must be accepted as law for all purposes. But after men have fought for centuries for what they regarded as an 'order of law', meaning thereby not any order enforced by authority but an order formed as a result of the individuals obeying universal rules of just conduct; after the term 'law' has for nearly as long determined the meaning of such political ideals as that of the Rule of Law, the *Rechtsstaat*, the Separation of Powers and the much older conception of law as the protection of individual freedom, and served in constitutional documents to limit the manner in which fundamental rights may be restricted; we cannot, if we are not to make nonsense of one of the determinants of Western civilization, like

Humpty Dumpty or Professor Glanville Williams,[43] insist that 'when I use a word it means just what I want it to mean,—neither more nor less!'[44] We must at least recognize that in certain contexts, including legal contexts, the word 'law' has a very specific meaning, different from that in which it is used in other contexts, and that what is called law in that specific sense may differ in origin, attributes, functions and possible content from some of the other statements also called 'law'.

Yet the definition of law as the product of the will of the legislator leads not only to the inclusion in 'law' of all the expressions of the will of the legislator, whatever its content ('Law may have any content whatever'[45]) but also to the view that content constitutes no significant distinction between different statements called law, and, in particular, that justice can in no sense be a determinant of what in fact is law but that it is rather the law which determines what is just. Contrary to the older tradition which had regarded justice as prior to law,[46] and at least certain parts of law as limited by conceptions of justice, the contention that the lawgiver was the creator of justice became the most characteristic tenet of legal positivism. From Thomas Hobbes' 'no law can be unjust'[47] to Hans Kelsen's 'just is only another word for legal or legitimate'[48] the efforts of the positivists have invariably been directed towards discrediting the conception of justice as a guide for determining what the law is.

The 'pure theory of law'

This central contention of legal positivism clearly implies the claim not merely that the legislator who sets up courts must indicate how these courts are to ascertain the law, but that the legislator creates the *content* of that law and in doing so has a completely free hand. In its most highly developed form, the 'pure theory of law' of Hans Kelsen, this result is made to appear plausible by a persistent but highly misleading use of words in an unusual special sense which evidently has become so habitual with the adherents of that school that they are no longer aware of it.

In the first instance, and most important, in order to serve the connection between 'law' and 'rule', Kelsen substitutes for 'rule' the term 'norm', and then, doing violence to language,[49] uses the latter term to include what he calls 'individual norms', i.e., every imperative and every ought-statement. In the second instance, he uses the term 'order' not for a factual state of affairs, but for the 'norms' prescribing a particular arrangement,[50] thus denying himself the insight that some, but only some, rules of conduct will in certain circumstances induce the formation of an order which for this reason must be distinguished from other rules.[51] Third, the term 'existence' is used of a norm as being synonymous with 'validity', and 'validity' is defined as being logically derivable from some act of will of the ultimate authority, or the 'basic norm'.[52] Fourth and finally, he uses the terms 'creating', 'setting' or 'positing' (*erzeugen* or *setzen*) to include everything that is 'constituted by human acts',[53] so that not only the products of human design but also such spontaneous growths as the rules of language or morals or etiquette must be regarded as 'set, that is, positive norms'.[54]

These last two usages produce together a *double* ambiguity. The assertion that a norm has arisen in a particular manner may not only mean *either* that the content of the rule has been formed in the particular way specified *or* that validity has been conferred in a particular manner on such an existing rule; it may also mean *either* that this content has been deliberately invented by a rational process, *or* that it is the 'result of human action but not of human design' (that is 'natural' in one of the senses in which the word has been used in the past).

It would exceed the scope of this book to examine the curious claim that the 'pure theory of law' is a 'normative science', or what this term means.[55] It is admittedly not an empirical science of fact and could claim at most to be a science in the sense in which logic or mathematics are sciences. What it in fact does is merely to elaborate the consequences of its definition of 'law', from which it follows that the 'existence' of a norm is the same as its 'validity', and that this validity is determined by its logical derivability from a hypothetical 'basic norm'—though the factual element of the 'efficacy' of the whole system of norms to which it belongs also enters in a manner never satisfactorily explained. This definition of the concept of law is postulated as the only possible and significant definition, and by representing as 'cognition' what are simply the consequences of the definition adopted, the 'pure theory' claims to be entitled to deny (or represent as meaningless) statements in which the term 'law' is used in a different and narrower sense. This is particularly true of the important assertion that no distinction can be drawn between a legal system in which the rule of law (or government under the law, or the *Rechtsstaat*) prevails and where this is not the case, and that therefore every legal order, even one where the powers of authority are wholly unlimited, is an instance of the rule of law.[56]

Conclusions drawn from a definition can never tell us anything about what is true of particular objects observable in the world of facts. The insistence that the term 'law' must be used only in that particular sense, and that no further distinctions between different kinds of law are relevant for a legal 'science' has, however, a definite purpose: this purpose is to discredit a certain conception which has for long guided legislation and the decisions of courts, and to whose influence we owe the growth of the spontaneous order of a free society. This is the conception that coercion is legitimate only if it is applied in the enforcement of universal rules of just conduct equally applicable to all citizens. The aim of legal positivism is to make coercion in the service of particular purposes or any special interests as legitimate as its use in preserving the foundations of a spontaneous order.

How little legal positivism in fact helps us to ascertain what is the law we see most clearly where this matters most, i.e. in the case of the judge who has to ascertain what rule he is to apply to a particular case. Whenever no specific prescription of the legislator tells him what to do (and often he is in effect told no more than that he ought to be just!), the fact that the authorization of the legislator confers on his decision 'the force of law' does not tell him what the law is which he ought to enforce. The judge is bound not merely by the designation by the legislator of some particular rules as valid, but by the internal requirements of a system which no one has deliberately designed as a whole, some parts of which may never yet have been articulated, and which, though tending to become consistent, is never in fact wholly so. There clearly does exist, independent of the will and even of the knowledge of the legislator, such a system of rules which is generally obeyed and to which the legislator often refers the judge. This is the wholly legitimate meaning of the contention that the judge may be bound by a law to which neither the legislator nor he himself has given its particular content, which thus exists independently of either, and which the judge may or may not be successful in finding, since it exists only implicitly in the whole system of rules and its relation to the factual order of actions. It is also clear that the judge may make a false decision which, though it may become valid (acquire 'the force of law'), will remain nevertheless in a meaningful sense contrary to the law. Evidently where a judicial decision has obtained the 'force of law' but is also 'contrary to the law', the term law is used in two different senses which must be distinguished but which are confused when the 'individual norm' set by the judge is treated as the same kind of thing as the rule which he infringes. For the judge the question whether a certain rule is valid cannot be answered by any logical derivation from the act which conferred upon him power to order enforcement of the rule, but only by reference of the implications of a system of rules which factually exists independently of either his will or that of a legislator.

The constant use, by Kelsen and his followers, of terms like 'creating' to describe a process by which validity is conferred upon rules and commands, even whole systems of rules which exist in the ordinary meaning of the word (i.e. are known and acted upon), and may have existed long before and independently of the legislator (and even be unknown to him), leads them constantly to assertions which do not follow from their premises. The fact that a system of rules on which a legislator confers validity may in its content not be a product of his design but may exist independently of his will, and that he neither contemplates, nor regards himself as capable of, replacing this existing system of recognized rules by a wholly new one, but accepts some of the established rules as beyond question, has an important consequence. It means that in many instances in which he would like to restate the law he will not be able to make whatever rules he likes, but will be bound by the requirements of the part of the system which is given to him. Or, to put this differently: *it will be the whole complex of rules which in fact are observed in a given society that will determine what particular rule it will be rational to enforce or which ought to be enforced.* Though those two sets of rules may in part be the same, yet the first set of rules may include some which need not be enforced because they are universally obeyed, while the second set of rules will contain some which would not voluntarily be obeyed but whose observance is important for the same reasons as the observance of the first, so that those who observe the first have good reasons for demanding that the second be also obeyed.

Of course, until validity is conferred upon such rules, they are according to the definition of the positivists not yet 'norms' or law, and do not 'exist' as legal norms. By this sleight of hand it is proved that they are 'created' by the arbitrary will of the legislator. But this assertion, which the unwary reader is apt to apply to the content of the rules, of which it would not be true, has been turned into a tautology which cannot be contradicted under the definitions adopted. It is nevertheless used to support such assertions as that the rules of positive law 'are derived from the arbitrary will of a human authority,'[57] that 'norms prescribing human behaviour can emanate only from human will, not from human reason',[58] or that '"positive" law means a law created by acts of human beings which take place in time and space.'[59]

The constant use of such expressions produces the *suggestio falsi*, to which apparently their users themselves frequently succumb, that it always is and must be an act of unfettered human will which determines the content of the law. Yet the basic question of what rule ought to be enforced in a particular instance can often not be answered by logical derivation from some expression of will, nor decided by an act of will, but only by a process ratiocination which shows which is the rule whose application in the particular case satisfies the requirement of being capable of universalization without conflicting with other recognized rules. In short, the original assertion that all valid law is set law is made good by re-defining 'set' as 'made valid' and 'made valid' as 'in fact enforced by authority'. This is certainly not what was meant when it was originally asserted that all valid law must be 'posited'; nor does this definition of law relieve the judge of the necessity of deciding what the law is—it may even require him to refer in that effort to a 'natural law' to which the legislator has directed him and which consists of rules existing (in the ordinary sense of this word) independently of the will of the legislator. The existence of a recognized procedure by which it is determined what is to be accepted as just thus does not exclude that this procedure may depend for its conclusions on a prevailing conception of justice— even if for most problems likely to arise such references to general principles of justice are precluded by the prescription of a particular answer.

The insistence that the word 'law' must always be used and interpreted in the sense given to it by the legal positivists, and especially that the difference between the functions of the two kinds of rules actually laid down by legislatures are irrelevant for legal science, has thus a definite purpose. It is to remove all limitations on the power of the legislator that would result from the assumption that he is entitled to make law only in a sense which substantively limits the content of what he can make into law. It is, in other words, directed against the doctrine, most explicitly expounded by John Locke, that 'the legislative authority is an authority to act *in a particular* way . . . those who wield this authority should make only general rules.' [60]

Legal positivism is in this respect simply the ideology of socialism —if we may use the name of the most influential and respectable form of constructivism to stand for all its various forms—and of the omnipotence of the legislative power. It is an ideology born out of the desire to achieve complete control over the social order, and the belief that it is in our power to determine deliberately in any manner we like, every aspect of this social order.

In the case of the pure theory of law this ideological character becomes most apparent in the fervour with which it is used by its adherents to represent as invalid and ideologically inspired certain important conclusions which others have drawn concerning the significance of law. Law, in the specific sense in which this term has, constantly if not always consistently, been used since antiquity, has been understood by a long line of modern writers from Grotius through Locke, Hume and Bentham down to Emil Brunner, as being inseparable from private property and at the same time the indispensable condition of individual freedom. But while such understanding is true of those generic rules of just conduct which are necessary for the formation of a spontaneous order, it is of course not true of the specific commands which the direction of an organization requires. For those, on the other hand, who make the power of the legislator necessarily unlimited, individual freedom becomes a matter 'beyond salvation' [61] and freedom comes to mean exclusively the collective freedom of the community, i.e. democracy. [62] Legal positivism has thereby also become the chief ideological support of the unlimited powers of democracy.

But if the will of the majority is to be unlimited, it will of course be only the particular aims of that majority which can determine what is the law. 'Hence', as Kelsen maintains, 'from the point of view of rational cognition, there are only interests of human beings and hence conflicts of interests. The solution of these can be brought about either by satisfying one interest at the expense of the other, or by a compromise between the conflicting interests. It is not possible to prove that the one or the other solution is just.' [63]

The demonstration that there is no *positive* test of justice is here used to prove that there can be no objective test of justice whatever which could be used to determine whether a rule of law is valid or not.[64] The possibility that there may exist a negative test which enables us to eliminate certain norms as unjust is not even considered.

Historically, however, it was the pursuit of justice that has created the system of generic rules which in turn became the foundation and preserver of the developing spontaneous order. To bring about such an order the ideal of justice need not determine the particular content of the rules which can be regarded as just (or at least not unjust). What is required is merely a negative test that enables us progressively to eliminate rules which prove to be unjust, because they are not universalizable within the system of other rules whose validity is not questioned. It is thus at least conceivable that several different systems of rules of just conduct may satisfy this test. The fact that there exist different ideas of what is just does not preclude the possibility that the negative test of injustice may be an objective test which several different but not all systems of such rules can satisfy. The pursuit of the ideal of justice (like the pursuit of the ideal of truth) does not presuppose that it is known what justice (or truth) is, but only that we know what we regard as unjust (or untrue). Absence of injustice is merely a necessary but not a sufficient determinant of appropriate rules. Whether, at least in a given state of knowledge of a certain physical environment, the persistent application of this negative test will, as we have suggested, produce a process of convergent evolution, so that only one such system will fully satisfy the test, must remain an open question.

The characterization of Kelsen's pure theory of law as an ideology is here not meant as a reproach, though its defenders are bound to regard it as such. Since every social order rests on an ideology, every statement of the criteria by which we can determine what is appropriate law in such an order must also be an ideology. The only reason why it is important to show that this is also true of the pure theory of law is that its author prides himself on being able to 'unmask' all other theories of law as ideologies[65] and to have provided the only theory which is not an ideology. This *Ideolologie-kritik* is even regarded by some of his disciples as one of Kelsen's greatest achievements.[66] Yet, since every cultural order can be maintained only by an ideology, Kelsen succeeds only in replacing one ideology with another that postulates that all orders maintained by force are orders of the same kind, deserving the description (and dignity) of an order of law, the term which before was used to describe a particular kind of order valued because it secured individual freedom. Though within his system of thought his assertion is tautologically true, he has no right to assert, as he constantly does, that other statements in which, as he knows, [67] the term 'law' is used in a different sense, are not true. What 'law' is to mean we can ascertain only from what those who used the word in shaping our social order intended it to mean, not by attaching to it some meaning which covers all the uses ever made of it. Those men certainly did *not* mean by law, as Kelsen does, any 'social technique' which employs force, but used it in order to distinguish a particular 'social technique', a particular kind of restraint on the use of force, which by the designation of law they tried to distinguish from others. The use of enforceable generic rules in order to induce the formation of a self-maintaining order and the direction of an organization by command towards particular purposes are certainly not the same 'social techniques'. And if, because of accidental historical developments, the term 'law' has come to be used in connection with both these different techniques, it should certainly not be the aim of analysis to add to the confusion by insisting that these different uses of the word must be brought under the same definition.

The fact that man has undesignedly brought about the self-maintaining factual order of the social cosmos by pursuing an ideal which he called justice, and which did not specifically designate as just particular acts, but merely required him to discover such rules as could be consistently applied to all, and persistently to revise the system of traditional rules so as to eliminate all conflicts between the several rules that would emerge as the result of their generalization, means that this system can be understood, interpreted, improved, and even its particular content ascertained, only with reference to this ideal of justice. It is this ideal which men had in mind when they distinguished an order of law from arbitrary government, and which they therefore required their judges to observe.

It is only too true, as not only determined opponents of positivism such as Emil Brunner, [68] but in the end even life-long positivists like Gustav Radbruch [69] have recognized, that it was the prevalence of positivism which made the guardians of the law defenceless against the new advance of arbitrary government. After having been persuaded to accept a definition of law under which every state was a state of law, they had no choice but to act on the view which Kelsen approves retrospectively by maintaining that 'from the point of view of the science of law, the law (*Recht*) under the Nazi-government was law (*Recht*). We may regret it but we cannot deny that it was law.' [70] Yes—it was so regarded because law was so defined by the predominant positivist view.

It must be admitted that in this respect the Communists were at least more frank than socialists like Kelsen who, by insisting that their peculiar definition of law was the only legitimate one, surreptitiously derived what appeared to be statements of fact from what is merely a definition of law different from that presupposed by those whose statements they pretended to refute. The early theorists of communist law at least openly admitted that communism means 'the victory of socialism over any law' and the 'gradual extinction of law as such', because 'in a socialist community . . . all law is transformed into administration, all fixed rules into discretion and considerations of utility.' [71]

Law and morals

While we cannot attempt here to review the whole complex of problems concerning the relation of law and morals which have recently been much discussed, [72] a few points must be considered, in the first instance the connection of this issue with legal positivism. For as a result of the work of Professor H. L. A. Hart, which in most regards appears to me one of the most effective criticisms of legal positivism, this name is now often used to mean 'the simple contention that it is in no sense a necessary truth that laws reproduce or satisfy certain demands of morality'; and Professor Hart himself, who maintains this position, is for this reason represented as a positivist. [73] Yet in spite of my rejection of those theses of positivism which we have considered in the preceding section, I see no reason to reject the statement of Professor Hart quoted above if every term in it is carefully noted. Certainly many rules of law have no relation to moral rules, and others may unquestionably be valid law although they are in conflict with recognized moral rules. His statement also does not exclude the possibility that in some instances the judge may have to refer to the existing moral rules in order to find out what the law is: namely in such cases where the recognized rules of law either explicitly refer to such moral conceptions as 'good faith' etc., or tacitly presuppose the observance of certain other rules of conduct which in the past have not had to be enforced but which must be generally obeyed if the already articulated rules of law are to secure the order which they serve. The law of all countries is full of such references to prevailing moral convictions to which the judge can give content only on the basis of his knowledge of these moral beliefs.

A wholly different question is that of whether the existence of strongly and widely held moral convictions in any matter is by itself a justification for their enforcement. The answer seems to be that within a spontaneous order the use of coercion can be justified only where this is necessary to secure the private domain of the individual against interference by others, but that coercion should not be used to interfere in that private sphere where this is not necessary to protect others. Law serves a social order, i.e. the relations between individuals, and actions which affect nobody but the individuals who perform them ought not to be subject to the control of law, however strongly they may be regulated by custom and morals. The importance of this freedom of the individual within his protected domain, and everywhere where his actions do not conflict with the aims of the actions of others, rests mainly on the fact that the development of custom and morals is an experimental process, in a sense in which the enforcement of uniform rules of law cannot be—a process in which alternative rules compete and the more effective are selected by the success of the group obeying them, and may ultimately provide the model for appropriate legislation. This is not to say that the private conduct of individuals may not in some respects, especially in so far as it affects propagation, be very important for the future of the particular group to which they belong. Yet it must remain questionable whether membership in a community can entitle one to a legitimate interest in the prospects of propagation of other members of the same community, or whether this matter is not better regulated by the different fertility of the groups which will be the consequence of freedom.

Another question of some importance is that of how far prevailing moral standards limit not only the powers of the legislator but even the extent to which the application of recognized principles of the law can and should be carried. This is particularly significant in connection with the ideal underlying the Open Society that the same rules should be applied to all human beings. It is an ideal which I, for one, hope we shall continue gradually to approach because it seems to me the indispensable condition of a universal order of peace. Yet I greatly fear that the achievement of this ideal will be delayed rather than speeded up by all too impatient attempts to press for it. Such attempts to push a principle further than general sentiment is yet ready to support it is apt to produce a reaction which may make impossible for a considerable period even what more modest attempts might have achieved. While I look forward, as an ultimate ideal, to a state of affairs in which national boundaries have ceased to be obstacles to the free movement of men, I believe that within any period with which we can now be concerned, any attempt to realize it would lead to a revival of strong nationalist sentiments and a retreat from positions already achieved. However far modern man accepts in principle the ideal that the same rules should apply to all men, in fact he does concede it only to those whom he regards as similar to himself, and only slowly learns to extend the range of those he does accept as his likes. There is little legislation can do to speed up this process and much it may do to reverse it by re-awakening sentiments that are already on the wane.

The main point, however, which in conclusion should be stressed once more, is that the difference between moral and legal rules is not one between rules which have spontaneously grown and rules which have been deliberately made; for most of the rules of law also have not been deliberately made in the first instance. Rather, it is a distinction between rules to which the recognized procedure of enforcement by appointed authority ought to apply and those to which it should not, and therefore a distinction which would lose all meaning if all recognized rules of conduct, including all the rules which the community regards as moral rules, were to be enforced. But which rules ought to be enforced and are therefore to be regarded as law is determined not only by specific designation of some particular rules as enforceable by authority, but often follows from the interdependence of some groups of rules where the observation of every one of them is required for the achievement of what those already designated as enforceable serve: namely, the preservation of an ongoing overall order of actions. If such rules are enforced because they serve an order on whose existence everybody relies, this provides of course no justification for the enforcement of other recognized rules which do not in the same manner affect the existence of this interpersonal order of actions.

There may, in other words, exist a body of rules the regular observance of which produces a factual order of actions and some of which have already had legal validity conferred upon them by authority, while some may only in fact have been observed, or may only have been implicit in those already validated in the sense that the latter will achieve their purpose only if the former are observed. The validation of certain rules must therefore be deemed to authorize the judge to treat as also valid those which are implicit in them, although they have never before been confirmed specifically by the legislator or through an enforcement by a court.

The 'law of nature'

One of the chief sources of confusion in the field is that all theories which oppose legal positivism are alike labelled and lumped together under the misleading name of 'natural law', though some of them have nothing in common with each other except their opposition to legal positivism. This false dichotomy is now insisted upon mainly by the positivists, because their constructivist approach allows only that the law should be either the product of the design of a human or the product of the design of a super-human intelligence. [74] But, as we have seen, the term 'natural' was used earlier to assert that law was the product not of any rational design but of a process of evolution and natural selection, an unintended product whose function we can learn to understand, but whose present significance may be wholly different from the intention of its creators.

The position maintained in this book is therefore likely also to be represented by the positivists as a natural law theory. But though it is true that it develops an interpretation which in the past has been called 'natural' by some of its defenders, the term as currently used is so misleading that it ought to be avoided. True, even today the terms 'natural' and 'nature' are used in several quite different senses, but this is a further reason for avoiding them in scientific discussion. When we use 'nature' or 'natural' to describe the permanent order of the external or material world, and contrast this with what is supernatural or with what is artificial, we clearly mean something different from what we mean when we use it to say that something is part of the nature of an object. [75] While in the former sense cultural phenomena are clearly not natural, in the latter a particular cultural phenomenon may clearly be part of the nature of, or inseparable from, certain cultural structures.

Though there can be no justification for representing the rules of just conduct as natural in the sense that they are part of an external and eternal order of things, or permanently implanted in an unalterable nature of man, or even in the sense that man's mind is so fashioned once and for all that he must adopt those particular rules of conduct, it does not follow from this that the rules of conduct which in fact guide him must be the product of a deliberate choice on his part; or that he is capable of forming a society by adopting any rules he decides upon; or that these rules may not be given to him independent of any particular person's will and in this sense exist 'objectively'. It is sometimes held that only what is universally true can be regarded as an objective fact and that everything which is specific to a particular society can therefore not be regarded as such.[76] But this certainly does not follow from the ordinary meaning of the term 'objective'. The views and opinions which shape the order of a society, as well as the resulting order of that society itself, are not dependent on any one person's decision and will often not be alterable by any concrete act of will; and in this sense they must be regarded as an objectively existing fact. Those results of human action which are not brought about by human design may therefore well be objectively given to us.

The evolutionary approach to law (and all other social institutions) which is here defended has thus as little to do with the rationalist theories of natural law as with legal positivism. It rejects both the interpretation of law as the construct of a super-natural force and its interpretation as the deliberate construct of any human mind. It does not stand in any sense between legal positivism and most natural law theories, but differs from either in a dimension different from that in which they differ from each other.

We must again refrain here from examining the methodological objection which the adherents of the pure theory of law are likely to raise against this position, namely that it is not a juristic 'science of norms', but what they would describe as a sociology of law.[77] In brief the answer to this contention is that even in order to ascertain what in a given community is in fact the law, not only the scientist but also the judge requires a theory which does not logically derive the validity of law from some fictitious 'basic norm', but which explains the function of this law; because the law which he often will have to find may consist in some yet unarticulated rule which serves the same function as the unquestioningly accepted rules of law—namely to assist the constant re-formation of a factually existing spontaneous order.[78]

Law and sovereignty

There is little we need to add now to what has been said earlier (volume I, chapter IV, pp. 92–3) on the concept of sovereignty which plays such a central role in positivist legal theory. It is of interest here chiefly because its interpretation by positivism as the necessarily unlimited power of some supreme legislative authority has become one of the chief supports of the theory of popular sovereignty or the unlimited powers of a democratic legislature. For a positivist who defines law so as to make its substantive content dependent on an act of will of the legislator, this conception becomes indeed a logical necessity. If the term law is used in this sense, any legal limitation of the power of the supreme legislator is by definition excluded. But if the power of the legislator is not derived from some fictitious basic norm, but from a state of widespread opinion concerning the kind of rules he is authorized to lay down, his power might well be limited without the intervention of a higher authority capable of expressing explicit acts of will.

The logic of the positivist argument would be compelling only if its assertion that all law derives from the will of a legislator did not merely mean, as it does in the system of Kelsen, that its validity is derived from some act of deliberate will, but that its content is so derived. This, however, is factually often not the case. A legislator, in trying to maintain a going spontaneous order, cannot pick and choose any rules he likes to confer validity upon them, if he wants to achieve his aim. His power is not unlimited because it rests on the fact that some of the rules which he makes enforceable are regarded as right by the citizens, and the acceptance by him of these rules necessarily limits his powers of making other rules enforceable.

The concept of sovereignty, like that of the 'state', may be an indispensable tool for international law—though I am not sure that if we accept the concept there as our starting point, we do not thereby make the very idea of an international law meaningless. But for the consideration of the problem of the internal character of a legal order, both concepts seem to be as unnecessary as they are misleading. Indeed the whole history of constitutionalism, at least since John Locke, which is the same as the history of liberalism, is that of a struggle against the positivist conception of sovereignty and the allied conception of the omnipotent state.

NINE

'SOCIAL' OR DISTRIBUTIVE
JUSTICE

So great is the uncertainty of merit, both from its natural
obscurity, and from the self-conceit of each individual, that no
determinate rule of conduct could ever follow from it.

David Hume*

Welfare, however, has no principle, neither for him who
receives it, nor for him who distributes it (one will place it here
and another there); because it depends on the material content
of the will, which is dependent upon particular facts and therefore incapable of a general rule.

Immanuel Kant*

The concept of 'social justice'

While in the preceding chapter I had to defend the conception of
justice as the indispensable foundation and limitation of all law, I
must now turn against an abuse of the word which threatens to
destroy the conception of law which made it the safeguard of
individual freedom. It is perhaps not surprising that men should
have applied to the joint effects of the actions of many people, even
where these were never foreseen or intended, the conception of
justice which they had developed with respect to the conduct of
individuals towards each other. 'Social' justice (or sometimes
'economic' justice) came to be regarded as an attribute which the
'actions' of society, or the 'treatment' of individuals and groups by
society, ought to possess. As primitive thinking usually does when
first noticing some regular processes, the results of the spontaneous
ordering of the market were interpreted as if some thinking being
deliberately directed them, or as if the particular benefits or harm
different persons derived from them were determined by deliberate
acts of will, and could therefore be guided by moral rules. This
conception of 'social' justice is thus a direct consequence of that
anthropomorphism or personification by which naive thinking tries

to account for all self-ordering processes. It is a sign of the immaturity of our minds that we have not yet outgrown these primitive concepts and still demand from an impersonal process which brings about a greater satisfaction of human desires than any deliberate human organization could achieve, that it conform to the moral precepts men have evolved for the guidance of their individual actions.[1]

The use of the term 'social justice' in this sense is of comparatively recent date, apparently not much older than a hundred years. The expression was occasionally used earlier to describe the organized efforts to enforce the rules of just individual conduct,[2] and it is to the present day sometimes employed in learned discussion to evaluate the effects of the existing institutions of society.[3] But the sense in which it is now generally used and constantly appealed to in public discussion, and in which it will be examined in this chapter, is essentially the same as that in which the expression 'distributive justice' had long been employed. It seems to have become generally current in this sense at the time when (and perhaps partly because) John Stuart Mill explicitly treated the two terms as equivalent in such statements as that

> society should treat all equally well who have deserved equally
> well of it, that is, who have deserved equally well absolutely.
> This is the highest abstract standard of social and distributive
> justice; towards which all institutions, and the efforts of all
> virtuous citizens should be made in the utmost degree to
> converge[4]

or that

> it is universally considered just that each person should obtain
> that (whether good or evil) which he deserves; and unjust that
> he should obtain a good, or be made to undergo an evil, which
> he does not deserve. This is perhaps the clearest and most
> emphatic form in which the idea of justice is conceived by the
> general mind. As it involves the idea of desert, the question
> arises of what constitutes desert.[5]

It is significant that the first of these two passages occurs in the description of one of five meanings of justice which Mill distinguishes, of which four refer to rules of just individual conduct while this one defines a factual state of affairs which may but need not have been brought about by deliberate human decision. Yet Mill appears to have been wholly unaware of the circumstance that in this meaning it refers to situations entirely different from those to which the four other meanings apply, or that this conception of 'social justice' leads straight to full-fledged socialism.

Such statements which explicitly connect 'social and distributive justice' with the 'treatment' by society of the individuals according to their 'deserts' bring out most clearly its difference from plain justice, and at the same time the cause of the vacuity of the concept: the demand for 'social justice' is addressed not to the individual but to society—yet society, in the strict sense in which it must be distinguished from the apparatus of government, is incapable of acting for a specific purpose, and the demand for 'social justice' therefore becomes a demand that the members of society should organize themselves in a manner which makes it possible to assign particular shares of the product of society to the different individuals or groups. The primary question then becomes whether there exists a moral duty to submit to a power which can co-ordinate the efforts of the members of society with the aim of achieving a particular pattern of distribution regarded as just.

If the existence of such a power is taken for granted, the question of how the available means for the satisfaction of needs ought to be shared out becomes indeed a question of justice—though not a question to which prevailing morals provide an answer. Even the assumption from which most of the modern theorists of 'social justice' start, namely that it would require equal shares for all in so far as special considerations do not demand a departure from this principle, would then appear to be justified. [6] But the prior question is whether it is moral that men be subjected to the powers of direction that would have to be exercised in order that the benefits derived by the individuals could be meaningfully described as just or unjust.

It has of course to be admitted that the manner in which the benefits and burdens are apportioned by the market mechanism would in many instances have to be regarded as very unjust *if* it were the result of a deliberate allocation to particular people. But this is not the case. Those shares are the outcome of a process the effect of which on particular people was neither intended nor foreseen by anyone when the institutions first appeared—institutions which were then permitted to continue because it was found that they improve for all or most the prospects of having their needs satisfied. To demand justice from such a process is clearly absurd, and to single out some people in such a society as entitled to a particular share evidently unjust.

The conquest of public imagination by 'social justice'

The appeal to 'social justice' has nevertheless by now become the most widely used and most effective argument in political discussion. Almost every claim for government action on behalf of particular groups is advanced in its name, and if it can be made to appear that a certain measure is demanded by 'social justice', opposition to it will rapidly weaken. People may dispute whether or not the particular measure is required by 'social justice'. But that this is the standard which ought to guide political action, and that the expression has a definite meaning, is hardly ever questioned. In consequence, there are today probably no political movements or politicians who do not readily appeal to 'social justice' in support of the particular measures which they advocate.

It also can scarcely be denied that the demand for 'social justice' has already in a great measure transformed the social order and is continuing to transform it in a direction which those who called for it never foresaw. Though the phrase has undoubtedly helped occasionally to make the law more equal for all, whether the demand for justice in distribution has in any sense made society juster or reduced discontent must remain doubtful.

The expression of course described from the beginning the aspirations which were at the heart of socialism. Although classical socialism has usually been defined by its demand for the socialization of the means of production, this was for it chiefly a means thought to be essential in order to bring about a 'just' distribution of wealth; and since socialists have later discovered that this redistribution could in a great measure, and against less resistance, be brought about by taxation (and government services financed by it), and have in practice often shelved their earlier demands, the realization of 'social justice' has become their chief promise. It might indeed be said that the main difference between the order of society at which classical liberalism aimed and the sort of society into which it is now being transformed is that the former was governed by principles of just individual conduct while the new society is to satisfy the demands for 'social justice'—or, in other words, that the former demanded just action by the individuals while the latter more and more places the duty of justice on authorities with power to command people what to do.

The phrase could exercise this effect because it has gradually been taken over from the socialist not only by all the other political movements but also by most teachers and preachers of morality. It seems in particular to have been embraced by a large section of the clergy of all Christian denominations, who, while increasingly losing their faith in a supernatural revelation, appear to have sought a refuge and consolation in a new 'social' religion which substitutes a temporal for a celestial promise of justice, and who hope that they can thus continue their striving to do good. The Roman Catholic church especially has made the aim of 'social justice' part of its official doctrine; [7] but the ministers of most Christian denominations appear to vie with each other with such offers of more mundane aims—which also seem to provide the chief foundation for renewed ecumenical efforts.

The various modern authoritarian or dictatorial governments have of course no less proclaimed 'social justice' as their chief aim. We have it on the authority of Mr Andrei Sakharov that millions of men in Russia are the victims of a terror that 'attempts to conceal itself behind the slogan of social justice'.

The commitment to 'social justice' has in fact become the chief outlet for moral emotion, the distinguishing attribute of the good man, and the recognized sign of the possession of a moral conscience. Though people may occasionally be perplexed to say which of the conflicting claims advanced in its name are valid, scarcely anyone doubts that the expression has a definite meaning, describes a high ideal, and points to grave defects of the existing social order which urgently call for correction. Even though until recently one would have vainly sought in the extensive literature for an intelligible definition of the term, [8] there still seems to exist little doubt, either among ordinary people or among the learned, that the expression has a definite and well understood sense.

But the near-universal acceptance of a belief does not prove that it is valid or even meaningful any more than the general belief in witches or ghosts proved the validity of these concepts. What we have to deal with in the case of 'social justice' is simply a quasi-religious superstition of the kind which we should respectfully leave in peace so long as it merely makes those happy who hold it, but which we must fight when it becomes the pretext of coercing other men. And the prevailing belief in 'social justice' is at present probably the gravest threat to most other values of a free civilization.

Whether Edward Gibbon was wrong or not, there can be no doubt that moral and religious beliefs can destroy a civilization and that, where such doctrines prevail, not only the most cherished beliefs but also the most revered moral leaders, sometimes saintly figures whose unselfishness is beyond question, may become grave dangers to the values which the same people regard as unshakeable. Against this threat we can protect ourselves only by subjecting even our dearest dreams of a better world to ruthless rational dissection.

It seems to be widely believed that 'social justice' is just a new moral value which we must add to those that were recognized in the past, and that it can be fitted within the existing framework of moral rules. What is not sufficiently recognized is that in order to give this phrase meaning a complete change of the whole character of the social order will have to be effected, and that some of the values which used to govern it will have to be sacrificed. It is such a transformation of society into one of a fundamentally different type which is currently occurring piecemeal and without awareness of the outcome to which it must lead. It was in the belief that something like 'social justice' could thereby be achieved, that people have placed in the hands of government powers which it can now not refuse to employ in order to satisfy the claims of the ever increasing number of special interests who have learnt to employ the open sesame of 'social justice'.

I believe that 'social justice' will ultimately be recognized as a will-o'-the-wisp which has lured men to abandon many of the values which in the past have inspired the development of civilization—an attempt to satisfy a craving inherited from the traditions of the small group but which is meaningless in the Great Society of free men. Unfortunately, this vague desire which has become one of the strongest bonds spurring people of good will to action, not only is bound to be disappointed. This would be sad enough. But, like most attempts to pursue an unattainable goal, the striving for it will also produce highly undesirable consequences, and in particular lead to the destruction of the indispensible environment in which the traditional moral values alone can flourish, namely personal freedom.

The inapplicability of the concept of justice to the results of a spontaneous process

It is now necessary clearly to distinguish between two wholly different problems which the demand for 'social justice' raises in a market order.

The first is whether within an economic order based on the market the concept of 'social justice' has any meaning or content whatever.

The second is whether it is possible to preserve a market order while imposing upon it (in the name of 'social justice' or any other pretext) some pattern of remuneration based on the assessment of the performance or the needs of different individuals or groups by an authority possessing the power to enforce it.

The answer to each of these questions is a clear no.

Yet it is the general belief in the validity of the concept of 'social justice' which drives all contemporary societies into greater and greater efforts of the second kind and which has a peculiar self-accelerating tendency: the more dependent the position of the individuals or groups is seen to become on the actions of government, the more they will insist that the governments aim at some recognizable scheme of distributive justice; and the more governments try to realize some preconceived pattern of desirable distribution, the more they must subject the position of the different individuals and groups to their control. So long as the belief in 'social justice' governs political action, this process must progressively approach nearer and nearer to a totalitarian system.

We shall at first concentrate on the problem of the meaning, or rather lack of meaning, of the term 'social justice', and only later consider the effects which the efforts to impose *any* preconceived pattern of distribution must have on the structure of the society subjected to them.

The contention that in a society of free men (as distinct from any compulsory organization) the concept of social justice is strictly empty and meaningless will probably appear as quite unbelievable to most people. Are we not all constantly disquieted by watching how unjustly life treats different people and by seeing the deserving suffer and the unworthy prosper? And do we not all have a sense of fitness, and watch it with satisfaction, when we recognize a reward to be appropriate to effort or sacrifice?

The first insight which should shake this certainty is that we experience the same feelings also with respect to differences in human fates for which clearly no human agency is responsible and which it would therefore clearly be absurd to call injustice. Yet we do cry out against the injustice when a succession of calamities befalls one family while another steadily prospers, when a meritorious effort is frustrated by some unforeseeable accident, and particularly if of many people whose endeavours seem equally great, some succeed brilliantly while others utterly fail. It is certainly tragic to see the failure of the most meritorious efforts of parents to bring up their children, of young men to build a career, or of an explorer or scientist pursuing a brilliant idea. And we will protest against such a fate although we do not know anyone who is to blame for it, or any way in which such disappointments can be prevented.

It is no different with regard to the general feeling of injustice about the distribution of material goods in a society of free men. Though we are in this case less ready to admit it, our complaints about the outcome of the market as unjust do not really assert that somebody has been unjust; and there is no answer to the question of *who* has been unjust. Society has simply become the new deity to which we complain and clamour for redress if it does not fulfil the expectations it has created. There is no individual and no co-operating group of people against which the sufferer would have a just complaint, and there are no conceivable rules of just individual conduct which would at the same time secure a functioning order and prevent such disappointments.

The only blame implicit in those complaints is that we tolerate a system in which each is allowed to choose his occupation and therefore nobody can have the power and the duty to see that the results correspond to our wishes. For in such a system in which each is allowed to use his knowledge for his own purposes[9] the concept of 'social justice' is necessarily empty and meaningless, because in it nobody's will can determine the relative incomes of the different people, or prevent that they be partly dependent on accident. 'Social justice' can be given a meaning only in a directed or 'command' economy (such as an army) in which the individuals are ordered what to do; and any particular conception of 'social justice' could be realized only in such a centrally directed system. It presupposes that people are guided by specific directions and not by rules of just individual conduct. Indeed, no system of rules of just individual conduct, and therefore no free action of the individuals, could produce results satisfying any principle of distributive justice.

We are of course not wrong in perceiving that the effects of the processes of a free society on the fates of the different individuals are not distributed according to some recognizable principle of justice. Where we go wrong is in concluding from this that they are unjust and that somebody is to be blamed for this. In a free society in which the position of the different individuals and groups is not the result of anybody's design—or could, within such a society, be altered in accordance with a generally applicable principle—the differences in reward simply cannot meaningfully be described as just or unjust. There are, no doubt, many kinds of individual action which are aimed at affecting particular remunerations and which might be called just or unjust. But there are no principles of individual conduct which would produce a pattern of distribution which as such could be called just, and therefore also no possibility for the individual to know what he would have to do to secure a just remuneration of his fellows.

The rationale of the economic game in which only the conduct of the players but not the result can be just

We have seen earlier that justice is an attribute of human conduct which we have learnt to exact because a certain kind of conduct is required to secure the formation and maintenance of a beneficial order of actions. The attribute of justice may thus be predicated about the intended results of human action but not about circumstances which have not deliberately been brought about by men. Justice requires that in the 'treatment' of another person or persons, i.e. in the intentional actions affecting the well-being of other persons, certain uniform rules of conduct be observed. It clearly has no application to the manner in which the impersonal process of the market allocates command over goods and services to particular people: this can be neither just nor unjust, because the results are not intended or foreseen, and depend on a multitude of circumstances not known in their totality to anybody. The conduct of the individuals in that process may well be just or unjust; but since their wholly just actions will have consequences for others which were neither intended nor foreseen, these effects do not thereby become just or unjust.

The fact is simply that we consent to retain, and agree to enforce, uniform rules for a procedure which has greatly improved the chances of all to have their wants satisfied, but at the price of all individuals and groups incurring the risk of unmerited failure. With the acceptance of this procedure the recompense of different groups and individuals becomes exempt from deliberate control. It is the only procedure yet discovered in which information widely dispersed among millions of men can be effectively utilized for the benefit of all—and used by assuring to all an individual liberty desirable for itself on ethical grounds. It is a procedure which of course has never been 'designed' but which we have learnt gradually to improve after we had discovered how it increased the efficiency of men in the groups who had evolved it.

It is a procedure which, as Adam Smith (and apparently before him the ancient Stoics) understood, [10] in all important respects (except that normally it is not pursued solely as a diversion) is wholly analogous to a game, namely a game partly of skill and partly of chance. We shall later describe it as the game of catallaxy. It proceeds, like all games, according to rules guiding the actions of individual participants whose aims, skills, and knowledge are different, with the consequence that the outcome will be unpredictable and that there will regularly be winners and losers. And while, as in a game, we are right in insisting that it be fair and that nobody cheat, it would be nonsensical to demand that the results for the different players be just. They will of necessity be determined partly by skill and partly by luck. Some of the circumstances which make the services of a person more or less valuable to his fellows, or which may make it desirable that he change the direction of his efforts, are not of human design or foreseeable by men.

We shall in the next chapter have to return to the rationale of the discovery procedure which the game of competition in a market in effect constitutes. Here we must content ourselves with emphasizing that the results for the different individuals and groups of a procedure for utilizing more information than any one person or agency can possess, must themselves be unpredictable, and must often be different from the hopes and intentions which determined the direction and intensity of their striving; and that we can make effective use of that dispersed knowledge only if (as Adam Smith was also one of the first to see clearly) [11] we allow the principle of negative feedback to operate, which means that some must suffer unmerited disappointment.

We shall also see later that the importance for the functioning of the market order of particular prices or wages, and therefore of the incomes of the different groups and individuals, is not due chiefly to the effects of the prices on all of those who receive them, but to the effects of the prices on those for whom they act as signals to change the direction of their efforts. Their function is not so much to reward people for what they *have* done as to tell them what in their own as well as in general interest they *ought* to do. We shall then also see that, to hold out a sufficient incentive for those movements which are required to maintain a market order, it will often be necessary that the return of people's efforts do *not* correspond to recognizable merit, but should show that, in spite of the best efforts of which they were capable, and for reasons they could not have known, their efforts were either more or less successful than they had reason to expect. In a spontaneous order the question of whether or not someone has done the 'right' thing cannot always be a matter of merit, but must be determined independently of whether the persons concerned ought or could have known what was required.

The long and the short of it all is that men can be allowed to decide what work to do only if the remuneration they can expect to get for it corresponds to the value their services have to those of their fellows who receive them; and that *these values which their services will have to their fellows will often have no relations to their individual merits or needs.* Reward for merit earned and indication of what a person should do, both in his own and in his fellows' interest, are different things. It is not good intentions or needs but doing what in fact most benefits others, irrespective of motive, which will secure the best reward. Among those who try to climb Mount Everest or to reach the Moon, we also honour not those who made the greatest efforts, but those who got there first.

The general failure to see that in this connection we cannot meaningfully speak of the justice or injustice of the results is partly due to the misleading use of the term 'distribution' which inevitably suggests a personal distributing agent whose will or choice determines the relative position of the different persons or groups.[12] There is of course no such agent, and we use an impersonal process to determine the allocation of benefits precisely because through its operation we can bring about a structure of relative prices and remunerations that will determine a size and composition of the total output which assures that the real equivalent of each individual's share that accident or skill assigns to him will be as large as we know to make it.

It would serve little purpose to enquire here at greater length into the relative importance of skill and luck in actually determining relative incomes. This will clearly differ a great deal between different trades, localities and times, and in particular between highly

competitive and less enterprising societies. I am on the whole in-
clined to believe that within any one trade or profession the correspondence between individual ability and industry is higher than
is commonly admitted, but that the relative position of all the
members of a particular trade or profession compared with others
will more often be affected by circumstances beyond their control
and knowledge. (This may also be one reason why what is called
'social' injustice is generally regarded as a graver fault of the existing order than the corresponding misfortunes of individuals.)[13] But
the decisive point is not that the price mechanism does on the
whole bring it about that rewards are proportioned to skill and
effort, but that even where it is clear to us that luck plays a great
part, and we have no idea why some are regularly luckier in guess-
ing than others, it is still in the general interest to proceed on the
presumption that the past success of some people in picking winners makes it probable that they will also do so in the future, and
that it is therefore worthwhile to induce them to continue their
attempts.

The alleged necessity of a belief in the justice of rewards

It has been argued persuasively that people will tolerate major inequalities of the material positions only if they believe that the
different individuals get on the whole what they deserve, that they
did in fact support the market order only because (and so long as)
they thought that the differences of remuneration corresponded
roughly to differences of merit, and that in consequence the maintenance of a free society presupposes the belief that some sort of
'social justice' is being done.[14] The market order, however, does
not in fact owe its origin to such beliefs, nor was originally justified
in this manner. This order could develop, after its earlier beginnings had decayed during the middle ages and to some extent been
destroyed by the restrictions imposed by authority, when a thous-
and years of vain efforts to discover substantively just prices or
wages were abandoned and the late schoolmen recognized them to
be empty formulae and taught instead that the prices determined
by just conduct of the parties in the market, i.e. the competitive
prices arrived at without fraud, monopoly and violence, was all that
justice required.[15] It was from this tradition that John Locke and
his contemporaries derived the classical liberal conception of justice
for which, as has been rightly said, it was only 'the way in which

competition was carried on, not its results',[16] that could be just or unjust.

It is unquestionably true that, particularly among those who were very successful in the market order, a belief in a much stronger moral justification of individual success developed, and that, long after the basic principles of such an order had been fully elaborated and approved by catholic moral philosophers, it had in the Anglo–Saxon world received strong support from Calvinist teaching. It certainly is important in the market order (or free enterprise society, misleadingly called 'capitalism') that the individuals believe that their well-being depends primarily on their own efforts and decisions. Indeed, few circumstances will do more to make a person energetic and efficient than the belief that it depends chiefly on him whether he will reach the goals he has set himself. For this reason this belief is often encouraged by education and governing opinion —it seems to me, generally much to the benefit of most of the members of the society in which it prevails, who will owe many important material and moral improvements to persons guided by it. But it leads no doubt also to an exaggerated confidence in the truth of this generalization which to those who regard themselves (and perhaps are) equally able but have failed must appear as a bitter irony and severe provocation.

It is probably a misfortune that, especially in the USA, popular writers like Samuel Smiles and Horatio Alger, and later the sociologist W. G. Sumner, have defended free enterprise on the ground that it regularly rewards the deserving, and it bodes ill for the future of the market order that this seems to have become the only defence of it which is understood by the general public. That it has largely become the basis of the self-esteem of the businessman often gives him an air of self-righteousness which does not make him more popular.

It is therefore a real dilemma to what extent we ought to encourage in the young the belief that when they really try they will succeed, or should rather emphasize that inevitably some unworthy will succeed and some worthy fail—whether we ought to allow the views of those groups to prevail with whom the over-confidence in the appropriate reward of the able and industrious is strong and who in consequence will do much that benefits the rest, and whether without such partly erroneous beliefs the large numbers will tolerate actual differences in rewards which will be based only partly on achievement and partly on mere chance.

There is no 'value to society'

The futile medieval search for the just price and just wage, finally
abandoned when it was recognized that only that 'natural' price
could be regarded as just which would be arrived at in a competitive
market where it would be determined not by any human laws or
decrees but would depend on so many circumstances that it could
be known beforehand only by God,[17] was not the end of the search
for that philosophers' stone. It was revived in modern times, not
only by the general demand for 'social justice', but also by the long
and equally abortive efforts to discover criteria of justice in connection with the procedures for reconciliation or arbitration in wage
disputes. Nearly a century of endeavours by public spirited men
and women in many parts of the world to discover principles by
which just wage rates could be determined have, as more and more
of them acknowledge, produced not a single rule which would do
this.[18] It is somewhat surprising in view of this when we find an
experienced arbitrator like Lady Wootton, after admitting that
arbitrators are 'engaged in the impossible task of attempting to do
justice in an ethical vacuum', because 'nobody knows in this context
what justice is', drawing from it the conclusion that the criteria
should be determined by legislation, and explicitly demand a political determination of all wages and incomes.[19] One can hardly carry
any further the illusion that Parliament can determine what is just,
and I don't suppose the writer would really wish to defend the
atrocious principle implied that all rewards should be determined
by political power.

Another source of the conception that the categories of just and
unjust can be meaningfully applied to the remunerations determined
by the market is the idea that the different services have a determined and ascertainable 'value to society', and that the actual
remuneration frequently differs from the value. But though the
conception of a 'value to society' is sometimes carelessly used even
by economists, there is strictly no such thing and the expression
implies the same sort of anthropomorphism or personification of
society as the term 'social justice'. Services can have value only to
particular people (or an organization), and any particular service
will have very different values for different members of the same
society. To regard them differently is to treat society not as a
spontaneous order of free men but as an organization whose members are all made to serve a single hierarchy of ends. This would

necessarily be a totalitarian system in which personal freedom would be absent.

Although it is tempting to speak of a 'value to society' instead of a man's value to his fellows, it is in fact highly misleading if we say, e.g., that a man who supplies matches to millions and thereby earns $200,000 a year is worth more 'to society' than a man who supplies great wisdom or exquisite pleasure to a few thousand and thereby earns $20,000 a year. Even the performance of a Beethoven sonata, a painting by Leonardo or a play by Shakespeare have no 'value to society' but a value only to those who know and appreciate them. And it has little meaning to assert that a boxer or a crooner is worth more to society than a violin virtuoso or a ballet dancer if the former renders services to millions and the latter to a much smaller group. The point is not that the true values are different, but that the values attached to the different services by different groups of people are incommensurable; all that these expressions mean is merely that one in fact receives a larger aggregate sum from a larger number of people than the other.[20]

Incomes earned in the market by different persons will normally not correspond to the relative values of their services to any one person. Although, in so far as any one of a given group of different commodities is consumed by any one person, he or she will buy so much of each that the relative values to them of the last units bought will correspond to their relative prices, many pairs of commodities will never be consumed by the same person: the relative price of articles consumed only by men and of articles consumed only by women will not correspond to the relative values of these articles to anybody.

The remunerations which the individuals and groups receive in the market are thus determined by what these services are worth to those who receive them (or, strictly speaking, to the last pressing demand for them which can still be satisfied by the available supply) and not by some fictitious 'value to society'.

Another source of the complaint about the alleged injustice of this principle of remuneration is that the remuneration thus determined will often be much higher than would be necessary to induce the recipient to render those services. This is perfectly true but necessary if all who render the same service are to receive the same remuneration, if the kind of service in question is to be increased so long as the price still exceeds costs, and if anyone who wishes to buy or sell it at the current price is to be able to do so.

The consequence must be that all but the marginal sellers make a gain in excess of what was necessary to induce them to render the services in question—just as all but the marginal buyers will get what they buy for less than they were prepared to pay. The remuneration of the market will therefore hardly ever seem just in the sense in which somebody might endeavour justly to compensate others for the efforts and sacrifice incurred for his benefit.

The consideration of the different attitudes which different groups will take to the remuneration of different services incidentally also shows that the large numbers by no means grudge all the incomes higher than theirs, but generally only those earned by activities the functions of which they do not understand or which they even regard as harmful. I have never known ordinary people grudge the very high earnings of the boxer or torero, the football idol or the cinema star or the jazz king—they seem often even to revel vicariously in the display of extreme luxury and waste of such figures compared with which those of industrial magnates or financial tycoons pale. It is where most people do not comprehend the usefulness of an activity, and frequently because they erroneously regard it as harmful (the 'speculator'—often combined with the belief that only dishonest activities can bring so much money), and especially where the large earnings are used to accumulate a fortune (again out of the erroneous belief that it would be desirable that it should be spent rather than invested) that the outcry about the injustice of it arises. Yet the complex structure of the modern Great Society would clearly not work if the remunerations of all the different activities were determined by the opinion which the majority holds of their value—or indeed if they were dependent on any one person's understanding or knowledge of the importance of all the different activities required for the functioning of the system.

The main point is not that the masses have in most instances no idea of the values which a man's activities have to his fellows, and that it is necessarily their prejudices which would determine the use of the government's power. It is that nobody knows except in so far as the market tells him. It is true enough that our esteem of particular activities often differs from the value given to them by the market; and we express this feeling by an outcry about the injustice of it. But when we ask what ought to be the relative remunerations of a nurse and a butcher, of a coal miner and a judge at a high court, of the deep sea diver or the cleaner of sewers, of the organizer of a new industry and a jockey, of the inspector of taxes and the inventor of a life-saving drug, of the jet pilot or the professor of mathematics, the appeal to 'social justice' does not give us the slightest help in deciding—and if we use it it is no more than an insinuation that the others ought to agree with our view without giving any reason for it.

It might be objected that, although we cannot give the term 'social justice' a precise meaning, this need not be a fatal objection because the position may be similar to that which I have earlier contended exists with regard to justice proper: we might not know what is 'socially just' yet know quite well what is 'socially unjust'; and by persistently eliminating 'social injustice' whenever we encounter it, gradually approach 'social justice'. This, however, does not provide a way out of the basic difficulty. There can be no test by which we can discover what is 'socially unjust' because there is no subject by which such an injustice can be committed, and there are no rules of individual conduct the observance of which in the market order would secure to the individuals and groups the position which as such (as distinguished from the procedure by which it is determined) would appear just to us.[21] It does not belong to the category of error but to that of nonsense, like the term 'a moral stone'.

The meaning of 'social'

One might hope to get some help in the search for the meaning of 'social justice' by examining the meaning of the attribute 'social'; but the attempt to do so soon leads into a quagmire of confusion nearly as bad as that which surrounds 'social justice' itself.[22] Originally 'social' had of course a clear meaning (analogous to formations like 'national', 'tribal', or 'organizational'), namely that of pertaining to, or characteristic of the structure and operations of society. In this sense justice clearly is a social phenomenon and the addition of 'social' to the noun a pleonasm[23] such as if we spoke of 'social language'—though in occasional early uses it might have been intended to distinguish the generally prevailing views of justice from that held by particular persons or groups.

But 'social justice' as used today is not 'social' in the sense of 'social norms', i.e. something which has developed as a practice of individual action in the course of social evolution, not a product of society or of a social process, but a conception to be imposed upon society. It was the reference of 'social' to the whole of society, or to the interests of all its members, which led to its gradually acquiring a predominant meaning of moral approbation. When it came into general use during the third quarter of the last century it was meant to convey an appeal to the still ruling classes to concern themselves more with the welfare of the much more numerous poor whose interests had not received adequate consideration.[24] The 'social question' was posed as an appeal to the conscience of the upper classes to recognize their responsibility for the welfare of the neglected sections of society whose voices had till then carried little weight in the councils of government. 'Social policy' (or *Socialpolitik* in the language of the country then leading in the movement) became the order of the day, the chief concern of all progressive and good people, and 'social' came increasingly to displace such terms as 'ethical' or simply 'good'.

But from such an appeal to the conscience of the public to concern themselves with the unfortunate ones and recognize them as members of the same society, the conception gradually came to mean that 'society' ought to hold itself responsible for the particular material position of all its members, and for assuring that each received what was 'due' to him. It implied that the processes of society should be deliberately directed to particular results and, by personifying society, represented it as a subject endowed with a conscious mind, capable of being guided in its operation by moral principles.[25] 'Social' became more and more the description of the pre-eminent virtue, the attribute in which the good man excelled and the ideal by which communal action was to be guided.

But while this development indefinitely extended the field of application of the term 'social', it did not give it the required new meaning. It even so much deprived it of its original descriptive meaning that American sociologists have found it necessary to coin the new term 'societal' in its place. Indeed, it has produced a situation in which 'social' can be used to describe almost any action as publicly desirable and has at the same time the effect of depriving any terms with which it is combined of clear meaning. Not only 'social justice' but also 'social democracy', 'social market economy'[26] or the 'social state of law' (or rule of law—in German *sozialer Rechtsstaat*) are expressions which, though justice, democracy, the market economy or the *Rechtsstaat* have by themselves perfectly good meanings, the addition of the adjective 'social' makes them capable of meaning almost anything one likes. The word has indeed become one of the chief sources of confusion of political discourse and can probably no longer be reclaimed for a useful purpose.

There is apparently no end to the violence that will be done to language to further some ideal and the example of 'social justice' has recently given rise to the expression 'global justice'! Its negative, 'global injustice', was defined by an ecumenical gathering of American religious leaders as 'characterized by a dimension of sin in the economic, political, social, sexual, and class structures and systems of global society'![27] It would seem as if the conviction that one is arguing in a good cause produced more sloppy thinking and even intellectual dishonesty than perhaps any other cause.

'Social justice' and equality

The most common attempts to give meaning to the concept of 'social justice' resort to egalitarian considerations and argue that every departure from equality of material benefits enjoyed has to be justified by some recognizable common interest which these differences serve.[28] This is based on a specious analogy with the situation in which some human agency has to distribute rewards, in which case indeed justice would require that these rewards be determined in accordance with some recognizable rule of general applicability. But earnings in a market system, though people tend to regard them as rewards, do not serve such a function. Their rationale (if one may use this term for a role which was not designed but developed because it assisted human endeavour without people understanding how), is rather to indicate to people what they ought to do if the order is to be maintained on which they all rely. The prices which must be paid in a market economy for different kinds of labour and other factors of production if individual efforts are to match, although they will be affected by effort, diligence, skill, need, etc., cannot conform to any one of these magnitudes; and considerations of justice just do not make sense[29] with respect to the determination of a magnitude which does not depend on anyone's will or desire, but on circumstances which nobody knows in their totality.

The contention that all differences in earnings must be justified by some corresponding difference in deserts is one which would certainly not have been thought to be obvious in a community of farmers or merchants or artisans, that is, in a society in which success or failure were clearly seen to depend only in part on skill and industry, and in part on pure accident which might hit anyone—although even in such societies individuals were known to complain to God or fortune about the injustice of their fate. But, though people resent that their remuneration should in part depend on pure accident, that is in fact precisely what it must if the market order is to adjust itself promptly to the unavoidable and unforeseen changes in circumstances, and the individual is to be allowed to decide what to do. The now prevalent attitude could arise only in a society in which large numbers worked as members of organizations in which they were remunerated at stipulated rates for time worked. Such communities will not ascribe the different fortunes of its members to the operation of an impersonal mechanism which serves to guide the directions of efforts, but to some human power that ought to allocate shares according to merit.

The postulate of material equality would be a natural starting point only if it were a necessary circumstance that the shares of the different individuals or groups were in such a manner determined by deliberate human decision. In a society in which this were an unquestioned fact, justice would indeed demand that the allocation of the means for the satisfaction of human needs were effected according to some uniform principle such as merit or need (or some combination of these), and that, where the principle adopted did not justify a difference, the shares of the different individuals should be equal. The prevalent demand for material equality is probably often based on the belief that the existing inequalities are the effect of somebody's decision—a belief which would be wholly mistaken in a genuine market order and has still only very limited validity in the highly interventionist 'mixed' economy existing in most countries today. This now prevalent form of economic order has in fact attained its character largely as a result of governmental measures aiming at what was thought to be required by 'social justice'.

When the choice, however, is between a genuine market order, which does not and cannot achieve a distribution corresponding to any standard of material justice, and a system in which government uses its powers to put some such standard into effect, the question is not whether government ought to exercise, justly or unjustly, powers it must exercise in any case, but whether government should possess and exercise additional powers which can be used to determine the shares of the different members of society. The demand for 'social justice', in other words, does not merely require government to observe some principle of action according to uniform rules in those actions which it must perform in any case, but demands that it undertake additional activities, and thereby assume new responsibilities—tasks which are not necessary for maintaining law and order and providing for certain collective needs which the market could not satisfy.

The great problem is whether this new demand for equality does not conflict with the equality of the rules of conduct which government must enforce on all in a free society. There is, of course, a great difference between government treating all citizens according to the same rules in all the activities it undertakes for other purposes, and government doing what is required in order to place the different citizens in equal (or less unequal) material positions. Indeed, there may arise a sharp conflict between these two aims. Since people will differ in many attributes which government cannot alter, to secure for them the same material position would require that government treat them very differently. Indeed, to assure the same material position to people who differ greatly in strength, intelligence, skill, knowledge and perseverance as well as in their physical and social environment, government would clearly have to treat them very differently to compensate for those disadvantages and deficiencies it could not directly alter. Strict equality of those benefits which government could provide for all, on the other hand, would clearly lead to inequality of the material positions.

This, however, is not the only and not even the chief reason why a government aiming to secure for its citizens equal material positions (or any determined pattern of material welfare) would have to treat them very unequally. It would have to do so because under such a system it would have to undertake to tell people what to do. Once the rewards the individual can expect are no longer an appropriate indication of how to direct their efforts to where they are most needed, because these rewards correspond not to the value which their services have for their fellows, but to the moral merit or desert the persons are deemed to have earned, they lose the guiding function they have in the market order and would have to be replaced by the commands of the directing authority. A central planning office would, however, have to decide on the tasks to be allotted to the different groups or individuals wholly on grounds of expediency or efficiency and, in order to achieve its ends, would have to impose upon them very different duties and burdens. The individuals might be treated according to uniform rules so far as their rewards were concerned, but certainly not with respect to the different kinds of work they would have to be made to do. In assigning people to their different tasks, the central planning authority would have to be guided by considerations of efficiency and expediency and not by principles of justice or equality. No less than in the market order would the individuals in the common interest have to submit to great inequality—only these inequalities would be determined not by the interaction of individual skills in an impersonal process, but by the uncontradictable decision of authority.

As is becoming clear in ever increasing fields of welfare policy, an authority instructed to achieve particular results for the individuals must be given essentially arbitrary powers to make the individuals do what seems necessary to achieve the required result. Full equality for most cannot but mean the equal submission of the great masses under the command of some élite who manages their affairs. While an equality of rights under a limited government is possible and an essential condition of individual freedom, a claim for equality of material position can be met only by a government with totalitarian powers.[30]

We are of course not wrong when we perceive that the effects on the different individuals and groups of the economic processes of a free society are not distributed according to some recognizable principle of justice. Where we go wrong is in concluding from this that they are unjust and that somebody is responsible and to be blamed for this. In a free society in which the position of the different individuals and groups is not the result of anybody's design—or could within such a society not be altered in accordance with a principle of general applicability—the differences in rewards cannot meaningfully be described as just or unjust. There are, no doubt, many kinds of individual actions which are aimed at affecting particular remunerations and which might be regarded as unjust. But there are no principles of individual conduct which would produce a pattern of distribution which as such could be called just, and therefore also no possibility for the individual to know what he would have to do to secure a just remuneration of his fellows.

Our whole system of morals is a system of rules of individual conduct, and in a Great Society no conduct guided by such rules, or by decisions of the individuals guided by such rules, could produce for the individuals results which would appear to us as just in the sense in which we regard designed rewards as just or unjust: simply because in such a society nobody has the power or the knowledge which would enable him to ensure that those affected by his actions will get what he thinks right for them to get. Nor could anyone who is assured remuneration according to some principle which is accepted as constituting 'social justice' be allowed to decide what he is to do: remuneration indicating how urgent it was that a certain work should be done could not be just in this sense, because the need for work of a particular kind would often depend on unforeseeable accidents and certainly not on the good intentions or efforts of those able to perform it. And an authority that fixed remunerations with the intention of thereby reducing the kind and number of people thought necessary in each occupation could not make these remunerations 'just', i.e. proportionate to desert, or need, or the merits of any other claim of the persons concerned, but would have to offer what was necessary to attract or retain the number of people wanted in each kind of activity.

'Equality of opportunity'

It is of course not to be denied that in the existing market order not only the results but also the initial chances of different individuals are often very different; they are affected by circumstances of their physical and social environment which are beyond their control but in many particular respects might be altered by some governmental action. The demand for equality of opportunity or equal starting conditions (*Startgerechtigkeit*) appeals to, and has been supported by, many who in general favour the free market order. So far as this refers to such facilities and opportunities as are of necessity affected by governmental decisions (such as appointments to public office and the like), the demand was indeed one of the central points of classical liberalism, usually expressed by the French phrase 'la carrière ouverte aux talents'. There is also much to be said in favour of the government providing on an equal basis the means for the schooling of minors who are not yet fully responsible citizens, even though there are grave doubts whether we ought to allow government to administer them.

But all this would still be very far from creating real equality of opportunity, even for persons possessing the same abilities. To achieve this government would have to control the whole physical and human environment of all persons, and have to endeavour to provide at least equivalent chances for each; and the more government succeeded in these endeavours, the stronger would become the legitimate demand that, on the same principle, any still remaining handicaps must be removed—or compensated for by putting extra burden on the still relatively favoured. This would have to go on until government literally controlled every circumstance which could affect any person's well-being. Attractive as the phrase of equality of opportunity at first sounds, once the idea is extended beyond the facilities which for other reasons have to be provided by government, it becomes a wholly illusory ideal, and any attempt concretely to realize it apt to produce a nightmare.

'Social justice' and freedom under the law

The idea that men ought to be rewarded in accordance with the assessed merits or deserts of their services 'to society' presupposes an authority which not only distributes these rewards but also assigns to the individuals the tasks for the performance of which they will be rewarded. In other words, if 'social justice' is to be brought about, the individuals must be required to obey not merely general rules but specific demands directed to them only. The type of social order in which the individuals are directed to serve a single system of ends is the organization and not the spontaneous order of the market, that is, not a system in which the individual is free because bound only by general rules of just conduct, but a system in which all are subject to specific directions by authority.

It appears sometimes to be imagined that a mere alteration of the rules of individual conduct could bring about the realization of 'social justice'. But there can be no set of such rules, no principles by which the individuals could so govern their conduct that in a Great Society the joint effect of their activities would be a distribution of benefits which could be described as materially just, or any other specific and intended allocation of advantages and disadvantages among particular people or groups. In order to achieve *any* particular pattern of distribution through the market process, each producer would have to know, not only whom his efforts will benefit (or harm), but also how well off all the other people (actually or potentially) affected by his activities will be as the result of the services they are receiving from other members of the society. As we have seen earlier, appropriate rules of conduct can determine only the formal character of the order of activities that will form itself, but not the specific advantages particular groups or individuals will derive from it.

This rather obvious fact still needs to be stressed since even eminent jurists have contended that the substitution of 'social' or distributive for individual or commutative justice need not destroy the freedom under the law of the individual. Thus the distinguished German legal philosopher Gustav Radbruch explicitly maintained that 'the socialist community would also be a *Rechtsstaat* [i.e., the Rule of Law would prevail there], although a *Rechtsstaat* governed not by commutative but by distributive justice.'[31] And of France it is reported that 'it has been suggested that some highly placed administrators should be given the permanent task of "pronouncing" on the distribution of national income, as judges pronounce on legal matters.'[32] Such beliefs, however, overlook the fact that no specific pattern of distribution can be achieved by making the individuals obey rules of conduct, but that the achievement of such particular pre-determined results requires deliberate co-ordination of all the different activities in accordance with the concrete circumstances of time and place. It precludes, in other words, that the several individuals act on the basis of their own knowledge and in the service of their own ends, which is the essence of freedom, but requires that they be made to act in the manner which according to the knowledge of the directing authority is required for the realization of the ends chosen by that authority.

The distributive justice at which socialism aims is thus irreconcilable with the rule of law, and with that freedom under the law which the rule of law is intended to secure. The rules of distributive justice cannot be rules for the conduct towards equals, but must be rules for the conduct of superiors towards their subordinates. Yet though some socialists have long ago themselves drawn the inevitable conclusion that 'the fundamental principles of formal law by which every case must be judged according to general rational principles . . . obtains only for the competitive phase of capitalism,'[33] and the communists, so long as they took socialism seriously, had even proclaimed that 'communism means not the victory of socialist law, but the victory of socialism over any law, since with the abolition of classes with antagonistic interests, law will disappear altogether',[34] when, more than thirty years ago, the present author made this the central point of a discussion of the political effects of socialist economic policies,[35] it evoked great indignation and violent protests. But the crucial point is implied even in Radbruch's own emphasis on the fact that the transition from commutative to distributive justice means a progressive displacement of private by public law,[36] since public law consists not of rules of conduct for private citizens but of rules of organization for public officials. It is, as Radbruch himself stresses, a law that subordinates the citizens to authority.[37] Only if one understands by law not the general rules of just conduct only but any command issued by authority (or any authorization of such commands by a legislature), can the measures aimed at distributive justice be represented as compatible with the rule of law. But this concept is thereby made to mean mere legality and ceases to offer the protection of individual freedom which it was originally intended to serve.

There is no reason why in a free society government should not assure to all protection against severe deprivation in the form of an assured minimum income, or a floor below which nobody need to descend. To enter into such an insurance against extreme misfortune may well be in the interest of all; or it may be felt to be a clear moral duty of all to assist, within the organized community, those who cannot help themselves. So long as such a uniform minimum income is provided outside the market to all those who, for any reason, are unable to earn in the market an adequate maintenance, this need not lead to a restriction of freedom, or conflict with the Rule of Law. The problems with which we are here concerned arise only when the remuneration for services rendered is determined by authority, and the impersonal mechanism of the market which guides the direction of individual efforts is thus suspended.

Perhaps the acutest sense of grievance about injustice inflicted on one, not by particular persons but by the 'system', is that about being deprived of opportunities for developing one's abilities which others enjoy. For this any difference of environment, social or physical, may be responsible, and at least some of them may be unavoidable. The most important of these is clearly inseparable from the institution of the family. This not only satisfies a strong psychological need but in general serves as an instrument for the transmission of important cultural values. There can be no doubt that those who are either wholly deprived of this benefit, or grew up in unfavourable conditions, are gravely handicapped; and few will question that it would be desirable that some public institution so far as possible should assist such unfortunate children when relatives and neighbours fail. Yet few will seriously believe (although Plato did) that we can fully make up for such a deficiency, and I trust even fewer that, because this benefit cannot be assured to all, it should, in the interest of equality, be taken from those who now enjoy it. Nor does it seem to me that even material equality could compensate for those differences in the capacity of enjoyment and of experiencing a lively interest in the cultural surroundings which a suitable upbringing confers.

There are of course many other irremediable inequalities which must seem as unreasonable as economic inequalities but which are less resented than the latter only because they do not appear to be man-made or the consequence of institutions which could be altered.

The spatial range of 'social justice'

There can be little doubt that the moral feelings which express themselves in the demand for 'social justice' derive from an attitude which in more primitive conditions the individual developed towards the fellow members of the small group to which he belonged. Towards the personally known member of one's own group it may well have been a recognized duty to assist him and to adjust one's actions to his needs. This is made possible by the knowledge of his person and his circumstances. The situation is wholly different in the Great or Open Society. Here the products and services of each benefit mostly persons he does not know. The greater productivity of such a society rests on a division of labour extending far beyond the range any one person can survey. This extension of the process of exchange beyond relatively small groups, and including large numbers of persons not known to each other, has been made possible by conceding to the stranger and even the foreigner the same protection of rules of just conduct which apply to the relations to the known members of one's own small group.

This application of the same rules of just conduct to the relations to all other men is rightly regarded as one of the great achievements of a liberal society. What is usually not understood is that this extension of the same rules to the relations to all other men (beyond the most intimate group such as the family and personal friends) requires an attenuation at least of some of the rules which are enforced in the relations to other members of the smaller group. If the legal duties towards strangers or foreigners are to be the same as those towards the neighbours or inhabitants of the same village or town, the latter duties will have to be reduced to such as can also be applied to the stranger. No doubt men will always wish to belong also to smaller groups and be willing voluntarily to assume greater obligations towards self-chosen friends or companions. But such moral obligations towards some can never become enforced duties in a system of freedom under the law, because in such a system the selection of those towards whom a man wishes to assume special moral obligations must be left to him and cannot be determined by law. A system of rules intended for an Open Society and, at least in principle, meant to be applicable to all others, must have a somewhat smaller content than one to be applied in a small group.

Especially a common agreement on what is the due status or material position of the different members is likely to develop only in the relatively small group in which the members will be familiar with the character and importance of each other's activities. In such small communities the opinion about appropriate status will also still be associated with a feeling about what one self owes to the other, and not be merely a demand that somebody provide the appropriate reward. Demands for the realization of 'social justice' are usually as a matter of course, though often only tacitly, addressed to national governments as the agencies which possess the necessary powers. But it is doubtful whether in any but the smallest countries standards can be applied nationally which are derived from the condition of the particular locality with which the individual is familiar, and fairly certain that few men would be willing to concede to foreigners the same right to a particular income that they tend to recognize in their fellow citizens.

It is true that in recent years concern about the suffering of large numbers in the poor countries has induced the electorates of the wealthier nations to approve substantial material aid to the former; but it can hardly be said that in this considerations of justice played a significant role. It is indeed doubtful whether any substantial help would have been rendered if competing power groups had not striven to draw as many as possible of the developing countries into their orbit. And it deserves notice that the modern technology which has made such assistance possible could develop only because some countries were able to build up great wealth while most of the world saw little change.

Yet the chief point is that, if we look beyond the limits of our national states, and certainly if we go beyond the limits of what we regard as our civilization, we no longer even deceive ourselves that we know what would be 'socially just', and that those very groups within the existing states which are loudest in their demands for 'social justice', such as the trade unions, are regularly the first to reject such claims raised on behalf of foreigners. Applied to the international sphere, the complete lack of a recognized standard of 'social justice', or of any known principles on which such a standard could be based, becomes at once obvious; while on a national scale most people still think that what on the level of the face-to-face society is to them a familiar idea must also have some validity for national politics or the use of the powers of government. In fact, it becomes on this level a humbug—the effectiveness of which with well-meaning people the agents of organized interests have learnt successfully to exploit.

There is in this respect a fundamental difference between what is possible in the small group and in the Great Society. In the small group the individual can know the effects of his actions on his several fellows, and the rules may effectively forbid him to harm them in any manner and even require him to assist them in specific ways. In the Great Society many of the effects of a person's actions on various fellows must be unknown to him. It can, therefore, not be the specific effects in the particular case, but only rules which define kinds of actions as prohibited or required, which must serve as guides to the individual. In particular, he will often not know who the individual people will be who will benefit by what he does, and therefore not know whether he is satisfying a great need or adding to abundance. He cannot aim at just results if he does not know who will be affected.

Indeed the transition from the small group to the Great or Open Society—and the treatment of every other person as a human being rather than as either a known friend or an enemy—requires a reduction of the range of duties we owe to all others.

If a person's legal duties are to be the same towards all, including the stranger and even the foreigner (and greater only where he has voluntarily entered into obligations, or is connected by physical ties as between parents and children), the legally enforceable duties to neighbour and friend must not be more than those towards the stranger. That is, all those duties which are based on personal acquaintance and familiarity with individual circumstances must cease to be enforceable. The extension of the obligation to obey certain rules of just conduct to wider circles and ultimately to all men must thus lead to an attenuation of the obligation towards fellow members of the same small group. Our inherited or perhaps in part even innate moral emotions are in part inapplicable to Open Society (which is an abstract society), and the kind of 'moral socialism' that is possible in the small group and often satisfies a deeply ingrained instinct may well be impossible in the Great Society. Some altruistic conduct aimed at the benefit of some known friend that in the small group might be highly desirable, need not be so in the Open Society, and may there even be harmful (as e.g. the requirement that members of the same trade refrain from competing with each other). [38]

It may at first seem paradoxical that the advance of morals should lead to a reduction of specific obligations towards others: yet whoever believes that the principle of equal treatment of all men, which is probably the only chance for peace, is more important than special help to visible suffering, must wish it. It admittedly means that we make our rational insight dominate over our inherited instincts. But the great moral adventure on which modern man has embarked when he launched into the Open Society is threatened when he is required to apply to all his fellow-men rules which are appropriate only to the fellow members of a tribal group.

Claims for compensation for distasteful jobs

The reader will probably expect me now to examine in greater detail the particular claims usually justified by the appeal to 'social justice'. But this, as bitter experience has taught me, would be not only an endless but also a bootless task. After what has been said already, it should be obvious that there are no practicable standards of merit, deserts, or needs, on which in a market order the distribution of material benefits could be based, and still less any principle by which these different claims could be reconciled. I shall therefore confine myself to considering two arguments in which the appeal to 'social justice' is very commonly used. The first case is usually quoted in theoretical argument to illustrate the injustice of the distribution by the market process, though little is done about it in practice, while the second is probably the most frequent type of situation in which the appeal to social justice leads to government action.

The circumstance which is usually pointed out to demonstrate

the injustice of the existing market order is that the most unpleasant jobs are commonly also the worst paid. In a just society, it
is contended, those who have to dig coal underground or to clean
chimneys or sewers, or who perform other unclean or menial
tasks, should be remunerated more highly than those whose work
is pleasurable.

It is of course true that it would be unjust if persons, although
equally able as others to perform other tasks, were without special
compensation assigned by a superior to such distasteful duties. If,
e.g., in such an organization as an army, two men of equal capacity
were made to perform different tasks, one of which was attractive
and the other very unpleasant, justice would clearly require that
the one who had regularly to perform the unpleasant duty should
in some way be specially compensated for it.

The situation is entirely different, however, where people earn
their living by selling their services to whoever pays best for them.
Here the sacrifice brought by a particular person in rendering the
service is wholly irrelevant and all that counts is the (marginal)
value the services have to those to whom they are rendered. The
reason for this is not only that the sacrifices different people bring
in rendering the same kind of service will often be very different, or
that it will not be possible to take account of the reason why some
will be capable of rendering only less valuable services than others.
But those whose aptitudes, and therefore also remunerations, will
be small in the more attractive occupations will often find that they
can earn more than they could otherwise by undertaking unpleasant
tasks that are scorned by their more fortunate fellows. The very fact
that the more unpleasant occupations will be avoided by those who
can render services that are valued more highly by the buyers, will
open to those whose skills are little valued opportunities to earn
more than they otherwise could.

That those who have to offer to their fellows little that is valuable
may have to incur more pain and effort to earn even a pittance than
others who perhaps actually enjoy rendering services for which they
are well paid, is a necessary concomitant of any system in which
remuneration is based on the values the services have to the user
and not on an assessment of merit earned. It must therefore prevail
in any social order in which the individual is free to choose whatever
occupation he can find and is not assigned to one by authority.

The only assumption on which it could be represented as just
that the miner working underground, or the scavenger, or slaughter-

house workers, should be paid more highly than those engaged in more pleasant occupations, would thus be that this was necessary to induce a sufficient number of persons to perform these tasks, or that they are by some human agency deliberately assigned to these tasks. But while in a market order it may be a misfortune to have been born and bred in a village where for most the only chance of making a living is fishing (or for the women the cleaning of fish), it does not make sense to describe this as unjust. Who is supposed to have been unjust?—especially when it is considered that, if these local opportunities had not existed, the people in question would probably never have been born at all, as most of the population of such a village will probably owe its existence to the opportunities which enabled their ancestors to produce and rear children.

The resentment of the loss of accustomed positions

The appeal to 'social justice' which in practice has probably had the greatest influence is not one which has been much considered in literary discussion. The considerations of a supposed 'social injustice' which have led to the most far-reaching interference with the functioning of the market order are based on the idea that people are to be protected against an unmerited descent from the material position to which they have become accustomed. No other consideration of 'social justice' has probably exercised as widespread an influence as the 'strong and almost universal belief that it is unjust to disappoint legitimate expectations of wealth. When differences of opinion arise, it is always on the question of what expectations are legitimate.' It is believed, as the same author says, 'that it is legitimate even for the largest classes to expect that no very great and sudden changes will be made to their detriment.'[39]

The opinion that long established positions create a just expectation that they will continue serves often as a substitute for more substantial criteria of 'social justice'. Where expectations are disappointed, and in consequence the rewards of effort often disproportionate to the sacrifice incurred, this will be regarded as an injustice without any attempt to show that those affected had a claim in justice to the particular income which they expected. At least when a large group of people find their income reduced as a result of circumstances which they could not have altered or foreseen, this is commonly regarded as unjust.

The frequent recurrence of such undeserved strokes of misfortune affecting some group is, however, an inseparable part of the steering mechanism of the market: it is the manner in which the cybernetic principle of negative feedback operates to maintain the order of the market. It is only through such changes which indicate that some activities ought to be reduced, that the efforts of all can be continuously adjusted to a greater variety of facts than can be known to any one person or agency, and that that utilization of dispersed knowledge is achieved on which the well-being of the Great Society rests. We cannot rely on a system in which the individuals are induced to respond to events of which they do not and cannot know without changes of the values of the services of different groups occurring which are wholly unrelated to the merits of their members. It is a necessary part of that process of constant adaptation to changing circumstances on which the mere maintenance of the existing level of wealth depends that some people should have to discover by bitter experience that they have misdirected their efforts and are forced to look elsewhere for a remunerative occupation. And the same applies to the resentment of the corresponding undeserved gains that will accrue to others for whom things have turned out better than they had reason to expect.

The sense of injury which people feel when an accustomed income is reduced or altogether lost is largely the result of a belief that they have morally deserved that income and that, therefore, so long as they work as industriously and honestly as they did before, they are in justice entitled to the continuance of that income. But the idea that we have morally deserved what we have honestly earned in the past is largely an illusion. What is true is only that it would have been unjust if anybody had taken from us what we have in fact acquired while observing the rules of the game.

It is precisely because in the cosmos of the market we all constantly receive benefits which we have not deserved in any moral sense that we are under an obligation also to accept equally undeserved diminutions of our incomes. Our only moral title to what the market gives us we have earned by submitting to those rules which makes the formation of the market order possible. These rules imply that nobody is under an obligation to supply us with a particular income unless he has specifically contracted to do so. If we were all to be consistently deprived, as the socialists propose to do, of all 'unearned benefits' which the market confers upon us, we would have to be deprived of most of the benefits of civilization.

It is clearly meaningless to reply, as is often done, that, since we owe these benefits to 'society', 'society' should also be entitled to allocate these benefits to those who in its opinion deserve them. Society, once more, is not an acting person but an orderly structure of actions resulting from the observation of certain abstract rules by its members. We all owe the benefits we receive from the operation of this structure not to anyone's intention to confer them on us, but to the members of society generally obeying certain rules in the pursuit of their interests, rules which include the rule that nobody is to coerce others in order to secure for himself (or for third persons) a particular income. This imposes upon us the obligation to abide by the results of the market also when it turns against us.

The chance which any individual in our society has of earning an income approximating that which he has now is the consequence of most individuals obeying the rules which secure the formation of that order. And though this order provides for most good prospects for the successful employment of their skills, this success must remain dependent also on what from the point of view of the individual must appear as mere luck. The magnitude of the chances open to him are not of his making but the result of others submitting to the same rules of the game. To ask for protection against being displaced from a position one has long enjoyed, by others who are now favoured by new circumstances, means to deny to them the chances to which one's own present position is due.

Any protection of an accustomed position is thus necessarily a privilege which cannot be granted to all and which, if it had always been recognized, would have prevented those who now claim it from ever reaching the position for which they now demand protection. There can, in particular, be no right to share equally in a general increase of incomes if this increase (or perhaps even their maintenance at the existing level) is dependent on the continuous adjustment of the whole structure of activities to new and unforeseen circumstances that will alter and often reduce the contributions some groups can make to the needs of their fellows. There can thus be in justice no such claims as, e.g., those of the American farmer for 'parity', or of any other group to the preservation of their relative or absolute position.

The satisfaction of such claims by particular groups would thus not be just but eminently unjust, because it would involve the denial to some of the chances to which those who make this claim owe their position. For this reason it has always been conceded only to some powerfully organized groups who were in the position to enforce their demands. Much of what is today done in the name of 'social justice' is thus not only unjust but also highly unsocial in the true sense of the word: it amounts simply to the protection of entrenched interests. Though it has come to be regarded as a 'social problem' when sufficiently large numbers clamour for protection of their accustomed position, it becomes a serious problem chiefly because, camouflaged as a demand for 'social justice', it can engage the sympathy of the public. We shall see in volume 3 why, under the existing type of democratic institutions, it is in practice inevitable that legislatures with unlimited powers yield to such demands when made by sufficiently large groups. This does not alter the fact that to represent such measures as satisfying 'social justice' is little more than a pretext for making the interest of the particular groups prevail over the general interest of all. Though it is now usual to regard every claim of an organized group as a 'social problem', it would be more correct to say that, though the long run interests of the several individuals mostly agree with the general interest, the interests of the organized groups almost invariably are in conflict with it. Yet it is the latter which are commonly represented as 'social'.

Conclusions

The basic contention of this chapter, namely that in a society of free men whose members are allowed to use their own knowledge for their own purposes the term 'social justice' is wholly devoid of meaning or content, is one which by its very nature cannot be *proved*. A negative assertion never can. One may demonstrate for any number of particular instances that the appeal to 'social justice' in no way assists the choices we have to make. But the contention that in a society of free men the term has no meaning whatever can only be issued as a challenge which will make it necessary for others to reflect on the meaning of the words they use, and as an appeal not to use phrases the meaning of which they do not know.

So long as one assumes that a phrase so widely used must have some recognizable meaning one may endeavour to prove that attempts to enforce it in a society of free individuals must make that society unworkable. But such efforts become redundant once it is recognized that such a society lacks the fundamental precondition for the application of the concept of justice to the manner in which material benefits are shared among its members, namely that this is determined by a human will—or that the determination of rewards by human will could produce a viable market order. One does not have to prove that something is impracticable which cannot exist.

What I hope to have made clear is that the phrase 'social justice' is not, as most people probably feel, an innocent expression of good will towards the less fortunate, but that it has become a dishonest insinuation that one ought to agree to a demand of some special interest which can give no real reason for it. If political discussion is to become honest it is necessary that people should recognize that the term is intellectually disreputable, the mark of demagogy or cheap journalism which responsible thinkers ought to be ashamed to use because, once its vacuity is recognized, its use is dishonest. I may, as a result of long endeavours to trace the destructive effect which the invocation of 'social justice' has had on our moral sensitivity, and of again and again finding even eminent thinkers thoughtlessly using the phrase, [40] have become unduly allergic to it, but I have come to feel strongly that the greatest service I can still render to my fellow men would be that I could make the speakers and writers among them thoroughly ashamed ever again to employ the term 'social justice'.

That in the present state of the discussion the continued use of the term is not only dishonest and the source of constant political confusion, but destructive of moral feeling, is shown by the fact that again and again thinkers, including distinguished philosophers, [41] after rightly recognizing that the term justice in its now predominant meaning of distributive (or retributive) justice is meaningless, draw from this the conclusion that the concept of justice itself is empty, and who in consequence jettison one of the basic moral conceptions on which the working of a society of free men rests. But it is justice in this sense which courts of justice administer and which is the original meaning of justice and must govern men's conduct if peaceful coexistence of free men is to be possible. While the appeal to 'social justice' is indeed merely an invitation to give moral approval to demands that have no moral justification, and which are in conflict with that basic rule of a free society that only such rules as can be applied equally to all should be enforced, justice in the sense of rules of just conduct is indispensable for the intercourse of free men.

We are touching here upon a problem which with all its ramifications is much too big to try to be examined here systematically, but which must at least be mentioned briefly. It is that we can't have any morals we like or dream of. Morals, to be viable, must satisfy certain requirements, requirements which we may not be able to specify but may only be able to find out by trial and error. What is required is not merely consistency, or compatibility of the rules as well as the acts demanded by them. A system of morals also must produce a functioning order, capable of maintaining the apparatus of civilization which it presupposes.

We are not familiar with the concept of non-viable systems of morals and certainly cannot observe them anywhere in practice since societies which try them rapidly disappear. But they are being preached, often by widely revered saintly figures, and the societies in decay which we can observe are often societies which have been listening to the teaching of such moral reformers and still revere the destroyers of their society as good men. More often, however, the gospel of 'social justice' aims at much more sordid sentiments: the dislike of people who are better off than oneself, or simply envy, that 'most anti-social and evil of all passions' as John Stuart Mill called it, [42] that animosity towards great wealth which represents it as a 'scandal' that some should enjoy riches while others have basic needs unsatisfied, and camouflages under the name of justice what has nothing to do with justice. At least all those who wish to despoil the rich, not because they expect that some more deserving might enjoy that wealth, but because they regard the very existence of the rich as an outrage, not only cannot claim any moral justification for their demands, but indulge in a wholly irrational passion and in fact harm those to whose rapacious instincts they appeal.

There can be no moral claim to something that would not exist but for the decision of others to risk their resources on its creation. What those who attack great private wealth do not understand is that it is neither by physical effort nor by the mere act of saving and investing, but by directing resources to the most productive uses that wealth is chiefly created. And there can be no doubt that most of those who have built up great fortunes in the form of new industrial plants and the like have thereby benefited more people through creating opportunities for more rewarding employment than if they had given their superfluity away to the poor. The suggestion that in these cases those to whom in fact the workers are most indebted do wrong rather than greatly benefit them is an absurdity. Though there are undoubtedly also other and less meritorious ways of acquiring large fortunes (which we can hope to control by improving the rules of the game), the most effective and important is by directing investment to points where they most enhance the productivity of labour—a task in which governments notoriously fail, for reasons inherent in non-competitive bureaucratic organizations.

But it is not only by encouraging malevolent and harmful prejudices that the cult of 'social justice' tends to destroy genuine moral feelings. It also comes, particularly in its more egalitarian forms, into constant conflict with some of the basic moral principles on which any community of free men must rest. This becomes evident when we reflect that the demand that we should equally esteem all our fellow men is irreconcilable with the fact that our whole moral code rests on the approval or disapproval of the conduct of others; and that similarly the traditional postulate that each capable adult is primarily responsible for his own and his dependants' welfare, meaning that he must not through his own fault become a charge to his friends or fellows, is incompatible with the idea that 'society' or government owes each person an appropriate income.

Though all these moral principles have also been seriously weakened by some pseudo-scientific fashions of our time which tend to destroy all morals—and with them the basis of individual freedom—the ubiquitous dependence on other people's power, which the enforcement of any image of 'social justice' creates, inevitably destroys that freedom of personal decisions on which all morals must rest.[43] In fact, that systematic pursuit of the *ignis fatuus* of 'social justice' which we call socialism is based throughout on the atrocious idea that political power ought to determine the material position of the different individuals and groups—an idea defended by the false assertion that this must always be so and socialism merely wishes to transfer this power from the privileged to the most numerous class. It was the great merit of the market order as it has spread during the last two centuries that it deprived everyone of such power which can be used only in arbitrary fashion. It had indeed brought about the greatest reduction of arbitrary power ever achieved. This greatest triumph of personal freedom the seduction of 'social justice' threatens again to take from us. And it will not be long before the holders of the power to enforce 'social justice' will entrench themselves in their position by awarding the benefits of 'social justice' as the remuneration for the conferment of that power and in order to secure to themselves the support of a praetorian guard which will make it certain that their view of what is 'social justice' will prevail.

Before leaving the subject I want to point out once more that the recognition that in such combinations as 'social', 'economic', 'distributive' or 'retributive' justice the term 'justice' is wholly empty should not lead us to throw the baby out with the bath water. Not only as the basis of the legal rules of just conduct is the justice which the courts of justice administer exceedingly important; there unquestionably also exists a genuine problem of justice in connection with the deliberate design of political institutions, the problem to which Professor John Rawls has recently devoted an important book. The fact which I regret and regard as confusing is merely that in this connection he employs the term 'social justice'. But I have no basic quarrel with an author who, before he proceeds to that problem, acknowledges that the task of selecting specific systems or distributions of desired things as just must be 'abandoned as mistaken in principle, and it is, in any case, not capable of a definite answer. Rather, the principles of justice define the crucial constraints which institutions and joint activities must satisfy if persons engaging in them are to have no complaints against them. If these constraints are satisfied, the resulting distribution, whatever it is, may be accepted as just (or at least not unjust).'[44] This is more or less what I have been trying to argue in this chapter.

JUSTICE AND INDIVIDUAL RIGHTS

The transition from the negative conception of justice as defined by rules of individual conduct to a 'positive' conception which makes it a duty of 'society' to see that individuals have particular things, is often effected by stressing the *rights* of the individual. It seems that among the younger generation the welfare institutions into which they have been born have engendered a feeling that they have a claim in justice on 'society' for the provision of particular things which it is the duty of that society to provide. However strong this feeling may be, its existence does not prove that the claim has anything to do with justice, or that such claims can be satisfied in a free society.

There is a sense of the noun 'right' in which every rule of just individual conduct creates a corresponding right of individuals. So far as rules of conduct delimit individual domains, the individual will have a right to his domain, and in the defence of it will have the sympathy and the support of his fellows. And where men have formed organizations such as government for enforcing rules of conduct, the individual will have a claim in justice on government that his right be protected and infringements made good.

Such claims, however, can be claims in justice, or rights, only in so far as they are directed towards a person or organization (such as government) which can act, and which is bound in its actions by rules of just conduct. They will include claims on people who have voluntarily incurred obligations, or between people who are connected by special circumstances (such as the relations between parents and children). In such circumstances the rules of just conduct will confer on some persons rights and on others corresponding obligations. But rules as such, without the presence of the particular circumstances to which they refer, cannot confer on anyone a right to a particular sort of thing. A child has a right to be fed, clad, and housed because a corresponding duty is placed on the parents or guardians, or perhaps a particular authority. But there can be no such right in the abstract determined by a rule of just conduct without the particular circumstances being stated which determine on whom the corresponding obligation rests. Nobody has a right to a particular state of affairs unless it is the duty of someone to secure it. We have no right that our houses do not burn down, nor a right that our products or services find a buyer, nor that any particular goods or services be provided for us. Justice does not impose on our fellows a general duty to provide for us; and a claim to such a provision can exist only to the extent that we are maintaining an organization for that purpose. It is meaningless to speak of a right to a condition which nobody has the duty, or perhaps even the power, to bring about. It is equally meaningless to speak of right in the sense of a claim on a spontaneous order, such as society, unless this is meant to imply that somebody has the duty of transforming that cosmos into an organization and thereby to assume the power of controlling its results.

Since we are all made to support the organization of government, we have by the principles determining that organization certain rights which are commonly called political rights. The existence of the compulsory organization of government and its rules of organization does create a claim in justice to shares in the services of government, and may even justify a claim for an equal share in determining what government shall do. But it does not provide a basis for a claim on what government does not, and perhaps could not, provide for all. We are not, in this sense, members of an organization called society, because the society which produces the means for the satisfaction of most of our needs is not an organization directed by a conscious will, and could not produce what it does if it were.

The time-honoured political and civil rights which have been embodied in formal Bills of Right constitute essentially a demand that so far as the power of government extends it ought to be used justly. As we shall see, they all amount to particular applications of, and might be effectively replaced by, the more comprehensive formula that no coercion must be used except in the enforcement of a generic rule applicable to an unknown number of future instances. It may well be desirable that these rights should become truly universal as a result of all governments submitting to them. But so long as the powers of the several governments are at all limited, these rights cannot produce a duty of the governments to bring about a particular state of affairs. What we can require is that so far as government acts it ought to act justly; but we cannot derive from them any positive powers government ought to have. They leave wholly open the question whether the organization for coercion which we call government can and ought in justice be used to determine the particular material position of the several individuals or groups.

To the negative rights which are merely a complement of the rules protecting individual domains and which have been institutionalized in the charters of organization of governments, and to the positive rights of the citizens to participate in the direction of this organization, there have recently been added new positive 'social and economic' human rights for which an equal or even higher dignity is claimed.[1] These are claims to particular benefits to which every human being as such is presumed to be entitled without any indication as to who is to be under the obligation to provide those benefits or by what process they are to be provided.[2] Such positive rights, however, demand as their counterpart a decision that somebody (a person or organization) should have the duty of providing what the others are to have. It is, of course, meaningless to describe them as claims on 'society' because 'society' cannot think, act, value, or 'treat' anybody in a particular way. If such claims are to be met, the spontaneous order which we call society must be replaced by a deliberately directed organization: the cosmos of the market would have to be replaced by a taxis whose members would have to do what they are instructed to do. They could not be allowed to use their knowledge for their own purposes but would have to carry out the plan which their rulers have designed to meet the needs to be satisfied. From this it follows that the old civil rights and the new social and economic rights cannot be achieved at the same time but are in fact incompatible; the new rights could not be enforced by law without at the same time destroying that liberal order at which the old civil rights aim.

The new trend was given its chief impetus through the proclamation by President Franklin Roosevelt of his 'Four Freedoms' which included 'freedom *from* want' and 'freedom *from* fear' together with the old 'freedom *of* speech' and 'freedom *of* worship'. But it found its definite embodiment only in the *Universal Declaration of Human Rights* adopted by the General Assembly of the United Nations in 1948. This document is admittedly an attempt to fuse the rights of the Western liberal tradition with the altogether different conception deriving from the Marxist Russian Revolution.[3] It adds to the list of the classical civil rights enumerated in its first twenty-one articles seven further guarantees intended to express the new 'social and economic rights'. In these additional clauses 'every one, as a member of society' is assured the satisfaction of positive claims to particular benefits without at the same time placing on anyone the duty or burden of providing them. The document also completely fails to define these rights in such a manner that a court could possibly determine what their contents are in a particular instance. What, for instance, can be the legal meaning of the statement that every one 'is entitled to the realization . . . of the economic, social, and cultural rights indispensible for his dignity and free development of his personality' (Art. 22)? Against whom is 'every one' to have a claim to 'just and favourable conditions of work' (Art. 23 (1)) and to 'just and favourable employment' (Art. 23 (3))? What are the consequences of the requirement that every one should have the right 'freely to participate in the cultural life of the community and to share in the scientific advances and its benefits' (Art. 27 (1))? 'Every one' is even said to be 'entitled to a social and international order in which the rights and freedoms set forth in this Declaration are fully realized' (Art. 28)—on the assumption apparently that not only is this possible but that there exists now a known method by which these claims can be satisfied for all men.

It is evident that all these 'rights' are based on the interpretation of society as a deliberately made organization by which everybody is employed. They could not be made universal within a system of rules of just conduct based on the conception of individual responsibility, and so require that the whole of society be converted into a single organization, that is, made totalitarian in the fullest sense of the word. We have seen that rules of just conduct which apply to everybody alike but subject nobody to the commands of a superior can never determine what particular things any person is to have. They can never take the form of 'everybody must have so and so.' In a free society what the individual will get must always depend in some measure on particular circumstances which nobody can foresee and nobody has the power to determine. Rules of just conduct can therefore never confer on any person as such (as distinct from the members of a particular organization) a claim to particular things; they can bring about only opportunities for the acquiring of such claims.

It apparently never occurred to the authors of the Declaration that not everybody is an employed member of an organization whose right 'to just and favourable remuneration, including reasonable limitations of working hours and periodic holidays with pay' (Art. 24) can be guaranteed. The conception of a 'universal right' which assures to the peasant, to the Eskimo, and presumably to the Abominable Snowman, 'periodic holidays with pay' shows the absurdity of the whole thing. Even the slightest amount of ordinary common sense ought to have told the authors of the document that what they decreed as universal rights were for the present and for any foreseeable future utterly impossible of achievement, and that solemnly to proclaim them as rights was to play an irresponsible game with the concept of 'right' which could result only in destroying the respect for it.

The whole document is indeed couched in that jargon of organization thinking which one has learnt to expect in the pronouncement of trade union officials or the International Labour Organization and which reflects an attitude business employees share with civil servants and the organization men of the big corporations, but which is altogether inconsistent with the principles on which the order of a Great Society rests. If the document were merely the production of an international group of social philosophers (as in origin it is), it would constitute only somewhat disturbing evidence of the degree to which organization thinking has permeated the thinking of these social philosophers and how much they have become total strangers to the basic ideals of a free society. But its acceptance by a body of presumably responsible statesmen, seriously concerned with the creation of a peaceful international order, gives cause for much greater apprehension.

Organization thinking, largely as a result of the sway of the rationalist constructivism of Plato and his followers, has long been the besetting vice of social philosophers; perhaps it should therefore not surprise us that academic philosophers in their sheltered lives as members of organizations should have lost all understanding of the forces which hold the Great Society together and, imagining themselves to be Platonic philosopher-kings, should propose a re-organization of society on totalitarian lines. If it should be true, as we are told, that the social and economic rights of the Universal Declaration of Human Rights would today be 'accepted by the vast majority of American and British moralists,'[4] this would merely indicate a sorry lack of critical acumen on the part of these thinkers.

The spectacle, however, of the General Assembly of the United

Nations solemnly proclaiming that *every* individual (!), 'keeping this Declaration constantly in mind' (!), should strive to insure the universal observation of those human rights, would be merely comic if the illusions which this creates were not so profoundly tragic. To see the most comprehensive authority which man has yet created undermining the respect it ought to command by giving countenance to the naive prejudice that we can create any state of affairs which we think to be desirable by simply decreeing that it ought to exist, and indulging in the self-deception that we can benefit from the spontaneous order of society and at the same time mould it to our own will, is more than merely tragic.[5]

The fundamental fact which these illusions disregard is that the availability of all those benefits which we wish as many people as possible to have depends on these same people using for their production their own best knowledge. To establish enforceable rights to the benefits is not likely to produce them. If we wish everybody to be well off, we shall get closest to our goal, not by commanding by law that this should be achieved, or giving everybody a legal claim to what we think he ought to have, but by providing inducements for all to do as much as they can that will benefit others. To speak of rights where what are in question are merely aspirations which only a voluntary system can fulfil, not only misdirects attention from what are the effective determinants of the wealth which we wish for all, but also debases the word 'right', the strict meaning of which it is very important to preserve if we are to maintain a free society.

TEN

THE MARKET ORDER OR CATALLAXY

> The judgement of mankind about what is equitable is liable to change, and . . . one of the forces which cause it to change is mankind's discovery from time to time that what was supposed to be quite just and equitable in some particular matter has become, or perhaps always was, uneconomical.
>
> Edwin Cannan*

The nature of the market order

In chapter 2 we have discussed the general character of all spontaneous orders. It is necessary now to examine more fully the special attributes possessed by the order of the market and the nature of the benefits we owe to it. This order serves our ends not merely, as all order does, by guiding us in our actions and by bringing about a certain correspondence between the expectations of the different persons, but also, in a sense which we must now make more precise, by increasing the prospects or chances of every one of a greater command over the various goods (i.e. commodities and services) than we are able to secure in any other way. We shall see, however, that this manner of co-ordinating individual actions will secure a high degree of coincidence of expectations and an effective utilization of the knowledge and skills of the several members only at the price of a constant disappointment of some expectations.

For a proper understanding of the character of this order it is essential that we free ourselves of the misleading associations suggested by its usual description as an 'economy'. An economy, in the strict sense of the word in which a household, a farm, or an enterprise can be called economies, consists of a complex of activities by which a given set of means is allocated in accordance with a unitary plan among the competing ends according to their relative importance. The market order serves no such single order of ends.

re P. Koslowski.

What is commonly called a social or national economy is in this sense not a single economy but a network of many interlaced economies.[1] Its order shares, as we shall see, with the order of an economy proper some formal characteristics but not the most important one: its activities are not governed by a single scale or hierarchy of ends. The belief that the economic activities of the individual members of society are or ought to be part of one economy in the strict sense of this term, and that what is commonly described as the economy of a country or a society ought to be ordered and judged by the same criteria as an economy proper, is a chief source of error in this field. But, whenever we speak of the economy of a country, or of the world, we are employing a term which suggests that these systems ought to be run on socialist lines and directed according to a single plan so as to serve a unitary system of ends.

While an economy proper is an organization in the technical sense in which we have defined that term, that is, a deliberate arrangement of the use of the means which are known to some single agency, the cosmos of the market neither is nor could be governed by such a single scale of ends; it serves the multiplicity of separate and incommensurable ends of all its separate members.

The confusion which has been created by the ambiguity of the word economy is so serious that for our present purposes it seems necessary to confine its use strictly to the original meaning in which it describes a complex of deliberately co-ordinated actions serving a single scale of ends, and to adopt another term to describe the system of numerous interrelated economies which constitute the market-order. Since the name 'catallactics' has long ago been suggested for the science which deals with the market order[2] and has more recently been revived,[3] it would seem appropriate to adopt a corresponding term for the market order itself. The term 'catallactics' was derived from the Greek verb *katallattein* (or *katallassein*) which meant, significantly, not only 'to exchange' but also 'to admit into the community' and 'to change from enemy into friend'.[4] From it the adjective 'catallactic' has been derived to serve in the place of 'economic' to describe the kind of phenomena with which the science of catallactics deals. The ancient Greeks knew neither this term nor had a corresponding noun; if they had formed one it would probably have been *katallaxia*. From this we can form an English term *catallaxy* which we shall use to describe the order brought about by the mutual adjustment of many individual economies in a market. A catallaxy is thus the special kind of spontaneous order produced by the market through people acting within the rules of the law of property, tort and contract.

A free society is a pluralistic society without a common hierarchy of particular ends

It is often made a reproach to the Great Society and its market order that it lacks an agreed ranking of ends. This, however, is in fact its great merit which makes individual freedom and all it values possible. The Great Society arose through the discovery that men can live together in peace and mutually benefiting each other without agreeing on the particular aims which they severally pursue. The discovery that by substituting abstract rules of conduct for obligatory concrete ends made it possible to extend the order of peace beyond the small groups pursuing the same ends, because it enabled each individual to gain from the skill and knowledge of others whom he need not even know and whose aims could be wholly different from his own.[5]

The decisive step which made such peaceful collaboration possible in the absence of concrete common purposes was the adoption of barter or exchange. It was the simple recognition that different persons had different uses for the same things, and that often each of two individuals would benefit if he obtained something the other had, in return for his giving the other what he needed. All that was required to bring this about was that rules be recognized which determined what belonged to each, and how such property could be transferred by consent.[6] There was no need for the parties to agree on the purposes which this transaction served. It is indeed characteristic of such acts of exchange that they serve different and independent purposes of each partner in the transaction, and that they thus assist the parties as means for different ends. The parties are in fact the more likely to benefit from exchange the more their needs differ. While within an organization the several members will assist each other to the extent that they are made to aim at the same purposes, in a catallaxy they are induced to contribute to the needs of others without caring or even knowing about them.

In the Great Society we all in fact contribute not only to the satisfaction of needs of which we do not know, but sometimes even to the achievement of ends of which we would disapprove if we knew about them. We cannot help this because we do not know for what purposes the goods or services which we supply to others will be used by them. That we assist in the realization of other people's aims without sharing them or even knowing them, and solely in order to achieve our own aims, is the source of strength of the Great Society. So long as collaboration presupposes common purposes, people with different aims are necessarily enemies who may fight each other for the same means; only the introduction of barter made it possible for the different individuals to be of use to each other without agreeing on the ultimate ends.

When this effect of exchange of making people mutually benefit each other without intending to do so was first clearly recognized,[7] too much stress was laid on the resulting division of labour and on the fact that it was their 'selfish' aims which led the different persons to render services to each other. This is much too narrow a view of the matter. Division of labour is extensively practised also within organizations; and the advantages of the spontaneous order do not depend on people being selfish in the ordinary sense of this word. The important point about the catallaxy is that it reconciles different knowledge and different purposes which, whether the individuals be selfish or not, will greatly differ from one person to another. It is because in the catallaxy men, while following their own interests, whether wholly egotistical or highly altruistic, will further the aims of many others, most of whom they will never know, that it is as an overall order so superior to any deliberate organization: in the Great Society the different members benefit from each other's efforts not only in spite of but often even because of their several aims being different.[8]

Many people regard it as revolting that the Great Society has no common concrete purposes or, as we may say, that it is merely means-connected and not ends-connected. It is indeed true that the chief common purpose of all its members is the purely instrumental one of securing the formation of an abstract order which has no specific purposes but will enhance for all the prospects of achieving their respective purposes. The prevailing moral tradition, much of which still derives from the end-connected tribal society, makes people often regard this circumstance as a moral defect of the Great Society which ought to be remedied. Yet it was the very restriction of coercion to the observance of the negative rules of just conduct that made possible the integration into a peaceful order of individuals and groups which pursued different ends; and it is the absence of prescribed common ends which makes a society of free men all that it has come to mean to us.

Though the conception that a common scale of particular values is a good thing which ought, if necessary, to be enforced, is deeply founded in the history of the human race, its intellectual defence today is based mainly on the erroneous belief that such a common *which ends* scale of ends is necessary for the integration of the individual *tacitly* activities into an order, and a necessary condition of peace. This *common ends* error is, however, the greatest obstacle to the achievement of those very ends. A Great Society has nothing to do with, and is in fact irreconcilable with 'solidarity' in the true sense of unitedness in the pursuit of known common goals.[9] If we all occasionally feel that it is a good thing to have a common purpose with our fellows, and enjoy a sense of elation when we can act as members of a group aiming at common ends, this is an instinct which we have inherited from tribal society and which no doubt often still stands us in good stead whenever it is important that in a small group we should act in concert to meet a sudden emergency. It shows itself conspicuously when sometimes even the outbreak of war is felt as satisfying a craving for such a common purpose; and it manifests itself most clearly in modern times in the two greatest threats to a free civilization: nationalism and socialism.[10]

Most of the knowledge on which we rely in the pursuit of our ends is the unintended by-product of others exploring the world in different directions from those we pursue ourselves because they are impelled by different aims; it would never have become available to us if only those ends were pursued which we regarded as desirable. To make it a condition for the membership of a society that one approved of, and deliberately supported, the concrete ends which one's fellow members serve, would eliminate the chief factor which makes for the advancement of such a society. Where agreement on concrete objects is a necessary condition of order and peace, and dissent a danger to the order of the society, where approval and censure depend on the concrete ends which particular actions serve, the forces for intellectual progress would be much confined. However much the existence of agreement on ends may in many respects smooth the course of life, the possibility of disagreement, or at least the lack of compulsion to agree on particular ends, is the basis of the kind of civilization which has grown up since the Greeks developed independent thought of the individual as the most effective method of advancement of the human mind.[11]

Though not a single economy, the Great Society is still held together
mainly by what vulgarly are called economic relations

The misconception that the market order is an economy in the strict
sense of the term is usually found combined with the denial that
the Great Society is held together by what are loosely called economic relations. These two views are frequently held by the same
persons because it is certainly true that those deliberate organizations which are properly called economies are based on an agreement on common ends which in turn mostly are non-economic;
while it is the great advantage of the spontaneous order of the
market that it is merely means-connected and that, therefore, it
makes agreement on ends unnecessary and a reconciliation of
divergent purposes possible. What are commonly called economic
relations are indeed relations determined by the fact that the use
of all means is affected by the striving for those many different
purposes. It is in this wide sense of the term 'economic' that the
interdependence or coherence of the parts of the Great Society is
purely economic.[12]

The suggestion that in this wide sense the only ties which hold
the whole of a Great Society together are purely 'economic' (more
precisely 'catallactic') arouse great emotional resistance. Yet the
fact can hardly be denied; nor the fact that, in a society of the
dimensions and complexity of a modern country or of the world, it
can hardly be otherwise. Most people are still reluctant to accept
the fact that it should be the disdained 'cash-nexus' which holds
the Great Society together, that the great ideal of the unity of mankind should in the last resort depend on the relations between the
parts being governed by the striving for the better satisfaction of
their material needs.

It is of course true that within the overall framework of the Great
Society there exist numerous networks of other relations that are in
no sense economic. But this does not alter the fact that it is the
market order which makes peaceful reconciliation of the divergent
purposes possible—and possible by a process which redounds to
the benefit of all. That interdependence of all men, which is now in
everybody's mouth and which tends to make all mankind One
World, not only is the effect of the market order but could not have
been brought about by any other means. What today connects the
life of any European or American with what happens in Australia,
Japan or Zaire are repercussions transmitted by the network of

market relations. This is clearly seen when we reflect how little, for instance, all the technological possibilities of transportation and communication would matter if the conditions of production were the same in all the different parts of the world.

The benefits from the knowledge which others possess, including all the advances of science, reach us through channels provided and directed by the market mechanism. Even the degree to which we can participate in the aesthetic or moral strivings of men in other parts of the world we owe to the economic nexus. It is true that on the whole this dependence of every man on the actions of so many others is not a physical but what we call an economic fact. It is therefore a misunderstanding, caused by the misleading terms used, if the economists are sometimes accused of 'pan-economism', a tendency to see everything from the economic angle, or, worse, wanting to make 'economic purposes' prevail over all others.[13] The truth is that catallactics is the science which describes the only overall order that comprehends nearly all mankind, and that the economist is therefore entitled to insist that conduciveness to that order be accepted as a standard by which all particular institutions are judged.

It is, however, a misunderstanding to represent this as an effort to make 'economic ends' prevail over others. There are, in the last resort, no economic ends. The economic efforts of the individuals as well as the services which the market order renders to them, consist in an allocation of means for the competing ultimate purposes which are always non-economic. The task of all economic activity is to reconcile the competing ends by deciding for which of them the limited means are to be used. The market order reconciles the claims of the different non-economic ends by the only known process that benefits all—without, however, assuring that the more important comes before the less important, for the simple reason that there can exist in such a system no single ordering of needs. What it tends to bring about is merely a state of affairs in which no need is served at the cost of withdrawing a greater amount of means from the use for other needs than is necessary to satisfy it. The market is the only known method by which this can be achieved without an agreement on the relative importance of the different ultimate ends, and solely on the basis of a principle of reciprocity through which the opportunities of any person are likely to be greater than they would otherwise be.

The aim of policy in a society of free men cannot be a maximum of foreknown results but only an abstract order

The erroneous interpretation of the catallaxy as an economy in the strict sense of this word frequently leads to attempts to evaluate the benefits which we derive from it in terms of the degree of satisfaction of a given order of ends. But, if the importance of the various demands is judged by the price offered, this approach, as has been pointed out innumerable times, by the critics of the market order even more frequently than by its defenders, involves us in a vicious circle: because the relative strength of the demand for the different goods and services to which the market will adjust their production is itself determined by the distribution of incomes which in turn is determined by the market mechanism. Many writers have concluded from this that if this scale of relative demands cannot without circular reasoning be accepted as the common scale of values, another scale of ends must be postulated if we are to judge the effectiveness of this market order.

The belief that there can be no rational policy without a common scale of concrete ends implies, however, an interpretation of the catallaxy as an economy proper and for this reason is misleading. Policy need not be guided by the striving for the achievement of particular results, but may be directed towards securing an abstract overall order of such character that it will secure for the members the best chance of achieving their different and largely unknown particular ends. The aim of policy in such a society would have to be to increase equally the chances for any unknown member of society of pursuing with success his equally unknown purposes, and to restrict the use of coercion (apart from the raising of taxes) to the enforcement of such rules as will, if universally applied, tend in this sense to improve everyone's opportunities.

A policy making use of the spontaneously ordering forces therefore cannot aim at a known maximum of particular results, but must aim at increasing, for any person picked out at random, the prospects that the overall effect of all changes required by that order will be to increase his chances of attaining his ends. We have seen[14] that the common good in this sense is not a particular state of things but consists in an abstract order which in a free society must leave undetermined the degree to which the several particular needs will be met. The aim will have to be an order which will increase everybody's chances as much as possible—

not at every moment, but only 'on the whole' and in the long run.

Because the results of any economic policy must depend on the use made of the operation of the market by unknown persons guided by their own knowledge and their own aims, the goal of such a policy must be to provide a multi-purpose instrument which at no particular moment may be the one best adapted to the particular circumstances, but which will be the best for the great variety of circumstances likely to occur. If we had known those particular circumstances in advance, we could probably have better equipped ourselves to deal with them; but since we do not know them beforehand, we must be content with a less specialized instrument which will allow us to cope even with very unlikely events.

The game of catallaxy

The best way to understand how the operation of the market system leads not only to the creation of an order, but also to a great increase of the return which men receive from their efforts, is to think of it, as suggested in the last chapter, as a game which we may now call the game of catallaxy. It is a wealth-creating game (and not what game theory calls a zero-sum game), that is, one that leads to an increase of the stream of goods and of the prospects of all participants to satisfy their needs, but which retains the character of a game in the sense in which the term is defined by the *Oxford English Dictionary*: 'a contest played according to rules and decided by superior skill, strength or good fortune'. That the outcome of this game for each will, because of its very character, necessarily be determined by a mixture of skill and chance will be one of the main points we must now try to make clear.

The chief cause of the wealth-creating character of the game is that the returns of the efforts of each player act as the signs which enable him to contribute to the satisfaction of needs of which he does not know, and to do so by taking advantage of conditions of which he also learns only indirectly through their being reflected in the prices of the factors of production which they use. It is thus a wealth-producing game because it supplies to each player information which enables him to provide for needs of which he has no direct knowledge and by the use of means of the existence of which without it he would have no cognizance, thus bringing about the satisfaction of a greater range of needs than would otherwise be possible. The manufacturer does not produce shoes because he knows that Jones needs them. He produces because he knows that dozens of traders will buy certain numbers at various prices because they (or rather the retailer they serve) know that thousands of Joneses, whom the manufacturer does not know, want to buy them. Similarly, a manufacturer will release resources for additional production by others by substituting, say, aluminium for magnesium in the production of his output, not because he knows of all the changes in demand and supply which on balance have made aluminium less scarce and magnesium more scarce, but because he learns the one simple fact that the price at which aluminium is offered to him has fallen relatively to the price of magnesium. Indeed, probably the most important instance of the price system bringing about the taking into account of conflicts of desires which otherwise would have been overlooked is the accounting of costs—in the interests of the community at large the most important aspect, i.e. the one most likely to benefit many other persons, and the one at which private enterprise excels but government enterprise notoriously fails.

Thus in the market order each is made by the visible gain to himself to serve needs which to him are invisible, and in order to do so to avail himself of to him unknown particular circumstances which put him in the position to satisfy these needs at as small a cost as possible in terms of other things which it is possible to produce instead. And where only a few know yet of an important new fact, the much maligned speculators will see to it that the relevant information will rapidly be spread by an appropriate change of prices. The important effect of this will of course be that all changes are currently taken account of as they become known to somebody connected with the trade, not that the adaptation to the new facts will ever be perfect.

The current prices, it must be specially noted, serve in this process as indicators of what ought to be done in the present circumstances and have no necessary relation to what has been done in the past in order to bring the current supply of any particular good on the market. For the same reason that the prices which guide the direction of the different efforts reflect events which the producer does not know, the return from his efforts will frequently be different from what he expected, and must be so if they are to guide production appropriately. The remunerations which the market determines are, as it were, not functionally related with what people *have* done, but only with what they *ought* to do. They are incentives which as a rule guide people to success, but will produce a viable order only because they often disappoint the expectations they have caused when relevant circumstances have unexpectedly changed. It is one of the chief tasks of competition to show which plans are false. The facts that full utilization of the limited information which the prices convey is usually rewarded, and that this makes it worth-while to pay the greatest attention to them, are as important as that in the case of unforeseen changes the expectations are disappointed. The element of luck is as inseparable from the operation of the market as the element of skill.

There is no need morally to justify specific distributions (of income or wealth) which have not been brought about deliberately but are the outcome of a game that is played because it improves the chances of all. In such a game nobody 'treats' people differently and it is entirely consistent with respecting all people equally that the outcome of the game for different people is very different. It would also be as much a gamble what the effects of any one man's efforts would be worth if they were directed by a planning authority, only that not his knowledge but that of the authority would be used in determining the success or failure of his efforts.

The sum of information reflected or precipitated in the prices is wholly the product of competition, or at least of the openness of the market to anyone who has relevant information about some source of demand or supply for the good in question. Competition operates as a discovery procedure not only by giving anyone who has the opportunity to exploit special circumstances the possibility to do so profitably, but also by conveying to the other parties the information that there is some such opportunity. It is by this conveying of information in coded form that the competitive efforts of the market game secure the utilization of widely dispersed knowledge.

Even more important, perhaps, than the information about wants that may be satisfied and for whose satisfaction an attractive price is offered, is the information about the possibility of doing so by a smaller outlay than is currently incurred of resources which are needed also elsewhere. And it is not merely, or perhaps even chiefly, the fact that prices will spread the knowledge that some technical possibilities exist to produce a commodity more efficiently, but above all the indication which of the available technical methods is the most economical in the given circumstances, and the changes in the relative scarcities of the different materials and other factors, which alter the relative advantages of the different methods, which is of decisive importance. Almost any product can be produced by a great many different quantitative combinations of the various factors of production, and which of them will be the least costly, i.e. will involve the least sacrifice of other goods that might be produced with them, is indicated by the relative prices of these factors.[15]

By thus endeavouring to produce their outputs as cheaply as possible the producers in a sense will indeed make the total product of the catallaxy as great as possible. The prices at which they can buy the different factors on the market will tell each which quantities of any two of them cost the same because they bring elsewhere the same marginal return; and he will thereby be induced so to adjust the relative amounts of any pair of factors he requires that such quantities of them will make the same marginal contributions to his output (be 'marginal substitutes' for each other) as will cost him the same amount of money. If this is generally done, and the marginal rates of substitution between any two factors have become the same in all their uses, the market has reached the horizon of catallactic possibilities at which the greatest possible quantity of the particular combination of goods is being produced which in the circumstances can be produced.

For the case of only two goods this horizon of catallactic possibilities can be illustrated by a simple diagram known in economic theory as a transformation curve: if the quantities of the two goods are measured along two rectangular co-ordinates, any straight line through the origin will represent the locus of all possible total quantities of two products in a given quantitative proportion, say $a+2b$, $2a+4b$, $3a+6b$, etc., etc., and there will be, for any given supply of factors, an absolute maximum that can be obtained if these two factors are distributed economically between the two uses. The convex curve connecting the points standing for the maxima of the different combinations of the two goods is the 'transformation curve' representing the horizon of catallactic possibilities for these two goods in the existing situation. The important point about this range of potential maxima is that it is not simply a technical fact but is determined by the momentary scarcity or plenty of the different factors, and that the horizon of catallactic possibilities will be reached only if the marginal rates of substitution between the different factors are made the same in all their uses—which, of course, in a catallaxy producing many goods, can be achieved only by all producers adjusting the relative quantities of the different factors which they use according to their uniform market prices.

The horizon of catallactic possibilities (which for a system producing n goods would be represented by an n-dimensional surface) would indicate the range of what are now usually described as Pareto-optima, i.e. all the combinations of different goods which can be produced for which it is impossible so to rearrange production that some consumer gets more of something without in consequence anybody else getting less of anything (which is always possible if the product corresponds to any point inside the horizon).

If there is no accepted order of rank of the different needs, there is no way of deciding which among the different combinations of goods corresponding to this horizon is larger than any other. Yet every one of these combinations is a 'maximum' in a peculiar limited sense which, however, is the only sense in which, for a society which has no agreed hierarchy of ends, we can speak of a maximum at all: it corresponds to the largest amount of the particular combination of goods which can be produced by the known techniques (a sense in which the largest quantity of one good only that could be produced if nothing else were produced would be one of the maxima included in the horizon of possibilities!). The combination in fact produced will be determined by the relative strength of the demand for the different goods—which in turn depends on the distribution of incomes, that is the prices paid for the contributions of the different factors of production, and these again serve merely (or are necessary in order) to secure that the horizon of catallactic possibilities be approached.

The effect of all this is thus that, while the share of each factor of production in the total output is determined by the instrumental necessities of the only known process by which we can secure a steady approach to that horizon, the material equivalent of any given individual share will be as large as it can possibly be made. In other words, while the share of each player in the game of catallaxy will be determined partly by skill and partly by chance, the content of the share which is allocated to him by that mixed game of chance and skill will be a true maximum.

It would, of course, be unreasonable to demand more from the operation of a system in which the several actors do not serve a common hierarchy of ends but co-operate with each other only because they can thereby mutually assist each other in their respective pursuit of their individual ends. Nothing else is indeed possible in an order in which the participants are free in the sense of being allowed to use their own knowledge for their own purposes. So long as the game is played by which alone all this knowledge can be utilized and all these ends taken into account, it would be inconsistent and unjust to divert some part of the stream of goods to some group of players whom some authority thinks deserves it. On the other hand, in a centrally directed system, it would be impossible to reward people in accordance with the value which their voluntary contributions have to their fellows, because, without an effective market, the individuals could neither know, nor be allowed to decide, where to apply their efforts. The responsibility for the use of his gifts and the usefulness of the results would rest entirely with the directing authority.

Men can be allowed to act on their own knowledge and for their own purposes only if the reward they obtain is dependent in part on circumstances which they can neither control nor foresee. And if they are to be allowed to be guided in their actions by their own moral beliefs, it cannot also be morally required that the aggregate effects of their respective actions on the different people should correspond to some ideal of distributive justice. In this sense freedom is inseparable from rewards which often have no connection with merit and are therefore felt to be unjust.

In judging the adaptations to changed circumstances comparisons of the new with the former position are irrelevant

While in the case of bilateral barter the reciprocal advantages to both parties are easy to see, the position may at first seem to be different in the conditions of multilateral or multiangular exchange which are the rule in modern society. Here a person will normally render services to one group of persons, but himself receive services from another group. And as every decision will usually be a question of from whom to buy and to whom to sell, though it is still true that in this case both parties of the new transaction will gain, we must consider also the effects on those with whom the participants in the new transactions have decided not to deal again because their new partners have offered them more favourable terms. The effects of such decisions on third persons will be felt particularly severely when these have come to count on the opportunity to deal with the persons with whom they have done so in the past, and now find their expectations disappointed and their incomes diminished. Must we not in this case count the loss of those from whom demand or supply has turned as an offset against the gain of those who have availed themselves of the new opportunities?

As we have seen in the last chapter, such undeserved diminutions of the material positions of whole groups are the source of a main complaint against the market order. Yet such diminutions of the relative, and often even of the absolute position of some will be a necessary and constantly recurring effect so long as in the several transactions the parties consider only their own advantage and not the effects of their decisions on others. Does this mean that something is disregarded that ought to be taken into account in the formation of a desirable order?

The conditions which prevailed earlier, however, are wholly irrelevant for what is appropriate after the external circumstances have changed. The past position of those who are now forced to descend from it was determined by the operation of the same process as that which now favours others. The action of the market takes account only of the conditions known to exist at present (or expected to prevail in the future); it adapts relative values to them without regard to the past. Those whose services were more valuable in the past were then accordingly paid for them. The new position is not an improvement over the past condition in the sense that it constitutes a better adaptation to the same circumstances; it represents the same kind of adaptation to new circumstances as the former position did with respect to the circumstances which existed then.

In the context of an order the advantage of which is that it continually adapts the use of resources to conditions unforeseen and unknown to most people, bygones are forever bygones[16]—the past conditions tell us nothing about what is appropriate now. Though to some extent past prices will serve as the chief basis for forming expectations about future prices, they will do so only where a large part of the conditions have remained unchanged, but not where extensive changes have occurred.

Any discovery of more favourable opportunities for satisfying their needs by some will thus be a disadvantage to those on whose services they would otherwise have relied. Yet in this respect the effects of new and more favourable opportunities for exchanging which appear for particular individuals are for society as a whole as beneficial as the discovery of new or hitherto unknown material resources. The parties to the new exchange transaction will now be able to satisfy their needs by the expenditure of a smaller part of their resources, and what they thereby save can be used to provide additional services to others. Of course, those who as a result will be deprived of their former customers will incur a loss which it would be in their interest to prevent. But like all others, they will have been profiting all the time from the repercussions of thousands of similar changes elsewhere which release resources for a better supply of the market. And though in the short run the unfavourable effect on them may out-balance the sum of the indirect beneficial effects, in the long run the sum of all those particular effects, although they always will harm some, are likely to improve the chances for all. This result, however, will occur only if the immediate and generally more visible effects are systematically disregarded and policy is governed by the probability that in the long run all will profit by the utilization of every opportunity of the kind.

The known and concentrated harm to those who lose part or all of the customary source of income must, in other words, not be allowed to count against the diffused (and, from the point of view of policy, usually unknown and therefore indiscriminate) benefits to many. We shall see that the universal tendency of politics is to give preferential consideration to few strong and therefore conspicuous effects over the numerous small and therefore neglected ones, and therefore to grant special privileges to groups threatened with the loss of positions they have achieved. But when we reflect that most of the benefits we currently owe to the market are the results of continuous adaptations which are unknown to us, and because of which only some but not all of the consequences of our deliberate decisions can be foreseen, it should be obvious that we will achieve the best results if we abide by a rule which, if consistently applied, is likely to increase everybody's chances. Though the share of each will be unpredictable, because it will depend only in part on his skill and opportunities to learn facts, and in part on accident, this is the condition which alone will make it the interest of all so to conduct themselves as to make as large as possible the aggregate product of which they will get an unpredictable share. Of the resulting distribution it cannot be claimed that it is materially just, but only that it is the result of a process which is known to improve the chances of all and not the consequence of specific directed measures which favour some on principles that could not be generally acted upon.

Rules of just conduct protect only material domains and not market values

The value which any person's products or services will have in the market, and therefore his share in the aggregate product, will always depend also on decisions which other persons make in the light of the changing possibilities known to them. A particular price or a particular share in the total output can therefore be assured to any person only by requiring particular other persons to buy from him at a certain price. This is clearly incompatible with the principle that coercion is to be limited to the enforcement of uniform rules of just conduct equally applicable to all. Rules of just conduct which are end-independent cannot determine what anyone must do (apart from the discharge of obligations voluntarily entered into), but only what he must not do. They merely lay down the principles determining the protected domain of each on which nobody must encroach.

In other words, rules of just conduct can enable us merely to determine which particular things belong to particular persons, but not what these things will be worth, or what benefit they will confer on those to whom they belong. The rules serve to provide information for the decision of individuals, and thus help to reduce uncertainty, but they cannot determine what use the individual can make of this information and therefore also not eliminate *all* uncertainty. They tell each individual only what are the particular things he can count on being able to use, but not what the results of his use will be so far as these depend on the exchange of the product of their efforts with others.

It is clearly misleading to express this by saying that the rules of just conduct allocate particular things to particular people. They state the conditions under which any person can acquire or give up particular things, but do not by themselves definitely determine the particular conditions in which he will find himself. His domain will at any moment depend on how successfully he has used these conditions, and on the particular opportunities he happens to have encountered. In a sense it is even true that such a system gives to those who already have. But this is its merit rather than its defect, because it is this feature which makes it worth-while for everybody to direct his efforts not only towards immediate results but also towards the future increase of his capacity of rendering services to others. It is the possibility of acquisition for the purpose of improving the capacity for future acquisition which engenders a continuous overall process in which we do not at every moment have to start from scratch, but can begin with equipment which is the result of past efforts in order to make as large as possible the earnings from the means which we control.

The correspondence of expectations is brought about by a disappointment of some expectations

The abstract rule of conduct can (and, in order to secure the formation of a spontaneous order, should) thus protect only the expectation of command over particular physical things and services, and not the expectations concerning their market value, i.e. the terms on which they can be exchanged for other things. This is a point of central importance which is frequently misunderstood. From it follow several significant corollaries. First, though it is the aim of law to increase certainty, it can eliminate only certain sources of uncertainty and it would be harmful if it attempted to eliminate all uncertainty: it can protect expectations only by prohibiting interference with a man's property (including claims on such future services of others as these others have voluntarily promised) and not by requiring others to take particular actions. It can, therefore, not assure any one that the goods and services which he has to offer will have a particular value, but only that he will be allowed to obtain for them what price he can.

The reason why the law can protect only some but not all expectations, or remove only some but not all sources of uncertainty, is that rules of just conduct can only limit the range of permitted actions in such a manner that the intentions of different persons will not clash, but cannot positively determine what actions those individuals must perform. By restraining the range of actions which any individual may take, the law opens for all the possibility of effective collaboration with others, but does not assure it. Rules of conduct that equally limit the freedom of each so as to assure the same freedom to all can merely make possible agreements for obtaining what is now possessed by others, and thereby channel the efforts for all towards seeking agreement with others. But they cannot secure the success of these efforts, or determine the terms on which such agreements can be concluded.

The correspondence of expectations that makes it possible for all parties to achieve what they are striving for is in fact brought about by a process of learning by trial and error which must involve a constant disappointment of some expectations. The process of adaptation operates, as do the adjustments of any self-organizing system, by what cybernetics has taught us to call negative feedback: responses to the differences between the expected and the actual results of actions so that these differences will be reduced. This will produce an increased correspondence of expectations of the different persons so long as current prices provide some indications of what future prices will be, that is, so long as, in a fairly constant framework of known facts, always only a few of them change; and so long as the price mechanism operates as a medium of communicating knowledge which brings it about that the facts which become known to some, through the effects of their actions on prices, are made to influence the decision of others.

It may at first appear paradoxical that in order to achieve the greatest attainable certainty it should be necessary to leave uncertain so important an object of expectations as the terms at which things can be bought and sold. The paradox disappears, however, when we remember that we can aim only at providing the best basis for judging what of necessity is uncertain and for securing continual adaptation to what has not been known before: we can strive only for the best utilization of partial knowledge that constantly changes, and that is communicated mainly through changes in prices, and not for the best utilization of a given and constant stock of knowledge. The best we can attain in such a situation is not certainty but the elimination of avoidable uncertainty—which cannot be attained by preventing unforeseen changes from spreading their effects, but only by facilitating the adaptation to such changes.

It is often contended that it is unjust to let the burden of such unforeseeable changes fall on people who could not foresee them, and that, if such risks are unavoidable, they ought to be pooled and the losses equally born by all. It can, however, hardly be known whether any particular change was unforeseeable for all. The whole system rests on providing inducements for all to use their skill to find out particular circumstances in order to anticipate impending changes as accurately as possible. This incentive would be removed if each decision did not carry the risk of loss, or if an authority had to decide whether a particular error in anticipation was excusable or not.[17]

Abstract rules of just conduct can determine only chances and not particular results

Rules of just conduct that apply equally to all members of society can refer only to some but not to all of the conditions under which their actions take place. It is a consequence of this that they can secure for all individuals only chances and not the certainty of a particular outcome. Even in a game with equal chances for all players there will be some winners and some losers. By assuring the individual of some of the elements of the situation in which he will have to act, his prospects will be improved, but necessarily many factors left undetermined on which his success depends. The aim of legislation, in laying down rules for an unknown number of future instances, can therefore be only to increase the chances of unknown persons whose opportunities will chiefly depend on their individual knowledge and skill as well as on the particular conditions in which accident will place them. The efforts of the legislator can thus be directed only towards increasing the chances for all, not in the sense that the incidence of the diffused effects of his decision on the various individuals will be known, but only in the sense that he can aim at increasing the opportunities that will become available to some unknown persons.

It is a corollary of this that each individual will have a claim in justice, not to an equal chance in general, but only that the principles guiding all coercive measures of government should be equally likely to benefit anybody's chances; and that these rules be applied in all particular instances irrespective of whether the effect on particular individuals seems desirable or not. So long as the positions of the different individuals are to be left at all dependent on their skill and on the particular circumstances they encounter, nobody can assure that they will all have the same chances.

In such a game in which the results for the individuals depend partly on chance and partly on their skill, there is evidently no sense in calling the outcome either just or unjust. The position is somewhat like that in a competition for a prize in which we shall attempt to make conditions such that we can say who performs best, but will not be able to decide whether the best actual performance is proof of higher merit. We shall not be able to prevent accidents from interfering, and in consequence cannot be sure that the results will be proportionate to the capacity of the competitors or their particular qualities that we desire to encourage. Though we want nobody to cheat, we cannot prevent anyone from stumbling. Although we employ competition to find out who performs best, the result will only show who did best on the particular occasion, but not that the victor will generally do best. Too often we shall find that 'the race is not to the swift, nor the battle to the strong, neither yet bread to the wise, nor yet riches to men of understanding, nor yet favour to men of skill; but time and chance happeneth to them all.'[18] It is our ignorance of the effects of the application of the rules on particular people which makes justice possible in a spontaneous order of free men.[19]

Consistent justice will even often demand that we act as if we were ignorant of circumstances which in fact we do know. Both freedom and justice are values that can prevail only among men with limited knowledge and would have no meaning in a society of omniscient men. Consistent use of the power which we do possess over the structure of the market order will require systematic disregard of the concrete foreseeable effects a judicial decision will have. As the judge can be just only if he follows the principles of the law and disregards all the circumstances not referred to by its abstract rules (but which may be highly relevant for the moral evaluation of the action), so the rules of justice must limit the circumstances which may be taken into account in all instances. If *tout comprendre est tout pardonner*, this is precisely what the judge must not attempt because he never knows all. The need to rely on abstract rules in maintaining a spontaneous order is a consequence of that ignorance and uncertainty; and the enforcement of rules of conduct will achieve its purpose only if we adhere to them consistently and do not treat them merely as a substitute for knowledge which in the particular case we do not possess. It is therefore not the effect of their application in the particular cases but only the effects of their universal application that will lead to the improvement of everybody's chances and will therefore be accepted as just.[20] In particular, all concern with short run effects is bound to increase the preponderance of the visible and predictable effects over the invisible and distant ones, while rules intended to benefit all alike must not allow effects which accident has brought to the knowledge of the judge to outweigh those which he cannot know.

In a spontaneous order undeserved disappointments cannot be avoided. They are bound to cause grievances and a sense of having been treated unjustly, although nobody has acted unjustly. Those affected will usually, in perfectly good faith and as a matter of justice, put forward claims for remedial measures. But if coercion is to be restricted to the enforcement of uniform rules of just conduct, it is essential that government should not possess the power to accede to such demands. The reduction of the relative position of some about which they complain is the consequence of their having submitted to the same chances to which not only some others now owe the rise in their position, but to which they themselves owed their past position. It is only because countless others constantly submit to disappointments of their reasonable expectations that every one has as high an income as he has; and it is therefore only fair that he accept the unfavourable turn of events when they go against him. This is no less true when not a single individual but members of a large group share—and mutually support—that sense of grievance, and the change in consequence comes to be regarded as constituting a 'social problem'.

Specific commands ('interference') in a catallaxy create disorder and can never be just

A rule of just conduct serves the reconciliation of the different purposes of many individuals. A command serves the achievement of particular results. Unlike a rule of just conduct, it does not merely limit the range of choice of the individuals (or require them to satisfy expectations they have deliberately created) but commands them to act in a particular manner not required of other persons.

The term 'interference' (or 'intervention') is properly applied only to such specific orders which, unlike the rules of just conduct, do not serve merely the formation of a spontaneous order but aim at particular results. It was in this sense only that the classical economists used the term. They would not have applied it to the establishment or improvement of those generic rules which are required for the functioning of the market order and which they explicitly presupposed in their analysis.

Even in ordinary language 'interference' implies the operation of a process that proceeds by itself on certain principles because its parts obey certain rules. We would not call it interference if we oiled a clockwork, or in any other way secured the conditions that a going mechanism required for its proper functioning. Only if we changed the position of any particular part in a manner which is not in accord with the general principle of its operation, such as shifting the hands of a clock, can it properly be said that we have interfered. The aim of interference thus is always to bring about a particular result which is different from that which would have been produced if the mechanism had been allowed unaided to follow its inherent principles.[21] If the rules on which such a process proceeds are determined beforehand, the particular results it will produce at any one time will be independent of the momentary wishes of men.

The particular results that will be determined by altering a particular action of the system will always be inconsistent with its overall order: if they were not, they could have been achieved by changing the rules on which the system was henceforth to operate. Interference, if the term is properly used, is therefore by definition an isolated act of coercion,[22] undertaken for the purpose of achieving a particular result, and without committing oneself to do the same in all instances where some circumstances defined by a rule are the same. It is, therefore, always an unjust act in which somebody is coerced (usually in the interest of a third) in circumstances where another would not be coerced, and for purposes which are not his own.

It is, moreover, an act which will always disrupt the overall order and will prevent that mutual adjustment of all its parts on which the spontaneous order rests. It will do this by preventing the persons to whom the specific commands are directed from adapting their actions to circumstances known to them, and by making them serve some particular ends which others are not required to serve, and which will be satisfied at the expense of some other unpredictable effects. Every act of interference thus creates a privilege in the sense that it will secure benefits to some at the expense of others, in a manner which cannot be justified by principles capable of general application. What in this respect the formation of a spontaneous order requires is what is also required by the confinement of all coercion to the enforcement of rules of just conduct: that coercion be used only where it is required by uniform rules equally applicable to all.

The aim of law should be to improve equally the chances of all

Since rules of just conduct can affect only the chances of success of the efforts of men, the aim in altering or developing them should be to improve as much as possible the chances of anyone selected at random. Since in the long run it cannot be predicted when and where the particular conjunction of circumstances will occur to which any rule refers, it must also be unknown who will benefit by such an abstract rule and how much different persons will benefit. Such universal rules intended to apply for an indefinite period can thus aim solely at increasing the *chances* of unknown persons.

We prefer to speak in this context of chances rather than of probabilities because the latter term suggests numerical magnitudes which will not be known. All the law can do is to add to the number of favourable possibilities likely to arise for some unknown person and thus to build up an increasing likelihood that favourable opportunities will come anyone's way. But though the aim ought to be to add to everyone's prospects, it will normally not be known whose prospects will be improved by a particular legislative measure, and how much.

It should be noted that the concept of the chance enters here in two ways. In the first instance the relative position of any given persons can be described only as a range of opportunities which, if precisely known, could be represented as a probability distribution. Second, there is the question of the probability that any one member of the society will occupy any of the positions thus described. The resulting concept of the chances of any member of the society to have a certain range of opportunities is thus a complex one to which it is difficult to give mathematical precision. This would be useful, however, only if the numerical magnitudes were known, which, of course, they are not.[23]

It is obvious that the endeavour to add indiscriminately to anyone's chances will not result in making everybody's chances the same. The chances will always depend not only on future events which the law does not control, but also on the initial position of any individual at the moment the rules in question are adopted. In a continuous process this initial position of any person will always be a result of preceding phases, and therefore be as much an undesigned fact and dependent on chance as the future development. And since a part of most people's efforts will normally be directed to the improvement of their chances for the future, rather than to the satisfaction of their current needs, and more so as they have already succeeded in making provisions for the latter, the initial position of anyone will always be as much the result of a series of past accidents as of his efforts and foresight. It appears, therefore, that it is because the individual is free to decide whether to use the results of his current efforts for current consumption or for increasing his future opportunities that the position he has already achieved will improve his chances of reaching a still better position, or that 'to those who have will be given'. The possibility of distributing the use of one's resources over time will therefore always also tend to increase the discrepancy between the merits of a person's current efforts and the benefits which he currently receives.

To the extent that we rely on the institution of the family for the launching of the individual in life, the chain of events affecting the prospects of anyone will necessarily extend even beyond the period of his individual life. It is therefore inevitable that in the ongoing process of the catallaxy the starting point, and therefore also the prospects, of the different individuals will be different.

This is not to say that there may not be a case in justice for correcting positions which have been determined by earlier unjust acts or institutions. But unless such injustice is clear and recent, it will generally be impracticable to correct it. It will on the whole seem preferable to accept the given position as due to accident and simply from the present onwards to refrain from any measures aiming at benefiting particular individuals or groups. Though it might seem reasonable so to frame laws that they will tend more strongly to improve the opportunities of those whose chances are relatively small, this can rarely be achieved by generic rules. There are, no doubt, instances where the past development of law has introduced a bias in favour or to the disadvantage of particular groups; and such provisions ought clearly to be corrected. But on the whole it would seem that the fact which, contrary to a widely held belief, has contributed most during the last two hundred years to increase not only the absolute but also the relative position of those in the lowest income groups has been the general growth of wealth which has tended to raise the income of the lowest groups more than the relatively higher ones. This, of course, is a consequence of the circumstance that, once the Malthusian devil has been exorcized, the growth of aggregate wealth tends to make labour more scarce than capital. But nothing we can do, short of establishing absolute equality of all incomes, can alter the fact that a certain percentage of the population must find itself in the bottom of the scale; and as a matter of logic the chance of any person picked out at random being among the lowest 10 per cent must be one tenth![24]

The Good Society is one in which the chances of anyone selected at random are likely to be as great as possible

The conclusion to which our considerations lead is thus that we should regard as the most desirable order of society one which we would choose if we knew that our initial position in it would be decided purely by chance (such as the fact of our being born into a particular family). Since the attraction such chance would possess for any particular adult individual would probably be dependent on the particular skills, capacities and tastes he has already acquired, a better way of putting this would be to say that the best society would be that in which we would prefer to place our children if we knew that their position in it would be determined by lot. Very few people would probably in this case prefer a strictly egalitarian order. Yet, while one might, for instance, regard the kind of life lived in the past by the landed aristocracy as the most attractive kind of life, and would choose a society in which such a class existed if he were assured that he or his children would be a member of that class, he would probably decide differently if he knew that that position would be determined by drawing lots and that in consequence it would be much more probable that he would become an agricultural labourer. He would then very likely choose that very type of industrial society which did not offer such delectable plums to a few but offered better prospects to the great majority.[25]

ELEVEN

THE DISCIPLINE OF ABSTRACT RULES AND THE EMOTIONS OF THE TRIBAL SOCIETY

Liberalism—it is well to recall this today—is the supreme form of generosity; it is the right which the majority concedes to minorities and hence it is the noblest cry that has ever resounded on this planet. It announces the determination to share existence with the enemy; more than that, with an enemy which is weak. It was incredible that the human species should have arrived at so noble an attitude, so paradoxical, so refined, so anti-natural. Hence it is not to be wondered at that this same humanity should soon appear anxious to get rid of it. It is a discipline too difficult and complex to take firm root on earth.

José Ortega y Gasset *

The pursuit of unattainable goals may prevent the achievement of the possible

It is not enough to recognize that 'social justice' is an empty phrase without determinable content. It has become a powerful incantation which serves to support deep-seated emotions that are threatening to destroy the Great Society. Unfortunately it is not true that if something cannot be achieved, it can do no harm to strive for it.[1] Like chasing any mirage it is likely to produce results which one would have done much to avoid if one had foreseen them. Many desirable aims will be sacrificed in the vain hope of making possible what must forever elude our grasp.

We live at present under the governance of two different and irreconcilable conceptions of what is right; and after a period of ascendancy of conceptions which have made the vision of an Open Society possible, we are relapsing rapidly into the conceptions of the tribal society from which we had been slowly emerging. We had hoped that with the defeat of the European dictators we had banished the threat of the totalitarian state; but all we have achieved was to put down the first flare-up of a reaction which is slowly spreading everywhere. Socialism is simply a re-assertion of that tribal ethics whose gradual weakening had made an approach to the Great Society possible. The submergence of classical liberalism under the inseparable forces of socialism and nationalism is the consequence of a revival of those tribal sentiments.

Most people are still unwilling to face the most alarming lesson of modern history: that the greatest crimes of our time have been committed by governments that had the enthusiastic support of millions of people who were guided by moral impulses. It is simply not true that Hitler or Mussolini, Lenin or Stalin, appealed only to the worst instincts of their people: they also appealed to some of the feelings which also dominate contemporary democracies. Whatever disillusionment the more mature supporters of these movements may have experienced as they came to see the effects of the policies they had supported, there can be no doubt that the rank and file of the communist, national-socialist or fascist movements contained many men and women inspired by ideals not very different from those of some of the most influential social philosophers in the Western countries. Some of them certainly believed that they were engaged in the creation of a just society in which the needs of the most deserving or 'socially most valuable' would be better cared for. They were led by a desire for a visible common purpose which is our inheritance from the tribal society and which we still find breaking through everywhere.

The causes of the revival of the organizational thinking of the tribe

One reason why in recent times we have seen a strong revival of organizational thinking and a decline in the understanding of the operation of the market order is that an ever growing proportion of the members of society work as members of large organizations and find their horizon of comprehension limited to what is required by the internal structure of such organizations. While the peasant and the independent craftsman, the merchant and the journeyman, were familiar with the market and, even if they did not understand its operation, had come to accept its dictates as the natural course of things, the growth of big enterprise and of the great administrative bureaucracies has brought it about that an ever increasing part of the people spend their whole working life as members of large organizations, and are led to think wholly in terms of the requirements of the organizational form of life. Even though in the pre-industrial society the great majority also spent most of their lives within the familial organization which was the unit of all economic activity,[2] the heads of the households saw society as a network of family units connected by the markets.

Today organizational thinking increasingly dominates the activities of many of the most powerful and influential figures of modern society, the organizers themselves.[3] The modern improvements in the technique of organization, and the consequent increase of the range of particular tasks which can be performed by means of large-scale organization far beyond what was possible before, have created the belief that there are no limits to what organization can achieve. Most people are no longer aware of the extent to which the more comprehensive order of society on which depends the very success of the organizations within it is due to ordering forces of an altogether different kind.

The other main reason for the growing dominance of organizational thinking is that the success of the deliberate creation of new rules for purposive organizations has in many respects been so great, that men no longer recognize that the more comprehensive order within which the organizations operate rests on a different type of rules which have not been invented with a definite foreseen purpose in mind, but are the product of a process of trial and error in the course of which more experience has been accumulated than any living person is aware of.

The immoral consequences of morally inspired efforts

Though in the long perspective of Western civilization the history of law is a history of a gradual emergence of rules of just conduct capable of universal application, its development during the last hundred years has become increasingly one of the destruction of justice by 'social justice', until even some students of jurisprudence have lost sight of the original meaning of 'justice'. We have seen how the process has mainly taken the form of a replacement of the rules of just conduct by those rules of organization which we call public law (a 'subordinating law'), a distinction which some socialist lawyers are trying hard to obliterate.[4] In substance this has meant that the individual is no longer bound only by rules which confine the scope of his private actions, but has become increasingly subject to the commands of authority. The growing technological possibilities of control, together with the presumed moral superiority of a society whose members serve the same hierarchy of ends, have made this totalitarian trend appear under a moral guise. It is indeed the concept of 'social justice' which has been the Trojan Horse through which totalitarianism has entered.

The values which still survive from the small end-connected groups whose coherence depended upon them, are, however, not only different from, but often incompatible with, the values which make possible the peaceful coexistence of large numbers in the Open Society. The belief that while we pursue the new ideal of this Great Society in which all human beings are regarded as equal, we can also preserve the different ideals of the small closed society, is an illusion. To attempt it leads to the destruction of the Great Society.

The possibility of men living together in peace and to their mutual advantage without having to agree on common concrete aims, and bound only by abstract rules of conduct,[5] was perhaps the greatest discovery mankind ever made. The 'capitalist' system which grew out of this discovery no doubt did not fully satisfy the ideals of liberalism, because it grew up while legislators and governments did not really understand the *modus operandi* of the market, and largely in spite of the policies actually pursued.[6] Capitalism as it exists today in consequence undeniably has many remediable defects that an intelligent policy of freedom ought to correct. A system which relies on the spontaneous ordering forces of the market, once it has reached a certain level of wealth, is also by no means incompatible with government providing, outside the market, some security against severe deprivation. But the attempt to secure to each what he is thought to deserve, by imposing upon all a system of common concrete ends towards which their efforts are directed by authority, as socialism aims to do, would be a retrograde step that would deprive us of the utilization of the knowledge and aspirations of millions, and thereby of the advantages of a free civilization. Socialism is not based merely on a different system of ultimate values from that of liberalism, which one would have to respect even if one disagreed; it is based on an intellectual error which makes its adherents blind to its consequences. This must be plainly said because the emphasis on the alleged difference of the ultimate values has become the common excuse of the socialists for shirking the real intellectual issue. The pretended difference of the underlying value judgments has become a protective cloak used to conceal the faulty reasoning underlying the socialist schemes.

In the Great Society 'social justice' becomes a disruptive force

Not only is it impossible for the Great Society to maintain itself while enforcing rules of 'social' or distributive justice; for its preservation it is also necessary that no particular groups holding common views about what they are entitled to should be allowed to enforce these views by preventing others to offer their services at more favourable terms. Though common interests of those whose position is affected by the same circumstances are likely to produce strong common opinions about what they deserve, and will provide a motive for common action to achieve their ends, any such group action to secure a particular income or position for its members creates an obstacle to the integration of the Great Society and is therefore anti-social in the true sense of this word. It must become a divisive force because it produces not a reconciliation of, but a conflict between, the interests of the different groups. As the active participants in the struggle for 'social justice' well know, it becomes in practice a struggle for power of organized interests in which arguments of justice serve merely as pretexts.

The chief insight we must hold on to is that not always when a group of people have strong views about what they regard as their claims in justice does this mean that there exists (or can be found) a corresponding rule which, if universally applied, would produce a viable order. It is a delusion to believe that whenever a question is represented as one of justice it must be possible to discover a rule capable of universal application which will decide that question.[7] Nor does the fact that a law endeavours to meet somebody's claim for justice prove that it is a rule of just conduct.

All groups whose members pursue the same or parallel aims will develop common views about what is right for members of those groups. Such views, however, will be right only for all those who pursue the same aims, but may be wholly incompatible with any principles by which such a group can be integrated into the overall order of society. The producers of any particular commodity or service who all aim at a good remuneration for their efforts will regard as unjust the action of any fellow producer who tends to reduce the incomes of the others. Yet it will be precisely the kind of actions by some members of the group that the rest regard as harmful which will fit the activities of the members of the group into the overall pattern of the Great Society and thereby benefit all.

It is certainly in itself not unjust if a barber in one city receives

$3 for a haircut while in another city only $2 is paid for the same work. But it would clearly be unjust if the barbers in the first prevented any from the second city from improving their position by offering their services in the first for, say, $2.50 and thus, while improving their position, lowering the income of the first group. Yet it is precisely against such efforts that established groups are today permitted to combine in defence of their established position. The rule 'do nothing which will decrease the income of the members of your own group' will often be regarded as an obligation of justice toward one's fellow members. But it cannot be accepted as a rule of just conduct in a Great Society where it will conflict with the general principles on which the activities of that society are co-ordinated. The other members of that society will have every interest and moral right to prevent the enforcement of such a rule that the members of a special group regard as just, because the principles of integration of the Great Society demand that the action of some of those occupied in a particular manner should often lead to a reduction of the incomes of their fellows. This is precisely the virtue of competition. The conceptions of group justice would often proscribe all effective competition as unjust—and many of the 'fair competition' demands aim in effect at little less.

It is probably true that in any group whose members know that their prospects depend on the same circumstances, views will develop that represent as unjust all conduct of any member which harms the others; and there will in consequence arise a desire to prevent such conduct. But by any outsider it will rightly be regarded as unjust if any member of such a group is prevented by his fellows from offering him more advantageous terms than the rest of the group are willing to offer. And the same is true when some 'interloper' who before was not recognized as a member of the group is made to conform to the standards of the group as soon as his efforts compete with theirs.

The important fact which most people are reluctant to admit, yet which is probably true in most instances, is that, though the pursuit of the selfish aims of the individual will usually lead him to serve the general interest, the collective actions of organized groups are almost invariably contrary to the general interest. What in fact leads to the condemnation as anti-social of that pursuit of individual interests which contributes to the general interest, and to the commendation as 'social' of the subservience to those sectional interests which destroy the overall order, are sentiments which we have inherited from earlier forms of society. The use of coercion in the service of this kind of 'social justice', meaning the interests of the particular group to which the individual belongs, will thus always mean the creation of particular preserves of special groups united against the outsiders—interest groups which exist because they are allowed to use force or pressure on government for the benefit of their members. But, however much the members of such groups may agree among themselves that what they want is just, there exists no principle which could make it appear as just to the outsider. Yet today, if such a group is only large enough, its representation of the demands of its members as just is commonly accepted as one view of justice which must be taken into account in ordering the whole, even though it does not rest on any principle which could be generally applied.

From the care of the most unfortunate to the protection of vested interests

We must not lose sight, however, of the fact that at the beginning of the striving for 'social justice' stood the laudable desire to abolish destitution, and that the Great Society has brilliantly succeeded in abolishing poverty in the absolute sense. [8] Nobody capable of useful work need today lack food and shelter in the advanced countries, and for those incapable of themselves earning enough these necessities are generally provided outside the market. Poverty in the relative sense must of course continue to exist outside of any completely egalitarian society: so long as there exists inequality, somebody must be the bottom of the scale. But the abolition of absolute poverty is not helped by the endeavour to achieve 'social justice'; in fact, in many of the countries in which absolute poverty is still an acute problem, the concern with 'social justice' has become one of the greatest obstacles to the elimination of poverty. In the West the rise of the great masses to tolerable comfort has been the effect of the general growth of wealth and has been merely slowed down by measures interfering with the market mechanism. It has been this market mechanism which has created the increase of aggregate income, which also has made it possible to provide outside the market for the support of those unable to earn enough. But the attempts to 'correct' the results of the market in the direction of 'social justice' have probably produced more injustice in the form of new privileges, obstacles to mobility and frustration of efforts than they have contributed to the alleviation of the lot of the poor.

This development is a consequence of the circumstance that the appeal to 'social justice' that was originally made on behalf of the most unfortunate was taken up by many other groups whose members felt that they did not get as much as they thought that they deserved, and particularly by those groups who felt threatened in their present positions. As a demand that political action should assign to the members of any group the position which in some sense it deserved, 'social justice' is irreconcilable with the ideal that coercion should be used only to enforce the same rules of just conduct which all could take into account in making their plans. Yet when those claims were first admitted in favour of groups with whose misfortune everybody sympathized, the floodgates were opened to the demand by all who found their relative position threatened that their position be protected by government action. Misfortune, however, cannot create a claim for protection against risks which all have had to run in order to attain the position they occupy. The very language in current use which at once labels as a 'social problem' anything which causes dissatisfaction of any group, and suggests that it is the duty of the legislature to do something about such 'social injustice', has turned the conception of 'social justice' into a mere pretext for claims for privileges by special interests.

Those who turn with indignation against a conception of justice which failed, e.g., to prevent 'the rapidly proceeding up-rooting of the peasantry which commenced already after the Napoleonic wars, or the decline of the artisanry after the middle of the century, or the pauperization of the wage labourers' [9] wholly misconceive what can be achieved by enforcement of rules of just conduct in a world of free men who reciprocally serve each other for their own benefit and to whom nobody assigns tasks or allocates benefits. Since today we can probably even feed the numbers to which mankind has grown only thanks to the intensive utilization of dispersed knowledge which is made possible by the market—not to speak of maintaining that level of comfort which the great majority has reached in some parts of the world—it certainly would not be just to exempt some from the necessity of accepting a less favourable position than they had already attained if an unforeseen turn of events diminishes the value of their services to the rest. However sorry we may be for those who, through no fault of their own but as a result of unforeseeable developments, find themselves in a reduced position, this does not mean that we can have both the progressive increase in the level of general wealth on which the future improvement of the conditions of the great masses depends and no such recurrent declines of the position of some groups.

'Social justice' has in practice become simply the slogan used by all groups whose status tends to decline—by the farmer, the independent craftsman, the coalminer, the small shopkeeper, the clerical worker and a considerable part of the old 'middle class', rather than the industrial workers on whose behalf it was first raised but who have in general been the beneficiaries of recent developments. That the appeal to justice by such groups frequently succeeds in mobilizing the sympathy of many who regard the traditional hierarchy of society as a natural one, and who resent the ascent of new types to that middle position to which once the bare capacity to read and write gave access, does not show that such demands have any connection with generally applicable rules of just conduct.

In the existing political order such claims will in fact be met only when such groups are large enough to count politically and especially when it is possible to organize their members for common action. We shall see later that only some but not all such interests can be thus organized, and that in consequence the resulting advantages can be achieved only by some and will harm the rest. Yet the more organizations of interests are used for this purpose, the more necessary does it become for each group to organize for pressure on government, since those who fail to do so will be left out in the cold. Thus the conception of 'social justice' has resulted in the assurance by government of an appropriate income to particular groups, which has made the progressive organization of all such 'interests' inevitable. But the protection of expectations which such assurance involves cannot possibly be granted to all in any but a stationary society. The only just principle is therefore to concede this privilege to none.

At one time this argument would have had to be directed chiefly against the trade unions, since they were the first of such groups who succeeded in clothing their demands with the aura of legitimacy (and in being allowed to use coercion for their enforcement) by representing them as a requirement of 'social justice'. But though it was initially the use in the service of relatively poor and unfortunate groups that made discrimination in their favour appear justifiable, such discrimination served as the thin end of the wedge by which the principle of equality under the law was destroyed. It is now simply those who are numerically strong, or can readily be organized to withhold essential services, who gain in the process of political bargaining which governs legislation in contemporary democracy. But the particular absurdities which arise when a democracy attempts to determine the distribution of incomes by majority vote will occupy us further only in the third volume of the present work.

Attempts to 'correct' the order of the market lead to its destruction

The predominant view today appears to be that we should avail ourselves in the main of the ordering forces of the market, indeed must in a great measure do so, but should 'correct' its results where they are flagrantly unjust. Yet so long as the earnings of particular individuals or groups are not determined by the decision of some agency, no particular distribution of incomes can be meaningfully described as more just than another. If we want to make it substantively just, we can do so only by replacing the whole spontaneous order by an organization in which the share of each is fixed by some central authority. In other words, 'corrections' of the distribution brought about in a spontaneous process by particular acts of interference can never be just in the sense of satisfying a rule equally applicable to all. Every single act of this kind will give rise to demands by others to be treated on the same principle; and these demands can be satisfied only if all incomes are thus allocated.

The current endeavour to rely on a spontaneous order corrected according to principles of justice amounts to an attempt to have the best of two worlds which are mutually incompatible. Perhaps an absolute ruler, wholly independent of public opinion, might confine himself to mitigating the hardships of the more unfortunate ones by isolated acts of intervention and let a spontaneous order determine the positions of the rest. And it is certainly possible to take entirely out of the market process those who cannot adequately maintain themselves on the market and support them by means set aside for the purpose. For a person at the beginning of an uncertain career, and for his children, it might even be perfectly rational to agree that all should insure for a minimum of sustenance in such an eventuality. But a government dependent on public opinion, and particularly a democracy, will not be able to confine such attempts to supplement the market to the mitigation of the lot of the poorest. Whether it intends to let itself be guided by principles or not, it is in fact, if it has the power to do so, certain to be driven on by the principles implicit in the precedents it sets. By the measures it takes it will produce opinions and set standards which will force it to continue on the course on which it has embarked.

It is possible to 'correct' an order only by assuring that the principles on which it rests are consistently applied, but not by applying to some part of the whole principles which do not apply to the rest. As it is the essence of justice that the same principles are universally applied, it requires that government assist particular groups only in conditions in which it is prepared to act on the same principle in all similar instances.

The revolt against the discipline of abstract rules

The rise of the ideal of impersonal justice based on formal rules has been achieved in a continuous struggle against those feelings of personal loyalty which provide the basis of the tribal society but which in the Great Society must not be allowed to influence the use of the coercive powers of government. The gradual extension of a common order of peace from the small group to ever larger communities has involved constant clashes between the demands of sectional justice based on common visible purposes and the requirements of a universal justice equally applicable to the stranger and to the member of the group.[10] This has caused a constant conflict between emotions deeply ingrained in human nature through millennia of tribal existence and the demands of abstract principles whose significance nobody fully grasped. Human emotions are attached to concrete objects, and the emotions of justice in particular are still very much connected with the visible needs of the group to which each person belongs—the needs of the trade or profession, of the clan or the village, the town or the country to which each belongs. Only a mental reconstruction of the overall order of the Great Society enables us to comprehend that the deliberate aim at concrete common purposes, which to most people still appears as more meritorious and superior to blind obedience to abstract rules, would destroy that larger order in which all human beings count alike.

As we have already seen, much that will be truly social in the small end-connected group because it is conducive to the coherence of the working order of that society, will be anti-social from the point of view of the Great Society. The demand for 'social justice' is indeed an expression of revolt of the tribal spirit against the abstract requirements of the coherence of the Great Society with no such visible common purpose. It is only by extending the rules of just conduct to the relations with all other men, and at the same time depriving of their obligatory character those rules which cannot be universally applied, that we can approach a universal order of peace which might integrate all mankind into a single society.

While in the tribal society the condition of internal peace is the devotion of all members to some common visible purposes, and therefore to the will of somebody who can decide what at any moment these purposes are to be and how they are to be achieved, the Open Society of free men becomes possible only when the individuals are constrained only to obey the abstract rules that demarcate the domain of the means that each is allowed to use for his purposes. So long as any particular ends, which in a society of any size must always be the ends of some particular persons or group, are regarded as a justification of coercion, there must always arise conflicts between groups with different interests. Indeed, so long as particular purposes are the foundation of political organization, those whose purposes are different are inevitably enemies; and it is true that in such a society politics necessarily is dominated by the friend-enemy relation.[11] Rules of just conduct can become the same for all only when particular ends are not regarded as justification for coercion (apart from such special passing circumstances as war, rebellion or natural catastrophes).

The morals of the open and of the closed society

The process we are describing is closely associated with, and indeed a necessary consequence of, the circumstance that in an extensive market order the producers are led to serve people without knowing of their individual needs. Such an order which relies on people working with the effect of satisfying the wants of people of whom they do not know presupposes and requires somewhat different moral views, from one in which people serve visible needs. The indirect guidance by an expected monetary return, operating as an indicator of the requirements of others, demanded new moral conceptions which do not prescribe particular aims but rather general rules limiting the range of permitted actions.

It did become part of the ethos of the Open Society that it was better to invest one's fortune in instruments making it possible to produce more at smaller costs than to distribute it among the poor, or to cater for the needs of thousands of unknown people rather than to provide for the needs of a few known neighbours. These views, of course, did not develop because those who first acted upon them understood that they thus conferred greater benefits on their fellows, but because the groups and societies which acted in this way prospered more than others; it became in consequence gradually the recognized moral duty of the 'calling' to do so. In its purest form this ethos regards it as the prime duty to pursue a self-chosen end as effectively as possible without paying attention to the role it plays in the complex network of human activities. It is the view which is now commonly but somewhat misleading described as the Calvinist ethic—misleading because it prevailed already in the mercantile towns of medieval Italy and was taught by the Spanish Jesuits at about the same time as by Calvin.[12]

We still esteem doing good only if it is done to benefit specific known needs of known people, and regard it as really better to help one starving man we know than to relieve the acute need of a hundred men we do not know; but in fact we generally are doing most good by pursuing gain. It was somewhat misleading, and did his cause harm, when Adam Smith gave the impression as if the significant difference were that between the egoistic striving for gain and the altruistic endeavour to meet known needs. The aim for which the successful entrepreneur wants to use his profits may well be to provide a hospital or an art gallery for his home town. But quite apart from the question of what he wants to do with his profits after he has earned them, he is led to benefit more people by aiming at the largest gain than he could if he concentrated on the satisfaction of the needs of known persons. He is led by the invisible hand of the market to bring the succour of modern conveniences to the poorest homes he does not even know.[13]

It is true, however, that the moral views underlying the Open Society were long confined to small groups in a few urban localities, and have come generally to govern law and opinion in the Western world so comparatively recently that they are often still felt to be artificial and unnatural in contrast to the intuitive, and in part perhaps even instinctive, sentiments inherited from the older tribal society. The moral sentiments which made the Open Society possible grew up in the towns, the commercial and trading centres, while the feelings of the large numbers were still governed by the parochial sentiments and the xenophobic and fighting attitudes governing the tribal group.[14] The rise of the Great Society is far too recent an event to have given man time to shed the results of a development of hundreds of thousands of years, and not to regard as artificial and inhuman those abstract rules of conduct which often conflict with the deeply ingrained instincts to let himself be guided in action by perceived needs.

The resistance against the new morals of the Open Society was strengthened also by the realization that it not only indefinitely enlarged the circle of other people in relation to whom one had to obey moral rules, but that this extension of the scope of the moral code necessarily brought with itself a reduction of its content. If the enforceable duties towards all are to be the same, the duties towards none can be greater than the duties towards all—except where special natural or contractual relations exist. There can be a general obligation to render assistance in case of need towards a circumscribed group of fellow-men, but not towards men in general. The moral progress by which we have moved towards the Open Society, that is, the extension of the obligation to treat alike, not only the members of our tribe but persons of ever wider circles and ultimately all men, had to be bought at the price of an attenuation of the enforceable duty to aim deliberately at the well-being of the other members of the same group. When we can no longer know the others or the circumstances under which they live, such a duty becomes a psychological and intellectual impossibility. Yet the disappearance of these specific duties leaves an emotional void by depriving men both of satisfying tasks and the assurance of support in case of need.[15]

It would therefore not be really surprising if the first attempt of man to emerge from the tribal into an open society should fail because man is not yet ready to shed moral views developed for the tribal society; or, as Ortega y Gasset wrote of classical liberalism in the passage placed at the head of this chapter, it is not to be wondered that 'humanity should soon appear anxious to get rid of . . . so noble an attitude, so paradoxical, so refined, so anti-natural . . . a discipline too difficult and complex to take firm root on earth.' At a time when the great majority are employed in organizations and have little opportunity to learn the morals of the market, their intuitive craving for a more humane and personal morals corresponding to their inherited instincts is quite likely to destroy the Open Society.

It should be realized, however, that the ideals of socialism (or of 'social justice') which in such a position prove so attractive, do not really offer a new moral but merely appeal to instincts inherited from an earlier type of society. They are an atavism, a vain attempt to impose upon the Open Society the morals of the tribal society which, if it prevails, must not only destroy the Great Society but would also greatly threaten the survival of the large numbers to which some three hundred years of a market order have enabled mankind to grow.

Similarly the people who are described as alienated or estranged from a society based on the market order are not the bearers of a new moral but the non-domesticated or un-civilized who have never learnt the rules of conduct on which the Open Society is based, but want to impose upon it their instinctive, 'natural' conceptions derived from the tribal society. What especially most of the members of the New Left do not appear to see is that that equal treatment of all men which they also demand is possible only under a system in which individual actions are restricted merely by formal rules rather than guided by their known effects.

The Rousseauesque nostalgia for a society guided, not by learnt moral rules which can be justified only by a rational insight into the principles on which this order is based, but by the unreflected 'natural' emotions deeply grounded on millennia of life in the small horde, leads thus directly to the demand for a socialist society in which authority ensures that visible 'social justice' is done in a manner which gratifies natural emotions. In this sense, however, of course all culture is unnatural and, though undesigned, still artificial because relying on obedience to learnt rules rather than on natural instincts. This conflict between what men still feel to be natural emotions and the discipline of rules required for the preservation of the Open Society is indeed one of the chief causes of what has been called the 'fragility of liberty': all attempts to model the Great Society on the image of the familiar small group, or to turn it into a community by directing the individuals towards common visible purposes, must produce a totalitarian society.

The old conflict between loyalty and justice

The persistent conflict between tribal morals and universal justice has manifested itself throughout history in a recurrent clash between the sense of loyalty and that of justice. It is still loyalty to such particular groups as those of occupation or class as well as those of clan, nation, race or religion which is the greatest obstacle to a universal application of rules of just conduct. Only slowly and gradually do those general rules of conduct towards all fellow men come to prevail over the special rules which allowed the individual to harm the stranger if it served the interest of his group. Yet while only this process has made possible the rise of the Open Society, and offers the distant hope of a universal order of peace, current morals do not yet wholeheartedly approve this development; indeed, there has in recent times taken place a retreat from positions which had already been largely achieved in the Western world.

If in the distant past perhaps altogether inhuman demands were sometimes made in the name of formal justice, as when in ancient Rome the father was praised who as a magistrate unflinchingly condemned his son to death, we have learned to avoid the gravest of such conflicts, and in general to reduce the requirements of formal justice to what is compatible with our emotions. The advance of justice continued until recent times as a progressive ascendancy of the general rules of just conduct applying to our relations to any fellow member of society over the special rules serving the needs of particular groups. It is true that this development in some measure stopped at national frontiers; but most nations were of such a size that it still brought about a progressive replacement of the rules of the purpose-connected organization by the rules of the spontaneous order of an Open Society.

The main resistance to this development was due to its requiring a predominance of abstract rational principles over those emotions that are evoked by the particular and the concrete, or the predominance of conclusions derived from abstract rules, whose significance was little understood, over the spontaneous response to the perception of concrete effects which touched the lives and conditions of those familiar to us. This does not mean that those rules of conduct which refer to special personal relations have lost their importance for the functioning of the Great Society. It merely means that, since in a society of free men the membership in such special groups will be voluntary, there must also be no power of enforcing the rules of such groups. It is in such a free society that a clear distinction between the moral rules which are not enforced and the rules of law which are enforced becomes so important. If the smaller groups are to be integrated into the more comprehensive order of society at large, it must be through the free movement of individuals between groups into which they may be accepted if they submit to their rules.

The small group in the Open Society

The revolt against the abstractness of the rules we are required to obey in the Great Society, and the predilection for the concrete which we feel to be human, are thus merely a sign that intellectually and morally we have not yet fully matured to the needs of the impersonal comprehensive order of mankind. To submit comprehendingly to those rules which have made the approach to the Open Society possible and which we have obeyed so long as we attributed them to the command of a higher personal authority, and not to blame some imagined personal agent for any misfortune that we encounter, evidently requires a degree of insight into the working of a spontaneous order which few persons have yet attained.

Even moral philosophers often appear simply to wallow in the emotions inherited from the tribal society without examining their compatibility with the aspirations of the universal humanism that they also champion. Most people indeed will watch with regret the decline of the small group in which a limited number of persons were connected by many personal ties, and the disappearance of certain sentiments connected with it. But the price we have to pay for the achievement of the Great Society in which all human beings have the same claims on us is that these claims must be reduced to the avoidance of harmful actions and cannot include positive duties. The individual's free choice of his associates will in general have the effect that for different purposes he will be acting with different companions and that none of these connections will be compulsory. This presupposes that none of these small groups has power to enforce its standards on any unwilling person.

The savage in us still regards as good what was good in the small group but what the Great Society must not only refrain from enforcing but cannot even allow particular groups to enforce. A peaceful Open Society is possible only if it renounces the method of creating solidarity that is most effective in the small group, namely acting on the principle that 'if people are to be in harmony, then let them strive for some common end'. This is the conception of creating coherence which leads straight to the interpretation of all politics as a matter of friend-enemy relations. It is also the device which has been effectively employed by all dictators.

Except when the very existence of a free society is threatened by an enemy, it must deny itself what in many respects is still the strongest force making for cohesion, the common visible purpose. It must bid farewell, so far as the use of coercion is concerned, to the use of some of the strong moral emotions which still stand us in good stead in the small group and which, though still needed within the small groups from which the Great Society is built up, must result in tension and conflict if enforced in the Great Society.

The conception through which the atavistic craving for visible common purposes which so well served the needs of the small group today chiefly expresses itself is that of 'social justice'. It is incompatible with the principles on which the Great Society rests and indeed the opposite of those forces making for its coherence which can truly be called 'social'. Our innate instincts are here in conflict with the rules of reason we have learned, a conflict we can resolve only by limiting coercion to what is required by abstract rules and by abstaining from enforcing what can be justified only by the desire for particular results.

The kind of abstract order on which man has learnt to rely and which has enabled him peacefully to co-ordinate the efforts of millions, unfortunately cannot be based on such feelings as love which constituted the highest virtue in the small group. Love is a sentiment which only the concrete evokes, and the Great Society has become possible through the individual's efforts being guided not by the aim of helping particular other persons, but the confinement of the pursuit of their purposes by abstract rules.

The importance of voluntary associations

It would be a sad misunderstanding of the basic principles of a free society if it were concluded that, because they must deprive the small group of all coercive powers, they do not attach great value to voluntary action in the small groups. In restricting all coercion to the agencies of government and confining its employment to the enforcement of general rules, these principles aim at reducing all coercion as much as possible and leaving as much as possible to voluntary efforts. The mischievous idea that all public needs should be satisfied by compulsory organization and that all the means that the individuals are willing to devote to public purposes should be under the control of government, is wholly alien to the basic principles of a free society. The true liberal must on the contrary desire as many as possible of those 'particular societies within the state', voluntary organizations between the individual and government, which the false individualism of Rousseau and the French Revolution wanted to suppress; but he wants to deprive them of all exclusive and compulsory powers. Liberalism is not individualistic in the 'everybody for himself' sense, though necessarily suspicious of the tendency of organizations to arrogate exclusive rights for their members.

We shall later (in chapter 15) have to consider more fully the problems raised by the consideration that such voluntary organizations, because their power is so much greater than that of any individual, may have to be restricted in their activities by law in ways in which the individual need not be restrained and, in particular, that they may have to be denied some of the rights to discriminate which for the individual are an important part of his freedom. What we wish to stress at this point, however, is not the necessary limits but rather the importance of the existence of numerous voluntary associations, not only for the particular purposes of those who share some common interest, but even for public purposes in the true sense. That government should have the monopoly of coercion is necessary in order to limit coercion; but this must not mean that government should have the exclusive right to pursue public purposes. In a truly free society, public affairs are not confined to the affairs of government (least of all of central government) and public spirit should not exhaust itself in an interest in government.[16]

It is one of the greatest weaknesses of our time that we lack the patience and faith to build up voluntary organizations for purposes which we value highly, and immediately ask the government to bring about by coercion (or with means raised by coercion) anything that appears as desirable to large numbers. Yet nothing can have a more deadening effect on real participation by the citizen than if government, instead of merely providing the essential framework for spontaneous growth, becomes monolithic and takes charge of the provision for all needs which can be provided for only by the common efforts of many. It is the great merit of the spontaneous order concerned only with means that it makes possible the existence of a large number of distinct and voluntary value communities serving such values as science, the arts, sports and the like. And it is a highly desirable development that in the modern world these groups tend to extend beyond national boundaries and that, e.g. a mountain climber in Switzerland may have more in common with a mountain climber in Japan than with the football fan in his own country; and that he may even belong to a common association with the former which is wholly independent of any political organization to which either belongs.

The present tendency of governments to bring all common interests of large groups under their control tends to destroy real public spirit; and as a result an increasing number of men and women are turning away from public life who in the past would have devoted much effort to public purposes. On the European continent the over-solicitude of governments has in the past largely prevented the development of voluntary organizations for public purposes and produced a tradition in which private efforts were often regarded as the gratuitous meddling of busybodies, and modern developments seem progressively to have produced a similar situation even in the Anglo-Saxon countries where at one time private efforts for public purposes were so characteristic a feature of social life.

NOTES

* David Hume, *Treatise, Works*, ed. T. H. Green and T. H. Grose (London, 1890), vol. II, p. 318.

1 On the meaning of the concepts of common or public utility (or interest) in classical antiquity, when their equivalents were extensively used both in Greek and in Latin, see A. Steinwenter, 'Utilitas publica—utilitas singulorum', *Festschrift Paul Koschaker* (Weimar, 1939), vol. I, and J. Gaudemet, 'Utilitas publica', *Revue historique de droit français et étranger*, 4e série, 29, 1951. The medieval use is discussed in W. Merk, 'Der Gedanke des gemeinen Besten in der deutschen Staats- und Rechtsentwicklung', *Festschrift für A. Schultze* (Weimar, 1934).

2 For the upshots of the extensive but not very fruitful discussion of this subject, mainly in the USA, see *Nomos V, The Public Interest*, ed. C. J. Friedrich (New York, 1962), and the earlier literature mentioned in that work.

3 J. Bentham, *An Introduction to the Principles of Morals and Legislation*, new ed. (London, 1823), vol. I, p. 4: 'The interest of the community then is, what?—the sum of the interests of the several members who compose it.'

4 James Harrington, *The Prerogative of Popular Government* (1658) in *The Oceana and his Other Works*, ed. J. Toland (London, 1771), p. 224: 'the public interest (which is no other than common right and justice) may be called the empire of laws and not of men.'

5 Cf. the Book of Proverbs, 18:18, 'The lot causes contentions to cease, and parteth between the mighty.'

6 In this sense the 'principle of subsidiarity' is much stressed in the social doctrines of the Roman Catholic Church.

7 I ought probably to have explained earlier why I prefer the expression 'each being allowed to use his own knowledge for his own purposes' to the essentially equivalent expression of Adam Smith that every one should be free 'to pursue his own interest in his own way' (*Wealth of Nations*, ed. E. Cannan, London, 1904 and later, vol. II, p. 43 and elsewhere). The reason is that to the modern ear Smith's

phrase suggests a spirit of selfishness which is probably not intended and certainly inessential to the argument.

8 Cf. my essays on 'Rules, Perception, and Intelligibility' in *Proceedings of the British Academy*, XLVIII, 1962 (London, 1963), reprinted in *Studies in Philosophy, Politics, and Economics* (London and Chicago, 1967) and 'The Primacy of the Abstract' in A. Koestler and J. R. Smithies (eds) *Beyond Reductionism* (London, 1969).

9 It would seem that the commendatory use of 'will' rather than opinion came only with the Cartesian tradition and became general only through J.-J. Rousseau. The ancient Greeks were protected against the underlying confusion by the fact that the only word corresponding to 'willing' which their language offered (*boulomai*) clearly referred to aiming at a particular concrete object (Cf. M. Pohlenz, *Der Hellenische Mensch* (Göttingen, 1946), p. 210). When Aristotle (*Politics*, 1287a) demands that 'reason' and not 'will' should govern, this clearly means that abstract rules and not particular ends should govern all acts of coercion. We find the contrast then in ancient Rome as one between *voluntas* and *habitus animi*, the latter a rendering of the Aristotelian *héxis psychēs*. (Cf. esp. the interesting contrast between Cicero's definition of justice: 'iustitia est habitus animi, communi utilitate conservata, suam cuique tribuens dignitatem' in *De inventione*, 2,53,161,—and Ulpian's better known formula: 'iustitia est constans et perpetua voluntas ius suum cuique tribuendi' in *Dig.* 1,1.) Throughout the Middle Ages and early modern times we find *ratio* and *voluntas* constantly contrasted and finally arbitrariness characterized by the brief formula 'stat pro ratione voluntas'. No doubt C. H. McIlwain is right when in *Constitutionalism and the Modern State* (rev. ed., Ithaca, New York, 1947, p. 145) he stressed in the old terms that 'even in a popular state, such as we trust ours is, the problem of law versus will remains the most important of all political problems'. It is perhaps of interest that G. W. F. Hegel (*Grundlinien der Philosophie des Rechts*, para. 258, in Leipzig edn, 1911, p. 196) credits Rousseau to have established the *will* as the principle of the state.

10 Cf. J. Bentham, *Introduction to the Principles of Morals and Legislation* (London, 1789) ch. XI, sect. I, p. 131 of Oxford 1889 edn: 'disposition is a kind of fictitious entity, feigned for the convenience of discourse, in order to express what there is supposed to be *permanent* in a man's frame of mind, where, on such and such an occasion, he has been influenced by such or such a motive, to engage in an act, which, as it appears to him, was of such and such a tendency.' It seems clear that Bentham can conceive of such a disposition only as the result of conscious processes of the mind which recurrently decide upon to act in a certain manner.

11 Cf. M. Polanyi, *The Logic of Liberty* (London, 1951).

12 D. Hume, *A Treatise on Human Nature, Works,* (London, 1890), vol. II, p. 269. The whole long paragraph from which these sentences are taken deserves careful reading.

13 Thomas Aquinas, *Summa Theologiae,* Ia IIae, q. 95, art. 3: 'Finis autem humanae legis est utilitas hominum.'

It is misleading to represent as utilitarians all authors who account for the existence of certain institutions by their utility, because writers like Aristotle or Cicero, Thomas Aquinas or Mandeville, Adam Smith or Adam Ferguson, when they spoke of utility, appear to have thought of this utility favouring a sort of natural selection of institutions, not determining their deliberate choice by men. When in the passage quoted in note 9 above Cicero speaks of justice as a 'habitus animi, communi utilitate conservata' this is certainly not meant in the sense of a constructivist but in that of a sort of evolutionary utilitarianism. On the derivation of both traditions in the modern world from Bernard Mandeville see my lecture 'Dr Bernard Mandeville', *Proceedings of the British Academy,* vol. 52, pp. 134ff.

14 For the use of the conception of utility by David Hume see particularly his discussion of the stability of possession in *Treatise,* vol. II, pp. 273ff., where he argues that these rules 'are not derived from any utility or advantage, which either the *particular* person or the public may reap from his enjoyment of any *particular* goods. . . .

'It follows, therefore, that the general rules, that *possession must be stable,* is not applied by particular judgements, but by other general rules, which must extend to the whole society, and be inflexible either by spite or favour.' I do not know whether Bentham did ever explicitly say, as C. W. Everett (*The Education of Jeremy Bentham* (London, 1931), p. 47) suggests, that Hume's idea of utility 'was a vague one, as it was used simply as synonymous with conduciveness to an end, and with no intimation of happiness as connected with the idea.' If he did so, he had a true sense of the meaning of the word.

15 Bentham himself was well aware of this intellectual ancestry and of the contrast of his constructivist approach to the evolutionary tradition of the common law; cf. his letter to Voltaire of about 1776 quoted in C. W. Everett, *The Education of Jeremy Bentham* (Columbia, 1931), pp. 110ff., in which he wrote: 'I have taken council of you much oftener than of our own Ld. Coke and Hale and Blackstone. . . . I have built solely on the foundation of utility, laid as it is by Helvetius. Beccaria has been *lucerna pedibus* or if you please *manibus meis.*' Much information on the influence of the Continental rationalists, especially Beccaria and Maupertius, is to be found in D. Baumgardt, *Bentham and the Ethics of Today* (Princeton, 1952), esp. pp. 85, 221–6, and particularly the revealing passage from a manuscript of Bentham of about 1782, quoted on p. 557: 'The idea of considering happiness as resoluble into a number of (individual) pleasures, I took from

Helvetius: before whom it can scarcely be said to have a meaning. (This is directly contrary to the doctrine laid down in Cicero's Tusculan disputation: which book, like most of the philosophical writings of that great master of language is nothing but a heap of nonsense.) The idea of estimating the value of each sensation by analysing it into these four ingredients, I took from Beccaria.'

16 Some of the most important of these studies (by J. O. Urmson, J. Harrison, John Rawls, J. J. C. Smart, H. J. McCloskey, R. B. Brandt, A. Donagan, B. J. Diggs, and T. L. S. Sprigge) have been conveniently brought together in a volume edited by M. D. Bayles, *Contemporary Utilitarianism* (Garden City, New York, 1968). To these ought to be added two articles by J. D. Mabbott, 'Interpretations of Mill's "Utilitarianism"', *Philosophical Quarterly*, vol. VI, 1956, and 'Moral Rules', *Proceedings of the British Academy*, vol. XXXIX, 1953, and the books by R. M. Hare, *Freedom and Reason* (Oxford, 1963), J. Hospers, *Human Conduct* (New York, 1961), M. G. Singer, *Generalisation in Ethics* (London, 1963) and S. E. Toulmin, *An Examination of the Place of Reason in Ethics* (Cambridge, 1950). Two more recent books of considerable importance, which for the time being ought to bring this discussion to a close, are David Lyons, *Forms and Limits of Utilitarianism* (Oxford, 1965), and D. H. Hodgson, *Consequences of Utilitarianism* (Oxford, 1967). A more complete bibliography will be found in N. Rescher, *Distributive Justice* (New York, 1966). Since the present chapter was completed the central issue was discussed in J. J. C. Smart and Bernard Williams, *Utilitarianism: For and Against* (Cambridge, 1973). What in the text is called 'particularistic' utilitarianism and is now most frequently described as 'act utilitarianism' has also been designated 'crude', 'extreme' and 'direct' utilitarianism, while what we call 'generic' and is more usually called 'rule'-utilitarianism has also been named 'modified', 'restricted' and 'indirect' utilitarianism.

17 Henry Sidgwick, *The Methods of Ethics* (London, 1874), p. 425.

18 G. E. Moore, *Ethics* (London, 1912), p. 232, but cf. his *Principia Ethica* (Cambridge, 1903), p. 162.

19 W. Paley, *The Principles of Moral and Political Philosophy* (1785; London, 1824 edn), p. 47, and cf. John Austin, *The Province of Jurisprudence* (1832; ed. H. L. A. Hart, London, 1954), lecture II, p. 38: 'Now the tendency of a human action (as its tendency is thus understood) is the whole of its tendency: the sum of its probable consequences, in so far as they are important and material: the sum of its remote and collateral, as well as of its direct consequences, in so far as any of its consequences may influence the general happiness ... we ... must look at the *class* of actions to which they belong. The probable *specific* consequences of doing that single act, are not the object of inquiry.'

20 The nearest approach to taking ignorance seriously in any discussion of utilitarianism known to me occurs in the article 'Utilitarianism' by J. J. C. Smart in the *Encyclopaedia of Philosophy*, vol. VIII, p. 210.

21 John W. Chapman, 'Justice and Fairness', in *Nomos VI, Justice* (New York, 1964), p. 153: 'Justice as reciprocity makes sense only if society is seen as a plurality of persons and not, as the utilitarian would have it, as a sort of single great person.'

22 Hastings Rashdall, *The Theory of Good and Evil* (London, 1907), vol. I, p. 184.

23 Cf. Gregory Vlastos, 'Justice', *Revue Internationale de la Philosophie*, XI, 1957, p. 338: 'The feature of Benthamism to which all of these would object most strenuously is that what we commonly call "acting on principle" has almost no place on this theory: one is supposed to live by applying the felicific calculus from act to act.' In the same article (p. 333) Vlastos quotes an interesting passage from Bishop Butler's *Dissertation Upon the Nature of Virtue* (an Appendix to *The Analogy of Religion*, 1736, reprinted as Appendix to *Five Sermons by Butler*, ed. S. M. Brown, New York, 1950) in which Butler argues against authors who imagine 'the whole of virtue to consist in simply aiming, according to the best of their judgement, at promoting the happiness of mankind in the present state.'

24 Theodor Geiger, *Vorstudien zu einer Soziologie des Rechts* (Copenhagen, 1947, 2nd edn, Darmstadt, 1964), p. 111: 'Es ist nun in der Tat so, dass die Ursachen für die So-Gestaltung eines gegebenen habituellen Ordnungsgefüges unbekannt sind—und es vorläufig wohl auch bleiben.'

25 This, I believe, is what Karl Popper (*The Open Society and its Enemies*, Princeton, 1963) means by 'piecemeal engineering', an expression which I feel reluctant to adopt because 'engineering' suggests to me too much a technological problem of reconstruction on the basis of the total knowledge of the physical data, while the essential point about the practicable improvement is an experimental attempt to improve the functioning of some part without a full comprehension of the structure of the whole.

26 Cf. E. Westermarck, *The Origin and Development of Moral Ideas*, vol. I (London, 1906), pp. 386ff. and 399ff., summarized in his *Ethical Relativity* (London, 1932), pp. 184ff.

27 Cf. M. G. Singer, *Generalization in Ethics* (New York, 1961).

CHAPTER EIGHT   THE QUEST FOR JUSTICE

* Paul Vinogradoff, *Common-Sense in Law* (London and New York, 1914), p. 70. Cf. also *ibid.*, pp. 46f.:

The problem consists in allowing such an exercise of each personal

will as is compatible with the exercise of other wills. . . . [A law] is
a limitation of one's freedom of action for the sake of avoiding
collision with others. . . . In social life, as we know, men have not
only to avoid collisions, but to arrange co-operation in all sorts of
ways, and the one common feature of all these forms of co-
operation is the limitation of individual wills in order to achieve a
common purpose.

And pp. 61f.: 'We can hardly define a right better than by saying that
it is the *range of action assigned to a particular will within the social
order established by law.*' In the third edition by H. G. Hambury
(London, 1959) the passages occur on pp. 51, 34f. and 45.

1 See Franz Boehm, 'Privatrechtsgesellschaft und Marktwirtschaft',
Ordo XVII, 1966, pp. 75–151, and 'Der Rechtsstaat und der soziale
Wohlfahrtsstaat' in *Reden und Schriften*, ed. E. S. Mestmäcker
(Karlsruhe, 1960), pp. 102f.

2 For interpretations of justice as an attribute of a factual state of affairs
rather than of human actions cf. Hans Kelsen, *What is Justice?*
(California, 1957) p. 1:

> Justice is primarily a possible, but not a necessary, quality of a
> social order regulating the mutual relations of men. Only second-
> arily it is a virtue of man, since a man is just, if his behaviour
> conforms to the norms of a social order supposed to be just. . . .
> Justice is social happiness. It is happiness guaranteed by a social
> order.

Similarly A. Brecht, *Political Theory* (Princeton, 1959), p. 146:
'Postulates of justice are generally expressed in terms of some desirable state of affairs, for instance one where equality, or "more"
equality, would be established. . . . Even when not expressed in such
terms, postulates of justice can be translated into them.'

3 Cf. H. L. A. Hart, *The Concept of Law* (Oxford, 1961), p. 195: 'There
are no settled principles forbidding the use of the word "law" of
systems where there are no centrally organized sanctions.' Hart draws
an important distinction between 'primary rules' under which 'human
beings are required to do or abstain from certain actions, whether
they wish or not' (p. 78) and 'secondary rules of recognition, change,
and adjudication', i.e. the rules of the organization which has been
set up to enforce the rules of conduct. Though this is of the greatest
importance, I find it difficult to regard the development of this
distinction as 'the decisive step from the pre-legal to the legal world'
(p. 91) or to characterize law 'as a union of primary rules of obligation
with secondary rules' (*ibid.*) as very helpful.

4 It would be possible to argue endlessly whether the law is or is not a

'system of rules', but this is largely a terminological question. If by 'system of rules' is understood a collection of articulated rules, this would certainly not constitute the whole law. Ronald M. Dworkin, who in an essay entitled 'Is Law a System of Rules?' (in R. S. Summers, ed., *Essays in Legal Philosophy*, Oxford and California, 1968) uses the term 'system' as equivalent to 'collection' (p. 52) and seems to accept only articulated rules as rules, shows convincingly that a system of rules so interpreted would be incomplete and requires for its completion what he calls 'principles'. (Cf. also Roscoe Pound, 'Why Law Day', *Harvard Law School Bulletin*, vol. x, no. 3, 1958, p. 4: 'The vital, the enduring part of the law is in principles—starting points for reasoning, not rules. Principles remain relatively constant or develop along constant lines. Rules have relatively short lives. They do not develop; they are repealed and are superseded by other rules.') I prefer to use the term *system* for a body of rules that are mutually adjusted to each other and possess an order of rank, and of course I include in 'rules' not only articulated but also not yet articulated rules which are implicit in the system or have yet to be found to make the several rules consistent. Thus, while I wholly agree with the substance of Professor Dworkin's argument, I should, in my terminology, affirm that the law *is* a system (and not a mere collection) of (articulated and unarticulated) rules.

5 In a general way this idea appears in the English literature at least in the eighteenth century and has been expressed especially by William Paley in his *Principles of Moral and Political Philosophy* (1785, new ed. London, 1824), p. 348: 'general laws are made . . . without forseeing whom they might affect' and recurs in its modern form in C. K. Allen, *Law in the Making* (6th ed., London, 1958), p. 367: 'a legal rule, like every kind of rule, aims at establishing a generalisation for an indefinite number of cases of a certain kind.' It was most systematically developed in that Continental (mainly German) discussion about the distinction between law in the 'material' and law in the merely 'formal' sense to which we have referred earlier (note 24 to chapter VI) and appears to have been established there by Hermann Schulze, *Das Preussische Staatsrecht* (Leipzig, 1877), vol. II, p. 209: 'Dem Merkmal der Allgemeinheit ist genügt, wenn sich nur der Regel überhaupt eine Zahl von nicht vorauszusehenden Fällen logisch unterzuordnen hat.' (See also *ibid.*, p. 205 for references to earlier relevant writings.) Of later works see particularly Ernst Seligmann, *Der Begriff des Gesetzes im materiellen und formellen Sinn* (Berlin, 1886), p. 63: 'In der Tat ist es ein Essentiale des Rechtsgesetzes, dass es abstrakt ist und eine nicht vorauszusehende Anzahl von Fällen ordnet.' M. Planiol, *Traité élémentaire de Droit Civil* (12th ed., Paris, 1937), p. 69: 'la loi est établie en permanence pour un nombre indéterminé d'actes et de faits, . . . un decision obligatoire d'une

manière permanente, pour un nombre de fois indéterminé.' Z. Giacometti, *Die Verfassungsgerichtsbarkeit des schweizerischen Bundesgerichts* (Zürich, 1933), p. 99: 'Generell abstrakt ist jede . . . an eine unbestimmte Vielheit von Personen für eine unbestimmte Vielheit von Fällen gerichtete Anordnung'; and the same author's *Allgemeine Lehre des rechtsstaatlichen Verwaltungsrechts* (Zürich, 1960), p. 5: 'Eine solche Bindung der staatlichen Gewaltenträger an generelle, abstrakte Vorschriften, die für eine unbestimmte Vielheit von Menschen gelten und die eine unbestimmte Vielheit von Tatbeständen regeln ohne Rücksicht auf einen bestimmten Einzelfall oder eine bestimmte Person. . . .' W. Burckhardt, *Einführung in die Rechtswissenschaft* (2nd ed., Zürich, 1948), p. 200: 'Die Pflichten, die das Gesetz den Privaten auferlegt, müssen (im Gegensatz zu den Pflichten der Beamten) zum Voraus für eine unbestimmte Anzahl möglicher Fälle vorgeschrieben sein.' H. Kelsen, *Reine Rechtslehre* (2nd ed., Vienna, 1960), pp. 362-3: 'Generell ist eine Norm, wenn sie . . . in einer von vornherein unbestimmten Zahl von gleichen Fällen gilt. . . . In dieser Beziehung ist sie dem abstrakten Begriff analog.' Donato Donati, 'I caratteri della legge in senso materiale,' *Rivista di Diritto Publico*, 1911 (and reprinted in *Scritti di Diritto Publico*, Padua, 1961, vol. II), p. 11 of the separate offprint: 'Questa generalità deve intendersi, non già nel senso, semplicemente, di *pluralità*, ma in quelle, invece, di universalità. Commando generale, in altre termini, sarebbe, non già quelle che concerne una *pluralità* di persone o di azioni, ma soltanto quello che concerne una universalità di persone o di azioni, vale a dire: non quello che concerne un numero di persone o di azioni *determinato* o *determinabile*, ma quello che concerne un numero di persone o di azioni *indeterminato* e *indeterminabile*.'

6 All these attributes of law in the narrow sense have been brought out in the extensive Continental discussion of the distinction between what was called law in the 'material' and law in the merely 'formal' sense, but were often wrongly treated as alternative or even incompatible criteria of law in the 'material' sense. See P. Laband, *Staatsrecht des deutschen Reiches* (5th ed., Tübingen, 1911-14), II, pp. 54-6; E. Seligmann, *Der Begriff des Gesetzes im materiellen und formellen Sinn* (Berlin, 1886); A. Haenel, *Studien zum deutschen Staatsrecht*, vol. II: *Gesetz im formellen und materiellen Sinne* (Leipzig, 1888); L. Duguit, *Traité de droit constitutionel* (2nd ed., Paris, 1921); R. Carré de Malberg, *La Loi: Expression de la volonté générale* (Paris, 1931); and Donato Donati, 'I caratteri della legge in senso materiale', *Rivista di Diritto Publico*, 1911, reprinted in the author's *Scritti di Diritto Publico* (Padua, 1961). The best known definition of law in the material sense is probably that given by Georg Jellinek, *Gesetz und Verordnung* (Freiburg, 1887), p. 240:

Hat ein Gesetz den nächsten Zweck, die Sphäre der freien
Tätigkeiten von Persönlichkeiten gegeneinander abzugrenzen, ist
es der sozialen Schrankenziehung halber erlassen, so enthält es
Anordnungen eines Rechtssatzes, ist daher auch ein Gesetz im
materiellen Sinn; hat es jedoch einen anderen Zweck, so ist es kein
materielles, sondern nur ein formelles Gesetz, das seinen Inhalt
nach als Anordnung eines Verwaltungsaktes, oder als ein Rechts-
spruch sich charakterisiert.

7 See, apart from the quotation from P. Vinogradoff placed at the head
of this chapter, particularly F. C. von Savigny, *System des heutigen
Römischen Rechts*, vol. I (Berlin, 1840), pp. 331–2:

Sollen nun in solcher Berührung freie Wesen nebeneinander
bestehen, sich gegenseitig fördernd, nicht hemmend, in ihrer
Entwicklung, so ist dieses nur möglich durch Anerkennung einer
unsichtbaren Grenze, innerhalb welcher das Dasein, und die
Wirksamkeit jedes einzelnen einen sichern, freien Raum gewinne.
Die Regel, wodurch jene Grenze und durch die dieser freie Raum
bestimmt wird, ist das Recht.

Also P. Laband, *Das Staatsrecht des Deutschen Reiches* (4th ed.,
Tübingen, 1901), vol. II, p. 64, where he ascribes to the state the task
of 'die durch das gesellige Zusammenleben der Menschen gebotenen
Schranken und Grenzen der natürlichen Handlungsfreiheit der
Einzelnen zu bestimmen.' J. C. Carter, *Law, Its Origin, Growth, and
Function* (New York and London, 1907), pp. 133–4: 'Custom thus
fostered and enforced became the beginning of law. The direct and
necessary tendency of this restraint was to trace out boundary lines of
individual action within which each person might freely move without exciting the opposition of others. Here we find exhibited in its
earliest and simplest form the function of law.' J. Salmond, *Jurisprudence* (10th ed. by G. Williams, London, 1947), p. 62: 'The rule
of justice determines the sphere of individual liberty within the limits
which are consistent with the general welfare of mankind. Within the
sphere of liberty so delimited for every man by the rule of justice,
he is left free to seek his own interest in accordance with the rule of
wisdom.' H. Lévy-Ullman, *La Définition du droit* (Paris, 1917), p.
165: 'Nous définions donc le droit: la delimitation de ce que les
hommes et leur groupements ont la liberté de faire et ne pas faire,
sans encourire une condemnation, une seizie, une mise en jeu particulière de la force.' Donato Donati, 'I caratteri della legge in senso
materiale', *Rivista di Diritto Publico*, 1911 and reprinted in the author's
Scritti di Diritto Publico (Padua, 1961), vol. II, p. 23 of the separate
offprint of the article:

La funzione del diritto e infatti sorge e si esplica per la deliminazione

delle diverse sfere spettanti a ciascun consociato. La società
umana si trasforma de società anarchica in società ordinata per
questo, che interviene una volontà ordinatrice a determinare la
cerchia dell' attività di ciascuno: dell' attività lecita come dell'
attività doverosa.

8 Adam Smith, *The Theory of Moral Sentiments* (London, 1801), Part
VI, sect. ii, introd. vol. II, p. 58:

> The wisdom of every state or commonwealth endeavours, as well
> as it can, to employ the force of the society to restrain those who
> are subject to its authority, from hurting or disturbing the happi-
> ness of one another. The rules which it establishes for this purpose,
> constitute the civil and criminal law of each particular state or
> country.

9 The emphasis on the primary character of injustice appears already
in Herakleitos (see J. Burnet, *Early Greek Philosophy*, 4th ed., London, 1930, p. 166) and it is clearly stated by Aristotle in the *Nico-
machean Ethics*, 1134 a: 'Law exists for men between whom there is
injustice.' In modern times it frequently reappears, e.g. in La Roche-
foucauld, *Maximes* (1665) no. 78: 'L'amour de la justice n'est que la
crainte de souffrir injustice' and becomes prominent with David
Hume, Immanuel Kant and Adam Smith, for whom the rules of just
conduct serve mainly the delimitation and protection of individual
domains. L. Bagolini, *La Simpatia nella morale e nel diritto* (Bologna,
1952), p. 60 even describes the treatment of 'il probleme de diritto e
della giustizia del punto di vista del ingiustizia' as specially characteristic of the thinking of Adam Smith. Cf. the latter's *Theory of Moral
Sentiments* (1759), part II, sect. II, chapter I, vol. I, p. 165 of ed. of
1801: 'Mere justice is, upon most occasions, but a negative virtue, and
only hinders us from hurting our neighbour. The man who barely
abstains from violating either the person, or the estate, or the reputation of his neighbours, has surely little positive merit. He fulfils, however, all the rules of what is peculiarly called justice, and does every
thing which his equals can with propriety force him to do, or which
they can punish him for not doing. We may often fulfil all the rules
of justice by sitting still and doing nothing.' Cf. also Adam Ferguson,
Institutes of Moral Philosophy (Edinburgh, 1785), p. 189: 'The fundamental law of morality, in its first application to the actions of men, is
prohibitory and forbids the commission of wrong'; John Millar, *An
Historical View of the English Government* (London, 1787), quoted in
W. C. Lehmann, *John Millar of Glasgow* (Cambridge, 1960), p. 340:
'Justice requires no more than that I abstain from hurting my
neighbour'; Similarly J.-J. Rousseau, *Émile* (1762) Book II: 'La plus
sublime vertu est negative; elle nous instruit de ne jamais faire de mal

à personne.' This view seems to have been widespread also among lawyers so that F. C. von Savigny, *System des Heutigen Römischen Rechts*, I (Berlin, 1840), p. 332 could say that 'Viele aber gehen, um den Begriff des Rechts zu finden, von dem entgegengesetzten Standpunkt aus, von dem Begriff des Unrechts. Unrecht ist ihnen Störung der Freiheit durch fremde Freiheit, die der menschlichen Entwicklung hinderlich ist, und daher als ein Übel abgewehrt werden muss.'

In the nineteenth century two outspoken representatives of this view are the philosopher Arthur Schopenhauer and the economist Frédéric Bastiat, who may possibly have been indirectly influenced by the former. See A. Schopenhauer, *Parerga und Paralipomena*, II, 9, 'Zur Rechtslehre und Politik', in *Sämtliche Werke*, ed. A. Hübscher (Leipzig, 1939), vol. VI, p. 257: 'Der Begriff des *Rechts* ist nämlich ebenso wie auch der der *Freiheit* ein *negativer*, sein Inhalt ist eine blosse Negation. Der Begriff des *Unrechts* ist der positive und gleichbedeutend mit Verletzung im weitesten Sinn, also laesio.' F. Bastiat, *La Loi* (1850), in *Oeuvres Complètes* (Paris, 1854), vol. IV, p. 35: 'Cela est si vrai qu'ainsi qu'un des mes amis me le faisait remarquer, dire que le but de la Loi est de faire régner la Justice, c'est de se servir d'une expression qui n'est pas vigoureusement exacte. Il faudrait dire: *La but de la Loi est d'empêcher l'Injustice de régner*. En effet, ce n'est pas la Justice qui a une existence propre, c'est l'Injustice. L'un résulte de la absence de l'autre.' Cf. also J. S. Mill, *Utilitarianism* (1861, ed. J. Plamenatz, Oxford, 1949), p. 206: 'for justice, like many other moral attributes, is best defined by its opposites.'

More recently, among philosophers, Max Scheler has emphasized the same point. See his *Der Formalismus in der Ethik und die materielle Wertethik* (3rd ed., 1927), p. 212: 'Niemals kann daher (bei genauer Reduktion) die Rechtsordnung sagen, was sein soll (oder was recht ist), sondern immer nur, was nicht sein soll (oder nicht recht ist). Alles, was innerhalb der Rechtsordnung *positiv* gesetzt ist, ist reduziert auf pure Rechtsein- und Unrechtseinverhalte, stets ein *Unrechtseinverhalt*.' Cf. also Leonhard Nelson, *Die Rechtswissenschaft ohne Recht*, (Leipzig, 1917), p. 133, about the 'Auffassung vom Recht . . . wonach das Recht . . . die Bedeutung einer negativen, den Wert möglicher positiver Zwecke einschränkenden Bedingung hat'; and *ibid.*, p. 151, about the 'Einsicht in den negativen (Werte nur beschränkenden) Charakter des Rechts'.

Among contemporary authors cf. further L. C. Robbins, *The Theory of Economic Policy* (London, 1952), p. 193: The classical Liberal 'proposes, as it were, a division of labour: the state shall prescribe what individuals shall not do, if they are not to get into each other's way, while citizens shall be left free to do anything which is not so forbidden. To the one is assigned the task of establishing formal rules, to the other responsibility for the substance of specific action.'

K. E. Boulding, *The Organisational Revolution* (New York, 1953), p. 83: 'The difficulty seems to be that "justice" is a negative concept; that is, it is not justice which leads to action, but injustice or discontent.' McGeorge Bundy, 'A Lay View of Due Process', in A. E. Sutherland (ed.), *Government under Law* (Harvard, 1956), p. 365: 'I suggest, then, that legal process is best understood not as a source of pure and positive justice, but rather as an imperfect remedy for gross wrongs. . . . Or perhaps we can think of the law not as something good in itself, but as an instrument which derives its value less from what it does than what it prevents. . . . What one asks of [the courts] is not that they do justice but that they give some protection against grave injustice.' Bernard Mayo, *Ethics and Moral Life* (London, 1958), p. 204: 'With certain apparent exceptions . . . the function of law is to prevent something.' H. L. A. Hart, *The Concept of Law* (Oxford, 1961), p. 190: 'The common requirement of law and morality consists for the most part not of active services to be rendered but of forbearances, which are usually formulated in negative form as prohibitions.' Lon L. Fuller, *The Morality of the Law* (Yale, 1964), p. 42: 'In what may be called the basic morality of social life, duties that run towards other persons generally . . . normally require only forbearances, or as we say, are negative in nature.' J. R. Lucas, *The Principles of Politics* (Oxford, 1966), p. 130:

> In the face of human imperfection, we articulate the Rule of law partly in terms of procedures designed not to secure that absolute Justice will be done but to be a safeguard against the worst sort of injustice. Injustice rather than Justice 'wears the trousers' in political philosophy, because, being fallible, we cannot say in advance what the just decision will always be, and, living among selfish men, we cannot always secure that it will be carried out, so, for the sake of definiteness, we adopt a negative approach, and lay down procedures to avoid certain likely forms of injustice, rather than aspire to all forms of Justice.

On the whole issue see particularly E. N. Cahn, *The Sense of Injustice* (New York, 1949) who defines 'justice' (pp. 13f.) as 'the active process of remedying or preventing what would arouse a sense of Injustice'. Cf. also the dictum of Lord Atkin, quoted by A. L. Goodhart, *English Law and the Moral Law* (London, 1953), p. 95: 'the rule that you are to love your neighbour becomes in law, you must not injure your neighbour.'

10 See A. L. Goodhart, *op. cit.*, p. 100 and J. B. Ames, 'Law and Morals', *Harvard Law Review*, XXII, 1908/9, p. 112.

11 See para. 330c of the German Penal Code, added in 1935, which provides punishment for 'anybody who in cases of accident, common danger or distress does not render help, although this is needed and

can be reasonably expected from him, especially if he can do so without himself incurring substantial danger or violating other important duties.'

12 That 'general obligation to help and sustain one another' which Max Gluckman (*Politics, Law and Ritual in Tribal Society*, London and Chicago, 1965, p. 54) describes as characteristic of the tribal society and especially the kinship group, and for the lack of which the Great Society is generally blamed, is incompatible with it and its abandonment part of the price we pay for the achievement of a more extensive order of peace. This obligation can exist only towards particular, known people—and though in a Great Society it may well be a moral obligation towards people of one's choice, it cannot be enforced under equal rules for all.

13 Cf. Paul A. Freund, 'Social Justice and the Law', in Richard B. Brandt, ed., *Social Justice* (Englewood Cliffs, New Jersey, 1962), p. 96: 'Reasonable expectations are more generally the ground rather than the product of law, as well as a basis for a critique of positive law and thus a ground of law in the process of becoming.'

14 I. Kant, *Metaphysik der Sitten, Rechtslehre.* I,2, para. 9: 'Bürgerliche Verfassung ist hier allein der rechtliche Zustand, durch welchen jedem das Seine nur gesichert, eigentlich aber nicht ausgemacht oder bestimmt wird.—Alle Garantie setzt also das Seine von jedem (dem es gesichert wird) schon voraus.' In the translation by John Ladd (*The Metaphysical Elements of Justice*, Indianapolis, 1965, p. 65): 'A civil constitution only provides the juridical condition under which each person's property is secured and guaranteed to him, but it does not actually stipulate and determine what that property shall be.'

15 R. L. Hale, *Freedom through Law* (California, 1952), p. 15.

16 Only through this interpretation the famous formula of Ulpian (*Dig.*, I,1.10) 'Iustitia est constans et perpetua voluntas suum cuique tribuere' is preserved from becoming a tautology. It is of some interest that Ulpian in this phrase has evidently substituted *voluntas* for an older term describing an attitude of mind: see Cicero, *De Inventione*, II, 35, 160: 'Iustitia est habitus animi, communi utilitate conservata, suum cuique tribuens dignitatem.'

17 John W. Chapman, 'Justice and Fairness', *Nomos* VI, 1963, p. 153.

18 D. Hume, *An Enquiry concerning the Principles of Morals, Works* IV, p. 274:

> All the laws of nature, which regulate property, as well as all civil laws, are general, and regard alone some essential circumstances of the case, without taking into consideration the characters, situations, and connexions of the person concerned, or any particular consequences which may result from the determination of these laws, in any particular case which offers. They deprive, without

scruple, a beneficient man of all his possessions, if acquired by mistake, without a good title; in order to bestow them on a selfish miser, who has already heaped up immense stores of superfluous riches. Public utility requires, that property should be regulated by general inflexible rules; and though such rules are adopted as best serve the same end of public utility, it is impossible for them to prevent all particular hardships, or make beneficial consequences flow from every individual case. It is sufficient, if the whole plan or scheme be necessary for the support of civil society, and if the balance of good, in the main, do thereby preponderate much above that of evil.

19 Cf. John Rawls, 'Constitutional Liberty and the Concept of Justice', *Nomos* VI, *Justice* (New York. 1963), p. 102:

Put another way, the principles of justice do not select specific distributions of desired things as just, given the wants of particular persons. This task is abandoned as mistaken in principle, and it is, in any case, not capable of a definite answer. Rather, the principles of justice define the constraints which institutions and joint activities must satisfy if persons engaging in them are to have no complaints against them. If these constraints are satisfied, the resulting distribution, whatever it is, may be accepted as just (or at least not unjust).

20 See note 16 above.
21 Cf. D. Hume, *Enquiry Works* IV, p. 195: 'all these institutions arise merely from the necessities of human society.'
22 D. Hume, *Treatise, Works* II, p. 293.
23 Leon Duguit as described by J. Walter Jones, *Historical Introduction to the Theory of Law* (Oxford, 1940), p. 114.
24 See M. J. Gregor, *Laws of Freedom* (London, 1964), p. 81: Cf. also the statement a few paragraphs earlier that 'juridical laws . . . merely forbid us to employ certain means of achieving whatever ends we have', and p. 42 for the description of the character of Kant's negative test for just law as 'merely the limitation of freedom through the formal condition of its thorough-going consistency with itself'.

I owe it to this excellent book that I became aware *how* closely my conclusions agree with Kant's philosophy of law, which, apart from occasional references, I had not seriously examined since my student days. What I had not seen before I read Miss Gregor's book was that in his legal philosophy Kant sticks consistently to the use of the categorical imperative as a negative test and that he does not attempt as he does in his philosophy of morals, to use it as a premise for a process of deduction through which the positive content of the moral rules is to be derived. This suggests to me very strongly, though I have no proof to offer, that Kant probably did not, as is generally assumed, discover the principle of the categorical imperative in morals and afterwards applied it to law, but that he rather found the basic conception in Hume's treatment of the rule of law and then applied it to morals. But while his brilliant treatment of development of the ideal of the rule of law with its stress on the negative and end-independent character of the legal rules seems to me to be one of his permanent achievements, his attempt to turn what in law is a test of justice to be applied to an existing body of rules into a premise from which the system of moral rules can be deductively derived was bound to fail.

25 Karl R. Popper, *The Logic of Scientific Discovery* (London, 1955), *The Open Society and its Enemies* (esp. 4th ed., Princeton, 1963), and *Conjectures and Refutations* (2nd ed., London, 1965).

26 Cf. e.g. G. Radbruch's statement quoted below, note 69.

27 See the full account of this development in John H. Hallowell, *The Decline of Liberalism as an Ideology with Particular Reference to German Politico-Legal Thought* (California, 1943), esp. pp. 77 and 111ff. Hallowell clearly shows how the leading liberal legal theorists in the Germany of the late nineteenth century by their acceptance of a legal positivism which regarded all law as the deliberate creation of a legislator and who were interested only in the constitutionality of an act of legislation and not in the character of the rules laid down, deprived themselves of any possibility of a resistance to the supersession of the 'material' by the merely 'formal' *Rechtsstaat* and at the same time discredited liberalism by this connection with a legal positivism with which it is fundamentally incompatible. A recognition of this fact can also be found in the early writings of Carl Schmitt, especially in his *Die geistesgeschichtliche Lage des deutschen Parlamentarismus* (2nd ed., Munich, 1926) p. 26:

> Konstitutionelles und absolutistisches Denken haben also an dem Gesetzesbegriff ihren Prüfstein, aber natürlich nicht an dem, was man in Deutschland seit Laband Gesetz im formellen Sinn nennt und wonach alles, was unter der Mitwirkung der Volksvertretung zustandekommt, Gesetz heisst, sondern an einem nach logischen Merkmalen bestimmten Satz. Das entscheidende Merkmal bleibt immer, ob das Gesetz ein genereller, rationaler Satz ist, oder Massnahme, konkrete Einzelverfügung, Befehl.

28 William James, *Pragmatism* (new impr., New York, 1940) p. 222: ' "The true", to put it briefly, is only the expedient in the way of our thinking, just as "the right" is only the expedient in the way of our behaving.'

29 John Dewey and James Tuft, *Ethics* (New York, 1908 and later); John

Dewey, *Human Nature and Conduct* (New York, 1922 and later); and *Liberalism and Social Action* (New York, 1963 edn).

30 Vilfredo Pareto, *The Mind and Society* (London and New York, 1935), para. 1210: 'When a person says: "That thing is unjust," what he means is that the thing is offensive to his sentiments as his sentiments stand in the state of social equilibrium to which he is accustomed.'

31 Cf. H. L. A. Hart, *op. cit.*, p. 253.

32 See vol. I, p. 20.

33 Thomas Hobbes, *Leviathan*, ch. 26, Latin ed. (London, 1651), p. 143.

34 Thomas Hobbes, *Dialogue of the Common Laws* (1681), in *Works*, vol. VI, p. 26.

35 Jeremy Bentham, *Constitutional Code* (1827), in *Works*, vol. IX, p. 8 and cf. *The Theory of Legislation*, ed. C. K. Ogden (London, 1931), p. 8: 'The primitive sense of the word *law*, and the ordinary meaning of the word, is . . . the will of command of a legislator.'

36 John Austin, *Lectures on Jurisprudence*, 4th ed. (London, 1879), vol. I, pp. 88 and 555. Cf. also I.c., p. 773: 'The rights and duties of political subordinates, and the rights and duties of private persons, are creatures of a common author, namely, the Sovereign State'; also *The Province of Jurisprudence Determined*, ed. H. L. A. Hart (London, 1954), p. 124: 'Strictly speaking, every law properly so called, is a *positive* law. For it is *put* or set by its individual or collective author, or it exists by the *position* or institution of its individual or collective author.'

37 Hans Kelsen, *What is Justice?* (California, 1967), p. 20. The works of Kelsen to which in the following we shall most frequently refer will be indicated by the year of publication only, namely:

1935, 'The Pure Theory of Law', *Law Quarterly Review*, 51.

1945, *General Theory of Law and State* (Harvard).

1957, *What is Justice?* (California).

1960, *Reine Rechtslehre*, 2nd ed. (Vienna).

38 Kelsen himself repeatedly stresses that 'it is impossible to "will" something of which one is ignorant' (1949, p. 34, similarly 1957, p. 273), but then circumvents, as we shall see, the difficulty this would create for less sophisticated forms of positivism by confining the 'will' of the legislator to the conferring of validity on a rule, so that the legislator who had made something into a 'norm' need not know the content of the law he has 'made'.

The first author to have made this shuffle was apparently Thomas Hobbes, See *Leviathan*, ch. XXVI: 'The legislator is he, not by whose authority the law was first made, but by whose authority they now continue to be laws.'

39 The objections of the legal historians at least since H. S. Maine are directed against the conception of law as the command of a sovereign. Cf. e.g., H. Kantorowicz, *The Definition of Law* (Cambridge, 1958),

p. 35: 'The whole history of legal science, particularly the work of the Italian glossators and the German pandectists, would become unintelligible if law were to be considered as a body of commands of the sovereign.'

40 Gustav Radbruch, *Rechtsphilosophie* (6th ed., Stuttgart, 1963), p. 179: 'Vermag niemand festzustellen, was gerecht ist, so muss jemand festsetzen, was rechtens sein soll.' Cf. also A. Brecht, *Political Theory* (Princeton, 1959), p. 147: 'Science . . . is unable to decide which state of affairs *is* really just. Opinions differ and science cannot decide between them in absolute terms.'

41 Gustav Radbruch, 'Vom individualistischen zum sozialen Recht' (1930), reprinted in *Der Mensch im Recht* (Göttingen, 1957), p. 39: 'Für eine soziale Rechtsordnung [ist] das Privatrecht . . . nur ein vorläufig ausgesparter und sich immer verkleinernder Spielraum für die Privatinitiative innerhalb des allumfassenden öffentlichen Rechts.' Cf. also in his *Rechtsphilosophie*, p. 224: 'Der Sozialismus würde ein fast völliges Aufgehen des privaten Rechts im öffentlichen Recht bedeuten.'

42 H. A. L. Hart, *The Concept of Law* (Oxford, 1961), p. 35, with reference to the statement by H. Kelsen, *Central Theory of Law and State* (Harvard, 1945), p. 63: 'One shall not steal; if somebody steals he shall be punished. . . . If at all existent, the first norm is contained in the second norm which is the only genuine norm. . . . Law is the primary norm which stipulates the sanction.' Cf. also Kelsen, 1957, p. 248 where private property is represented as 'a public function *par excellence*', and the conception of 'a specific sphere of "private" interest' as an 'ideological' conception.

43 Glanville Williams, 'The Controversy concerning the Word "Law" ', *British Year Book of International Law*, XXII, 1945, revised version in P. Laslett (ed.), *Philosophy, Politics, and Society* (Oxford, 1956); and 'Language and the Law', *Law Quarterly Review* LXI and LXII, 1945 and 1946.

44 Lewis Carroll, *Through the Looking Glass*, chapter VI.

45 H. Kelsen, 'The Pure Theory of Law', *Harvard Law Review*, LI, 1935, p. 517: 'Any content whatever can be legal; there is no human behaviour which could not function as the content of a legal norm'; also *General Theory of Law and State*, (Harvard, 1945) p. 113: 'Legal norms may have any kind of content.'

46 Cf. the quotations from Paulus and Accursius above, vol. 1, chapter IV, note to quotation at head of chapter.

47 Thomas Hobbes, *Leviathan*, Pt 1, ch. 13.

48 H. Kelsen, 'The Pure Theory of Law', *Law Quarterly Review*, vol. 50, 1934, p. 482.

49 E. Bodenheimer, *Jurisprudence* (Harvard, 1962), p. 169 describes this use with some justification as a *contradictio in adjecto* (a contradiction in terms).

50 This, of course, has long been legal usage and was made popular among social scientists by Max Weber, whose influential discussion of the relation between 'Legal Order and Economic Order' (in *Max Weber of Law in Economy and Society*, ed. Max Rheinstein (Harvard, 1954), ch. I, sec. 5; cf. also ch. II. sec. I) is for our purposes wholly useless and rather characteristic of a widespread confusion. For Weber 'order' is throughout something which is 'valid' or 'binding', which is to be enforced or contained in a maxim of law. In other words, order exists for him only as organization and the existence of a spontaneous order never becomes a problem. Like most positivists or socialists he thinks in this respect anthropomorphically and knows order only as *taxis* but not as *kosmos* and thereby blocks for himself the access to the genuine theoretical problems of a science of society.

51 Cf. e.g., Kelsen, 1945, p. 3: 'Law is an order of human behavior and "order" is a system of rules'; *ibid.*, p. 98: 'an order, a system of norms. It is this order—or what amounts to the same thing, this organisation— . . .'; 1960, p. 32: 'Eine "Ordnung" ist ein System von Normen, deren Einheit dadurch konstituiert wird, dass sie alle denselben Geltungsgrund haben'; and *Demokratie und Sozialismus* (Vienna, 1967), p. 100, note: 'So wie ja die Jurisprudenz nicht sanderes ist als eine Ordnungslehre.'

In one place at least Kelsen gives a quite adequate and defensible description of a 'natural' order, but evidently believes that with this description he has already demonstrated its metaphysical and non-factual character. In the essay on 'Die Idee des Naturrechts' (1928), reprinted in his *Aufsätze zur Ideologiekritik*, ed. E. Topitsch (Neuwied, 1964), p. 75, he writes:

> Unter einer 'natürlichen' Ordnung ist eine solche gemeint, die nicht auf dem menschlichen und darum unzulänglichen Willen beruht, die nicht 'willkürlich' geschaffen ist, sondern die sich gleichsam 'von selbst', aus einer irgendwie objektiv gegebenen, d.h. aber unabhängig vom subjektiv-menschlichen Willen existenten, dem Menschen aber doch irgendwie fassbaren, vom Menschen erkannten Grundtatsache, aus einem vom menschlichen Verstand nicht ursprünglich produzierten, aber von ihm doch reproduzierbaren Grundprinzip ergibt. Diese objektive Tatsache, dieses Grundprinzip, ist die 'Natur', oder in einem religiös-personifikativen Ausdruck 'Gott'.

If 'order' is here interpreted as a factual order of actions, 'objective' as given independently of the will of *any one* person, and 'not produced by human will' as not the result of human action but of human design, this (except for the last sentence) becomes not only an empirically meaningful statement but a statement which is factually true of spontaneous social orders.

52 Kelsen, 1945, p. 40: 'The existence of a legal norm is its validity.' Cf. also *ibid.*, pp. 30, 155 and 170 as well as 1957, p. 267: 'If we say a norm "exists" we mean that a norm is valid.' Similarly 1960, p. 9: 'Mit dem Worte "Geltung" bezeichnen wir die spezifische Existenz einer Norm.'

53 Kelsen 1945, pp. 115–22.

54 Kelsen 1960, p. 9: 'Da der Tatbestand der Gewohnheit durch Akte menschlichen Verhaltens konstituiert wird, sind auch die durch die Gewohnheit erzeugten Normen durch Akte menschlichen Verhaltens gesetzt, und sohin, wie die Normen, die der subjektive Sinn von Gesetzgebungsakten sind, *gesetzte*, das heisst *positive* Normen.'
 I find it difficult to believe that in such phrases as the following the words I have italicized are consistently used to mean either the conferring of validity or the determination of the content of a rule: 1945, p. 113: 'A norm is a valid legal norm by virtue of the fact that it has been created according to a definite rule and by virtue thereof only'; *ibid.*, p. 392: the rules of positive law 'are *derived from* the arbitrary will of human authority'; 1957, p. 138: 'positive law . . . *created* by man'; *ibid.*, p. 25: 'A norm belongs to a certain legal order only if it has *come into being* in a certain way'; *ibid.*, p. 251: 'customary law—law *created* by a specific method'; *ibid.*, p. 289: 'the social order, termed "law", tries to *bring about a certain behavior of men*, considered by the *lawmaker* as desirable', which clearly appears to refer to the determination of the *content* of the law; 'On the Pure Theory of Law', *Israel Law Review*, I, 1966, p. 2: 'In order to be "positive" a legal norm . . . must be "posited", that is to say, stated, established or— as formulated in a figure of speech—"created" by an act of a human being', and *Aufsätze zur Ideologiekritik*, ed. E. Topitsch (Neuwied, 1965), p. 85: 'Die Normen des positiven Rechtes gelten . . . weil sie auf eine bestimmte Art erzeugt, von einem bestimmten Menschen *gesetzt* sind.' And I confess myself completely baffled by the meaning of a statement like that in 'Die Lehre von den drei Gewalten oder Funktionen des Staates', *Kant-Festschrift der Internationalen Vereinigung für Rechts- und Wirtschaftsphilosophie* (Berlin, 1924), p. 220: 'Auch das sogenannte Gewohnheitsrecht wird gesetzt, ist "positiv", ist Produkt einer Rechtserzeugung, Rechtsschöpfung, wenn auch keiner Rechts*satzung*', which literally says that customary law, although 'set', is not the product of a setting of law.

55 Such an examination would show that Kelsen's conception of a 'science' which 'seeks to discover the nature of law itself' (1957, p. 226) rests on what Karl Popper has called 'methodological essentialism, i.e. the theory that it is the aim of science to reveal essences and to describe them by means of definitions' (K. Popper, *The Open Society and its Enemies*, new ed. Princeton, 1963, vol. 1, p. 32). The consequence is that Kelsen represents as 'cognition' what are merely

consequences of a definition and regards himself as entitled to represent as false (or meaningless) all statements in which the term 'law' is used in a different and narrower sense than the one he gives it and represents as the only legitimate one. The 'pure theory of law' is thus one of those pseudo-sciences like Marxism and Freudianism which are represented as irrefutable because all their statements are true by definition but tell us nothing about what is the fact. Kelsen has therefore also no business to represent, as he constantly does, as false or meaningless statements in which the term law is used in a different sense.

56 The assertion that every state is a state of law (*Rechtsstaat*) or that the rule of law prevails of necessity in every state is one of the most frequently reiterated throughout Kelsen's work. See e.g. *Hauptprobleme der Staatsrechtslehre* (Tübingen, 1911), p. 249, *Der soziologische und der juristische Staatsbegriff* (Tübingen, 1922), p. 190; 1935, p. 486; 1960, p. 314.

57 Kelsen, 1946, p. 392.

58 Kelsen, 1957, p. 20.

59 Kelsen, 1957, p. 295.

60 M. J. C. Vile, *Constitutionalism and the Separation of Powers* (Oxford, 1967), p. 63, based chiefly on John Locke, *Second Treatise of Government*, XI, para. 142: 'They are to govern by *promulgated established Laws*, not to be varied in particular cases, but to have one Rule for Rich and Poor, for the Favourite at Court, and the Country Man at Plough.'

61 Hans Kelsen, *Vom Wesen und Wert der Demokratie* (Tübingen, 1920), p. 10: 'Die im Grunde genommen unrettbare Freiheit des Individuums', which in the second edition of 1929, p. 13 becomes the 'im Grunde unmögliche Freiheit des Individuums'.

62 Kelsen, 1957, p. 23: 'democracy, by its very nature, means freedom.'

63 Kelsen, 1957, pp. 21f. Almost literally the same statement also in 1945, p. 13.

64 Cf. *ibid.*, p. 295: 'He who denies the justice of such [i.e. any positive] "law" and asserts that the so-called law is not "true" law, has to prove it; and this proof is practically impossible since there is no objective criterion of justice.'

65 E.g. in 'Was ist die Reine Rechtslehre?' in *Demokratie und Rechtsstaat, Festschrift für Z. Giacometti* (Zürich, 1953), p. 155: 'Von den vielen in der traditionellen Jurisprudenz vorgetragenen Doktrinen, die die Reine Rechtslehre als politische Ideologien aufgezeigt hat. . . .'

66 See the editor's Introduction to Hans Kelsen, *Aufsätze zur Ideologiekritik*, ed. E. Topitsch (Neuwied, 1964).

67 E.g. in 'Die Lehre von den drei Gewalten oder Funktionen des Staates' in *Kant-Festschrift zu Kant's 200 Geburtstag*, ed. by the Internationale Vereinigung für Rechts- und Wirtschaftsphilosophie

(Berlin, 1924), p. 219: 'Dagegen muss angenommen werden, dass im Gesetzgebungsbegriff der Gewaltenlehre unter "Gesetz" nur die generelle Norm verstanden sein soll. . . . Bei dem Worte "Gesetz" denkt man eben nur oder doch vornehmlich an generelle oder abstrakte Normen'; and 1945, p. 270: 'By "legislation" as a function we can hardly understand anything other than the creation of general legal norms.'

68 E. Brunner, *Justice and the Social Order* (New York, 1945), p. 7: 'The totalitarian state is simply and solely legal positivism in political practice.'

69 G. Radbruch, *Rechtsphilosophie* (4th ed. by E. Wolf, Stuttgart, 1950), p. 355: 'Diese Auffassung vom Gesetz und seiner Geltung (wir nennen sie die positivistische Lehre) hat die Juristen wie das Volk wehrlos gemacht gegen Gesetze noch so willkürlichen und verbrecherischen Inhalts. Sie setzt letzten Endes das Recht der Macht gleich, nur wo die Macht ist, ist das Recht.' See also in the same work, p. 352:

> Der Positivismus hat in der Tat mit seiner Überzeugung 'Gesetz ist Gesetz' den deutschen Juristenstand wehrlos gemacht gegen Gesetze willkürlichen und verbrecherischen Inhalts. Dabei ist der Positivismus gar nicht in der Lage, aus eigener Kraft die Geltung von Gesetzen zu begründen. Er glaubt die Geltung von Gesetzen schon damit erwiesen zu haben, dass es die Macht besessen hat, sich durchzusetzen.

70 Hans Kelsen in *Das Naturrecht in der politischen Theorie*, ed. F. M. Schmoelz (Salzburg, 1963), p. 148.

According to this view every judge in history who was not legally independent and who obeyed an order of an absolute king to decide in a manner contrary to generally recognized rules of justice would still have to be described as acting in accordance with the law. The judges under the Nazis which obeyed such commands under what they regarded as authoritative compulsion may deserve our commiseration; but only confusion is produced when it is maintained that their action was governed by the law.

Characteristically this conception was taken over (presumably via the British socialist lawyers—cf. *The Constitution of Liberty*, chapter 16, section 5) by H. J. Laski, *The State in Theory and Practice*, London, 1934, p. 177: 'The Hitlerite State, equally with that of Britain or France, is a Rechtsstaat in the sense that dictatorial power has been transferred to the Führer by legal order.'

71 For references and further quotations see my book *The Constitution of Liberty* (London and Chicago, 1960), p. 240 and notes, and for Kelsen's comments his *The Communist Theory of Law* (New York, 1955).

72 Mainly in connection with the British *Report of the Committee on Homosexual Offences and Prostitution* (London, Cmd 247, 1957), generally known as the Wolfenden Report, and its discussion by Lord Devlin in his British Academy Lecture on 'The Enforcement of Morals', *Proceedings of the British Academy*, XLV, 1959 (also separately issued). See particularly H. L. A. Hart, *Law, Liberty, and Morality* (Oxford, 1963), and Lon L. Fuller, *The Morality of Law* (Yale, 1964).

73 R. M. Dworkin, 'The Model of Rules', *University of Chicago Law Review*, vol. 35, 1967, reprinted in Robert S. Summers, *Essays in Legal Philosophy* (Oxford, 1968).

74 The incapacity of the philosophical positivists to conceive of a third possibility in addition to the conception of rules being invented by a human mind and their having been invented by a superhuman intelligence is shown very clearly in Auguste Comte's phrase in his *Système de la Politique Positive* (Paris, 1854), vol. 1, p. 356, about 'La superiorité nécessaire de la moral demontré sur la moral revellée'. It is still the same conception when we find Kelsen, 'On the Pure Theory of Law', *Israel Law Review*, I, 1966, p. 2, note, asserting that 'Natural law is—in the last analysis—divine law, because if nature is supposed to create law it must have a will and the will can only be the will of God which manifests itself in the nature created by Him.' This comes out even more clearly in the essay to which Kelsen refers at this place, namely 'Die Grundlage der Naturrechtslehre', *Österreichische Zeitschrift für öffentliches Recht*, XIII, 1963.

75 Cf. David Hume, *Treatise* Part II, sec. II, *Works* II, p. 258:

> where an invention is obvious and absolutely necessary, it may as properly be said to be natural as anything that proceeds immediately from original principles, without the intervention of thought or reflection. Though the rules of justice be *artificial*, they are not *arbitrary*. Nor is the expression improper to call them *Laws of Nature*; if by natural we understand what is common to any species, or even if we confine it to mean what is inseparable from the species.

Cf. also K. R. Popper, *The Open Society and its Enemies* (4th ed., Princeton, 1963), I, pp. 60ff., esp. p. 64: 'Nearly all misunderstandings can be traced back to one fundamental misapprehension, namely, to the belief that "convention" implies "arbitrariness" '.

76 Cf., e.g., E. Westermarck, *Ethical Relativity* (London, 1932), p. 183: 'objectivity implies universality'.

77 On these matters Kelsen's early works *Über Grenzen juristischer und soziologischer Methode* (Tübingen, 1911) and *Der soziologische und der juristische Staatsbegriff* (Tübingen, 1922) have still to be consulted to obtain a picture of his conception of a legal 'science'.

78 Cf. Maffeo Pantaleoni, *Erotemi di Economia* (Bari, 1925), vol. I, p. 112.
'Quella disposizione che crea un *ordine*, è la disposizione giusta; essa
è quella che crea un stato di diritto. Ma, la creazione di un ordine, or
di un ordinamento, è appunto ciò stesso che esclude il caso, l'arbitrio.
o il cappricio l'incalcolabile l'insaputo il mutevole senza regola.'
Also Ludwig von Mises. *Theory and History* (Yale 1957) p. 54: 'The
ultimate yardstick of justice is conduciveness to the preservation of
social cooperation'; and Max Rheinstein, 'The Relations of Morals
and Law', *Journal of Public Law*, I, 1952, p. 298: 'The just law is that
which reason shows us as being apt to facilitate, or at least not to
impede, the achievement of and preservation of a peaceful order of
society.'

CHAPTER NINE 'SOCIAL' OR DISTRIBUTIVE JUSTICE

* The first quotation is taken from David Hume, *An Enquiry Concerning the Principles of Morals*, sect. III, part II, *Works* IV, p. 187, and
ought to be given here in its context: the

> most obvious thought would be, to assign the largest possessions
> to the most extensive virtue, and give every one the power of doing
> good proportioned to his inclination. . . . But were mankind to
> execute such a law; so great is the uncertainty of merit, both from
> its natural obscurity, and from the self-conceit of each individual,
> that no determinate rule of conduct would ever follow from it; and
> the total dissolution of society must be the immediate consequence.

The second quotation is translated from Immanuel Kant (*Der Streit
der Fakultäten* (1798), sect. 2, para. 6, note 2) and reads in the
original: 'Wohlfahrt aber hat kein Prinzip, weder für den der sie
empfängt, noch für den der sie austeilt (der eine setzt sie hierin, der
andere darin); weil es dabei auf das *Materiale* des Willens ankommt,
welches empirisch und so einer allgemeinen Regel unfähig ist.' An
English translation of this essay in which the passage is rendered
somewhat differently will be found in *Kant's Political Writings*, ed.
H. Reiss, trs. H. B. Nisbett (Cambridge, 1970), p. 183, note.

1 Cf. P. H. Wicksteed, *The Common Sense of Political Economy*
(London, 1910), p. 184: 'It is idle to assume that ethically desirable
results will necessarily be produced by an ethically indifferent instrument.'

2 Cf. G. del Vecchio, *Justice* (Edinburgh, 1952), p. 37. In the eighteenth
century the expression 'social justice' was occasionally used to
describe the enforcement of rules of just conduct within a given
society, so e.g. by Edward Gibbon, *Decline and Fall of the Roman
Empire*, chapter 41 (World's Classics edn, vol. IV, p. 367).

3 E.g. by John Rawls, *A Theory of Justice* (Harvard, 1971).

4 John Stuart Mill, *Utilitarianism* (London, 1861), chapter 5, p. 92; in
H. Plamenatz, ed., *The English Utilitarians* (Oxford, 1949), p. 225.

5 *Ibid.*, pp. 66 and 208 respectively. Cf. also J. S. Mill's review of
F. W. Newman, *Lectures on Political Economy*, originally published
in 1851 in the *Westminster Review* and republished in *Collected Works*,
vol. v (Toronto and London, 1967), p. 444: 'the distinction between
rich and poor, so slightly connected as it is with merit and demerit,
or even with exertion and want of exertion, is obviously unjust.' Also
Principles of Political Economy, book II, ch. 1, §, ed. W. J. Ashley
(London, 1909), pp. 211ff.: 'The proportioning of remuneration to
work done is really just only in so far as the more or less of the work
is a matter of choice: when it depends on natural differences of
strength and capacity, this principle of remuneration is itself an
injustice, it gives to those who have.'

6 See e.g. A. M. Honoré, 'Social Justice' in *McGill Law Journal*, VIII,
1962 and revised version in R. S. Summers, ed., *Essays in Legal
Philosophy* (Oxford, 1968), p. 62 of the reprint: 'The first [of the two
propositions of which the principle of social justice consists] is the
contention that *all men considered merely as men and apart from their
conduct or choice have a claim to an equal share in all those things, here
called advantages, which are generally desired and are in fact conducive
to well-being.'* Also W. G. Runciman, *Relative Deprivation and Social
Justice* (London, 1966), p. 261.

7 Cf. especially the encyclicals *Quadragesimo Anno* (1931) and *Divini
Redemptoris* (1937) and Johannes Messner, 'Zum Begriff der sozialen
Gerechtigkeit' in the volume *Die soziale Frage und der Katholizismus*
(Paderborn, 1931) issued to commemorate the fortieth anniversary
of the encyclical *Rerum Novarum*.

8 The term 'social justice' (or rather its Italian equivalent) seems to
have been first used in its modern sense by Luigi Taparelli d'Azeglio,
Saggio teoretico di diritto naturale (Palermo, 1840) and to have
been made more generally known by Antonio Rosmini-Serbati, *La
costitutione secondo la giustizia sociale* (Milan, 1848). For more recent
discussions cf. N. W. Willoughby, *Social Justice* (New York, 1909);
Stephen Leacock, *The Unsolved Riddle of Social Justice* (London and
New York, 1920); John A. Ryan, *Distributive Justice* (New York,
1916); L. T. Hobhouse, *The Elements of Social Justice* (London and
New York, 1922); T. N. Carver, *Essays in Social Justice* (Harvard,
1922); W. Shields, *Social Justice, The History and Meaning of the
Term* (Notre Dame Ind. 1941); Benevuto Donati 'Che cosa è
giustizia sociale?', *Archivio giuridico*, vol. 134, 1947; C. de Pasquier,
'La notion de justice sociale', *Zeitschrift für Schweizerisches Recht*,
1952; P. Antoine, 'Qu-est-ce la justice sociale?', *Archives de Philosophie*, 24, 1961; For a more complete list of this literature see G. del
Vecchio, *op. cit.*, pp. 37–9.

In spite of the abundance of writings on the subject, when about ten years ago I wrote the first draft of this chapter, I found it still very difficult to find any serious discussion of what people meant when they were using this term. But almost immediately afterwards a number of serious studies of the subject appeared, particularly the two works quoted in note 6 above as well as R. W. Baldwin, *Social Justice* (Oxford and London, 1966), and R. Rescher, *Distributive Justice* (Indianapolis, 1966). Much the most acute treatment of the subject is to be found in a German work by the Swiss economist Emil Küng, *Wirtschaft und Gerechtigkeit* (Tübingen, 1967) and many sensible comments in H. B. Acton, *The Morals of the Market* (London, 1971), particularly p. 71: 'Poverty and misfortune are evils but not injustices'. Very important is also Bertrand de Jouvenel, *The Ethics of Redistribution* (Cambridge, 1951) as well as certain passages in his *Sovereignty* (London, 1957), two of which may here be quoted. P. 140: 'The justice now recommended is a quality not of a man and a man's actions, but of a certain configuration of things in social geometry, no matter by what means it is brought about. Justice is now something which exists independently of just men.' P. 164: 'No proposition is likelier to scandalise our contemporaries than this one: it is impossible to establish a just social order. Yet it flows logically from the very idea of justice, on which we have, not without difficulty, thrown light. To do justice is to apply, when making a share-out, the relevant serial order. But it is impossible for the human intelligence to establish a relevant serial order for all resources in all respects. Men have needs to satisfy, merits to reward, possibilities to actualize; even if we consider these three aspects only and assume that—what is not the case—there are precise *indicia* which we can apply to these aspects, we still could not weight correctly among themselves the three sets of *indicia* adopted.'

The at one time very famous and influential essay by Gustav Schmoller on 'Die Gerechtigkeit in der Volkswirtschaft' in that author's *Jahrbuch für Volkswirtschaft etc.*, vol. v, 1895 is intellectually most disappointing—a pretentious statement of the characteristic muddle of the do-gooder foreshadowing some unpleasant later developments. We know now what it means if the great decisions are to be left to the 'jeweilige Volksbewusstsein nach der Ordnung der Zwecke, die im Augenblick als die richtige erscheint'!

9 Cf. note 7 to chapter VII above.

10 Cf. Adam Smith, *The Theory of Moral Sentiments* (London, 1801), vol. II, part VII, sect. ii, ch. I, p. 198: 'Human life the Stoics appear to have considered as a game of great skill, in which, however, there was a mixture of chance or of what is vulgarly understood to be chance.' See also Adam Ferguson *Principles of Moral and Political Science* (Edinburgh 1792) vol. I p. 7: 'The Stoics conceived of

human life under the image of a Game, at which the entertainment and merit of the players consisted in playing attentively and well whether the stake was great or small.' In a note Ferguson refers to the *Discourses of Epictetus* preserved by Arrian, book II, ch. 5.

11 Cf. G. Hardin, *Nature and Man's Fate* (New York, 1961), p. 55: 'In a free market, says Smith in effect, prices are regulated by negative feedback.' The much ridiculed 'miracle' that the pursuit of self-interest serves the general interest reduces to the self-evident proposition that an order in which the action of the elements is to be guided by effects of which they cannot know can be achieved only if they are induced to respond to signals reflecting the effects of those events. What was familiar to Adam Smith has belatedly been rediscovered by scientific fashion under the name of 'self-organizing systems'.

12 See L. von Mises, *Human Action* (Yale, 1949), p. 255 note: 'There is in the operation of the market economy nothing which could properly be called distribution. Goods are not first produced and then distributed, as would be the case in a socialist state.' Cf. also M. R. Rothbard, 'Towards a Reconstruction of Utility and Welfare Economics' in M. Sennholz (ed.), *On Freedom and Free Enterprise* (New York, 1965), p. 231.

13 Cf. W. G. Runciman, *op. cit.*, p. 274: 'Claims for social justice are claims on behalf of a group, and the person relatively deprived within an individual category will, if he is the victim of an unjust inequality, be a victim only of individual injustice.'

14 See Irving Kristol, 'When Virtue Loses all Her Loveliness—Some Reflections on Capitalism and "The Free Society"', *The Public Interest*, no. 21 (1970), reprinted in the author's *On the Democratic Idea in America* (New York, 1972), as well as in Daniel Bell and Irving Kristol (eds), *Capitalism Today* (New York, 1970).

15 Cf. J. Höffner, *Wirtschaftsethik und Monopole im 15. und 16. Jahrhundert* (Jena, 1941) und 'Der Wettbewerb in der Scholastik', *Ordo*, V, 1953; also Max Weber, *On Law in Economy and Society*, ed. Max Rheinstein (Harvard, 1954) pp. 295ff., but on the latter also H. M. Robertson, *Aspects on the Rise of Economic Individualism* (Cambridge, 1933) and B. Groethuysen, *Origines de l'esprit bourgeois en France* (Paris, 1927). For the most important expositions of the conception of a just price by the late sixteenth century Spanish Jesuits see particularly L. Molina, *De iustitia et de iure*, vol. 2, *De Contractibus* (Cologne, 1594), disp. 347, no. 3 and especially disp. 348, no. 3, where the just price is defined as that which will form 'quando absque fraude, monopoliis, atque aliis versutiies, communiter res aliqua vendi consuevit pretio in aliqua regione, aut loco, it habendum est pro mensura et regula judicandi pretium iustum rei illius in ea regione.' About man's inability to determine beforehand what a just price would see also particularly Johannes de Salas, *Commentarii in*

Secundum Secundae D. Thomas de Contractibus (Lyon, 1617), *Tr. de empt. et Vend.* IV, n. 6, p. 9: '. . . quas exacte comprehendere, et ponderare Dei est, not hominum'; and J. de Lugo, *Disputationes de Iustitia et Iure* (Lyon, 1643), vol. II, d. 26, s. 4, n. 40; 'pretium iustum matematicum, licet soli Deo notum.' See also L. Molina, *op. cit.*, disp. 365, no. 9: 'omnesque rei publicae partes ius habent conscendendi ad gradum superiorem, si cuiusque sors id tulerit, neque cuiquam certus quidam gradus debitur, qui descendere et conscendere possit.' It would seem that H. M. Robertson (*op. cit.*, p. 164) hardly exaggerates when he writes 'It would not be difficult to claim that the religion which favoured the spirit of capitalism was Jesuitry, not Calvinism.'

16 John W. Chapman, 'Justice and Fairness', *Nomos VI, Justice* (New York, 1963), p. 153. This Lockean conception has been preserved even by John Rawls, at least in his earlier work, 'Constitutional Liberty and the Concept of Justice', *Nomos VI, Justice* (New York, 1963), p. 117, note: 'If one assumes that law and government effectively act to keep markets competitive, resources fully employed, property and wealth widely distributed over time, and maintains a reasonable social minimum, then, if there is equality of opportunity, the resulting distribution will be just or at least not unjust. It will have resulted from the working of a just system . . . a social minimum is simply a form of rational insurance and prudence.'

17 See passages quoted in note 15 above.

18 See M. Fogarty, *The Just Wage* (London, 1961).

19 Barbara Wootton, *The Social Foundation of Wage Policy* (London, 1962), pp. 120 and 162, and now also her *Incomes Policy, An Inquest and a Proposal* (London, 1974).

20 Surely Samuel Butler (*Hudibras*, II,1) was right when he wrote

> For what is worth in any thing
> But so much money as 'twill bring.

21 On the general problem of remuneration according to merit, apart from the passages by David Hume and Immanuel Kant placed at the head of this chapter, see chapter VI of my book *The Constitution of Liberty* (London and Chicago, 1960) and cf. also Maffeo Pantaleoni, 'L'atto economico' in *Erotemi di Economia* (2 vols, Padua, 1963), vol. I, p. 101:

> E tre sono le proposizioni che conviene comprendere bene:
> La prima è che il merito è una parola vuota di senso.
> La seconda è che il concetto di giustizia è un polisenso che si presta a quanti paralogismi si vogliono ex amphibologia.
> La terza è che la remunerazione non può essere commisurata da una produttività (marginale) capace di determinazione isolamente,

cioè senza la simultanea determinazione della produttività degli altri fattori con i quali entra in una combinazione di complimentarità.

22 On the history of the term 'social' see Karl Wasserrab, *Sozialwissenschaft und soziale Frage* (Leipzig, 1903); Leopold von Wiese, *Der Liberalismus in Vergangenheit und Zukunft* (Berlin, 1917), and *Sozial, Geistig, Kulturell* (Cologne, 1936); Waldemar Zimmermann, 'Das "Soziale" im geschichtlichen Sinn- und Begriffswandel' in *Studien zur Soziologie, Festgabe für L. von Wiese* (Mainz, 1948); L. H. A. Geck, *Über das Eindringen des Wortes 'sozial' in die deutsche Sprache* (Göttingen, 1963); and Ruth Crummenerl, 'Zur Wortgeschichte von "sozial" bis zur englischen Aufklärung', unpublished essay for the State examination in philology (Bonn, 1963). Cf. also my essay 'What is "Social"? What does it Mean?' in a corrected English version in my *Studies in Philosophy, Politics and Economics* (London and Chicago, 1967).

23 Cf. G. del Vecchio, *op. cit.*, p. 37.

24 Very instructive on this is Leopold von Wiese, *Der Liberalismus in Vergangenheit und Zukunft* (Berlin, 1917) pp. 115ff.

25 Characteristic for many discussions of the issue by social philosophers is W. A. Frankena, 'The Concept of Social Justice', in *Social Justice*, ed. R. B. Brandt (New York, 1962), p. 4, whose argument rests on the assumption that 'society' *acts* which is a meaningless term if applied to a spontaneous order. Yet this anthropomorphic interpretation of society seems to be one to which utilitarians are particularly prone, although this is not often as naively admitted as by J. W. Chapman in the statement quoted before in note 21 to chapter VII.

26 I regret this usage though by means of it some of my friends in Germany (and more recently also in England) have apparently succeeded in making palatable to wider circles the sort of social order for which I am pleading.

27 Cf. the 'Statement of Conscience' received by the 'Aspen Consultation on Global Justice', an 'ecumenical gathering of American religious leaders' at Aspen, Colorado, 4–7 June 1974, which recognized that 'global injustice is characterised by a dimension of sin in the economic, political, social, racial, sexual and class structures and systems of global society.' *Aspen Institute Quarterly* (New York), no. 7, third quarter, 1974, p. 4.

28 See particularly A. M. Honoré, *op. cit.* The absurdity of the contention that in a Great Society it needs moral justification if A has more than B, as if this were the result of some human artifice, becomes obvious when we consider not only the elaborate and complex apparatus of government which would be required to prevent this, but also that this apparatus would have to possess power to direct the

NOTES TO PAGES 80-6

efforts of all citizens and to claim the products of those efforts.

29 One of the few modern philosophers to see this clearly and speak out plainly was R. G. Collingwood. See his essay on 'Economics as a philosophical science,' *Ethics* 36, 1926, esp. p. 74: 'A just price, a just wage, a just rate of interest, is a contradiction in terms. The question of what a person ought to get in return for his goods and labour is a question absolutely devoid of meaning.'

30 If there is any one fact which all serious students of the claims for equality have recognized it is that material equality and liberty are irreconcilable. Cf. A. de Tocqueville, *Democracy in America*, book II, ch. I (New York, edn 1946, vol. II, p. 87): democratic communities 'call for equality in freedom, and if they cannot obtain that, they still call for equality in slavery'; William S. Sorley, *The Moral Life and the Moral Worth* (Cambridge, 1911), p. 110: 'Equality is gained only by constant interference with liberty'; or more recently Gerhard Leibholz, 'Die Bedrohung der Freiheit durch die Macht der Gesetzgeber', in *Freiheit der Persönlichkeit* (Stuttgart, 1958), p. 80: 'Freiheit erzeugt notwendig Ungleichheit und Gleichheit notwendig Unfreiheit', are merely a few instances which I readily find in my notes. Yet people who claim to be enthusiastic supporters of liberty still clamour constantly for material equality.

31 Gustav Radbruch, *Rechtsphilosophie* (Stuttgart, 1956), p. 87: 'Auch das sozialistische Gemeinwesen wird also ein Rechtsstaat sein, ein Rechtsstaat freilich, der statt von der ausgleichenden von der austeilenden Gerechtigkeit beherrscht wird.'

32 See M. Duverger, *The Idea of Politics* (Indianapolis, 1966), p. 201.

33 Karl Mannheim, *Man and Society in an Age of Reconstruction* (London, 1940), p. 180.

34 P. J. Stuchka (President of the Soviet Supreme Court) in *Encyclopedia of State and Law* (in Russian, Moscow, 1927), quoted by V. Gsovski, *Soviet Civil Law* (Ann Arbor, Michigan, 1948), I, p. 70. The work of E. Paschukanis the Soviet author who has most consistently developed the idea of the disappearance of law under socialism, has been described by Karl Korsch in *Archiv sozialistischer Literatur*, III, (Frankfurt, 1966) as the only consistent development of the teaching of Karl Marx.

35 *The Road to Serfdom* (London and Chicago, 1944), chapter IV. For discussions of the central thesis of that book by lawyers see W. Friedmann, *The Planned State and the Rule of Law* (Melbourne, 1948), reprinted in the same author's *Law and Social Change in Contemporary Britain* (London, 1951): Hans Kelsen, 'The Foundations of Democracy', *Ethics* 66, 1955; Roscoe Pound, 'The Rule of Law and the Modern Welfare State', *Vanderbilt Law Review*, 7, 1953; Harry W. Jones, 'The Rule of Law and the Modern Welfare State', *Columbia Law Review*, 58, 1958; A. L. Goodhart, 'The Rule

of Law and Absolute Sovereignty', *University of Pennsylvania Law Review*, 106, 1958.

36 G. Radbruch, *op. cit.*, p. 126.

37 Radbruch's conceptions of these matters are concisely summed up by Roscoe Pound (in his introduction to R. H. Graves, *Status in the Common Law*, London, 1953, p. XI): Radbruch

> starts with a distinction between commutative justice, a correcting justice which gives back to one what has been taken away from him or gives him a substantial substitute, and distributive justice, a distribution of the goods of existence not equally but according to a scheme of values. Thus there is a contrast between co-ordinating law, which secures interests by reparation and the like, treating all individuals as equal, and subordinating law, which prefers some or the interests of some according to its measure of value. Public law, he says, is a law of subordination, subordinating individual to public interests but not the interests of other individuals with those public interests.

38 Cf. Bertrand de Jouvenel, *Sovereignty* (Chicago, 1957), p. 136:

> The small society, as the milieu in which man is first found, retains for him an infinite attraction; he undoubtedly goes to it to renew his strength; but ... any attempt to graft the same features on a large society is utopian and leads to tyranny. With that admitted, it is clear that as social relations become wider and more various, the common good conceived as reciprocal trustfulness cannot be sought in methods which the model of the small, closed society inspires; such a model is, in the contrary, entirely misleading.

39 Edwin Cannan, *The History of Local Rates in England*, 2nd edn (London, 1912), p. 162.

40 While one has become used to find the confused minds of social philosophers talking about 'social justice', it greatly pains me if I find a distinguished thinker like the historian Peter Geyl (*Encounters in History*, London, 1963, p. 358) thoughtlessly using the term. J. M. Keynes (*The Economic Consequences of Mr. Churchill*, London, 1925, *Collected Writings*, vol. IX, p. 223) also writes unhesitatingly that 'on grounds of social justice no case can be made for reducing the wages of the miners.'

41 Cf. e.g. Walter Kaufmann, *Without Guilt and Justice* (New York, 1973) who, after rightly rejecting the concepts of distributive and retributive justice, believes that this must lead him to reject the concept of justice altogether. But this is not surprising after even *The Times* (London) in a thoughtful leading article (1 March 1957) apropos the appearance of an English translation of Josef Pieper's

Justice (London, 1957) had observed that 'roughly, it may be said that in so far as the notion of justice continues to influence political thinking, it has been reduced to the meaning of the phrase "distributive justice" and that the idea of commutative justice has almost entirely ceased to influence our calculations except in so far it is embodied in laws and customs—in the maxims for instance of the Common Law—which are preserved from sheer conservatism.' Some contemporary social philosophers indeed beg the whole issue by so *defining* 'justice' that it includes *only* distributive justice. See e.g. Brian M. Barry, 'Justice and the Common Good', *Analysis*, 19, 1961, p. 80: 'although Hume uses the expression "rules of justice" to cover such things as property rules, *"justice" is now analytically tied to "desert" and "need"*, so that one could quite properly say that some of what Hume calls "rules of justice" were unjust' (italics added). Cf. *ibid.*, p. 89.

42 J. S. Mill, *On Liberty*, ed. McCallum (Oxford, 1946), p. 70.

43 On the destruction of moral values by scientific error see my discussion in my inaugural lecture as Visiting Professor at the University of Salzburg, *Die Irrtümer des Konstruktivismus und die Grundlagen legitimer Kritik gesellschaftlicher Gebilde* (Munich, 1970, now reprinted for the Walter Eucken Institute at Freiburg i.Brg. by J. C. B. Mohr, Tübingen, 1975).

44 John Rawls, 'Constitutional Liberty and the Concept of Justice', *Nomos IV, Justice* (New York, 1963), p. 102, where the passage quoted is preceded by the statement that 'It is the system of institutions which has to be judged and judged from a general point of view.' I am not aware that Professor Rawls' later more widely read work *A Theory of Justice* (Harvard, 1971) contains a comparatively clear statement of the main point, which may explain why this work seems often, but as it appears to me wrongly, to have been interpreted as lending support to socialist demands, e.g. by Daniel Bell, 'On Meritocracy and Equality', *Public Interest*, Autumn 1972, p. 72, who describes Rawls' theory as 'the most comprehensive effort in modern philosophy to justify a socialistic ethic.'

APPENDIX TO CHAPTER NINE

This appendix has been published as an article in the 75th anniversary issue of the Norwegian journal *Farmand* (Oslo, 1966).

1 For discussions of the problem cf. the papers assembled in the *Philosophical Review*, April 1955 and in D. D. Raphael (ed.), *Political Theory and the Rights of Man* (London, 1967).

2 See the *Universal Declaration of Human Rights* adopted by the General Assembly of the United Nations on 10 December 1948. It is reprinted, and the intellectual background of this document can be

found, in the volume entitled *Human Rights, Comments and Interpretations*, a symposium edited by UNESCO (London and New York, 1945). It contains in the Appendix not only a 'Memorandum Circulated by UNESCO on the Theoretical Bases of the Rights of Men' (pp. 251–4), but also a 'Report of the UNESCO Committee on the Theoretical Bases of the Human Rights' (in other places described as the 'UNESCO Committee on the Principles of the Rights of Men'), in which it is explained that their efforts were directed towards reconciling the two different 'complementary' working concepts of human rights, of which one 'started, from the premises of inherent individual rights . . . while the other was based on Marxist principles', and at finding 'some common measure of the two tendencies'. 'This common formulation,' it is explained, 'must by some means reconcile the various divergent or opposing formulations now in existence'! (The British representatives on that committee were Professors H. J. Laski and E. H. Carr!).

3 *Ibid.*, p. 22, Professor E. H. Carr, the chairman of the UNESCO Committee of experts, explains that 'If the new declaration of the rights of man is to include provisions for social services, for maintenance in childhood, in old age, in incapacity or in unemployment, it becomes clear that no society can guarantee the enjoyment of such rights unless it in turn has the right to call upon and direct the productive capacities of the individuals enjoying them'!

4 G. Vlastos, 'Justice', *Revue Internationale de la Philosophie*, 1957, p. 331.

5 On the whole document cf. Maurice Cranston, 'Human Rights, Real and Supposed' in the volume edited by D. D. Raphael quoted in note 1 above, where the author argues that 'a philosophically respectable concept of human rights has been muddied, obscured, and debilitated in recent years by an attempt to incorporate in it specific rights of a different logical category.' See also the same author's *Human Rights Today* (London, 1955).

CHAPTER TEN   THE MARKET ORDER OR CATALLAXY

* Edwin Cannan, *The History of Local Rates in England* (London, 2nd ed., 1912), p. 173. The term 'uneconomical' is used in it in that wide sense in which it refers to what is required by the market order, a sense in which it is somewhat misleading and had better be avoided.

1 Cf. Carl Menger, *Problems of Economics and Sociology* (Illinois, 1963), p. 93:

The *nation* as such is not a large subject that has needs, that works, practices economy, and consumes; and what is called 'national economy' is therefore not the economy of a nation in the true sense of the word. 'National economy' is not a phenomenon analogous to the singular economies in the nation to which also the economy of finance belongs. It is not a large singular economy; just as little as it is one opposed to or existing along with the singular economies in the nation. It is in its most general form of phenomena a peculiar complication of singular economies.

Cf. also Appendix I to that work.

2 Richard Whately, *Introductory Lectures on Political Economy* (London, 1855), p. 4.

3 Especially by L. von Mises, *Human Action* (Yale, 1949), *passim.*

4 H. G. Liddell and R. A. Scott, *A Greek-English Dictionary* (London, new ed., 1940), s.v. *katallagden, katallage, katallagma, katallaktikos, katallasso (-tto), katallakterios* and *katallaxis.*

5 In the Greek terms we have used an economy proper is thus a *taxis* and a *teleocracy*, while the katallaxy is a *kosmos* and a *nomocracy.*

6 It was these rules to which David Hume and Adam Smith emphatically referred as 'rules of justice' and which Adam Smith meant when (*The Theory of Moral Sentiments, part I, sect. ii, chap. iii*) he spoke of justice as 'the main pillar of the whole edifice. If it is removed, the great, the immense fabric of human society, the fabric which to raise and support seems in this world, if I may say so, to have been the peculiar and darling care of Nature, must in a moment crumble into atoms.'

7 At the beginning of the eighteenth century, when Bernard Mandeville with his *Fable of the Bees* became its most influential expositor. But it seems to have been more widespread and is to be found, e.g., in the early Whig literature such as in Thomas Gordon, 'Cato's Letter' no. 63, dated 27 January 1721 (in the reprint in *The English Libertarian Heritage*, ed. David L. Jacobson, Indianapolis, 1965, pp. 138–9): 'Every Man's honest Industry and useful Talents, while they are employed for the Publick, will be employed for himself; and while he serves himself, he will serve the Publick; Publick and private Interest will secure each other; all will chearfully give a Part to secure the Whole—and be brave to defend it.' It then found first expression in classical works (in both instances probably under the influence of Mandeville) in C. de S. de Montesquieu, *The Spirit of the Laws*, Book III, sect. 7 (trs. T. Nugent, New York, 1949), p. 35: 'Each individual advances the public good, while he only thinks of promoting his own interest', and in David Hume, *Treatise* in *Works* II, p. 289: 'I learn to do a service to another, without bearing him any real kindness'; and *ibid.*, p. 291: 'advantage to the public, though it not be intended for that purpose'; cf. also *Essays, Works* III, p. 99: 'made it not the interest, even of bad men, to act for the public good.' It occurs later in Josiah Tucker, *Elements of Commerce* (London, 1756), in

Adam Smith, *Theory of Moral Sentiments* (London, 1759), part IV, chapter I, where he speaks of men being 'led by an invisible hand . . . without intending it, without knowing it, [to] advance the interest of society', and of course in its most famous formulation in Smith's *Wealth of Nations* (ed. Cannan, London, 1910), vol. I, p. 421: 'By directing that industry in such a manner as its produce may be of the greatest value, he intends only his own gain, and he is in this, as in many other cases, led by an invisible hand to promote an end which was no part of his intention. Nor is it always the worse for the society that it was no part of it. By pursuing his own interest he frequently promotes that of the society more effectually than when he really intends to promote it.' Cf. also Edmund Burke, *Thoughts and Details of Scarcity* (1795), in *Works* (World's Classics ed.), vol. VI, p. 9: 'The benign and wise disposer of all things, who obliges men whether they will or not, in pursuing their own selfish interest, to connect the general good with their own individual success.'

8 Cf. Adam Smith, *Wealth of Nations*, I, p. 16: 'It is not from the benevolence of the butcher, the brewer, or the baker, that we expect our dinner, but from their regard to their own interest.'

9 It is in the insistence on social 'solidarity' that the constructivist approach to sociology of Auguste Comte, Emile Durkheim and Léon Duguit shows itself most clearly.

10 Both of which were characteristically regarded by John Stuart Mill as the only 'elevated' feelings left in modern man.

11 On the significance of the development of criticism by the ancient Greeks see particularly Karl R. Popper, *The Open Society and Its Enemies* (London and Princeton, 1947 and later), *passim*.

12 Cf. already A. L. C. Destutt de Tracy, *A Treatise on Political Economy* (Georgetown, 1817), pp. 6ff.: 'Society is purely and solely a continual series of exchanges. . . . *Commerce is the whole of society.*' Before the term 'society' came into general use, 'economy' was often used where we would now speak of 'society'. Cf. for instance John Wilkins, *Essay toward a Real Character and a Philosophical Language* (London, 1668) as quoted by H. R. Robbins, *A Short History of Linguistics* (London, 1967), pp. 114–15, who appears to use 'economical' as equivalent to 'interpersonal'. At that time 'economy' seems also to have been used generally to mean what we call here a spontaneous order, as such frequently recurring phrases as the 'economy of creation' and the like show.

13 The chief objections to the 'allocational' approach or the 'economicism' of much of current economic theory from very different angles comes, on the one side, from J. M. Buchanan, most recently restated in the essay 'Is Economics the Science of Choice' in E. Streissler (ed.), *Roads to Freedom* (London, 1969), and G. Myrdal, especially in *The Political Element in the Development of Economic*

Theory (London, 1953) and *Beyond the Welfare State* (Yale, 1960). Cf. also Hans Peter, *Freiheit der Wirtschaft* (Cologne, 1953); Gerhard Weisser, 'Die Überwindung des Ökonomismus in der Wirtschaftswissenschaft' in *Grundfragen der Wirtschaftsordnung* (Berlin, 1954); and Hans Albert, *Ökonomische Theorie und Politische Ideologie* (Göttingen, 1954).

What is often inexactly though perhaps conveniently described as 'economic ends' are the most general and yet undifferentiated means such as money or general purchasing power which in the course of the ordinary process of earning a living are the immediate ends, because the particular purpose for which they will be used is not yet known. On the fact that there are strictly speaking no economic ends and for the clearest statement of economics seen as a theory of choice see L. C. Robbins, *The Nature and Significance of Economic Science* (London, 1930 and later).

14 See also chapter 7 above.

15 It is a point which cannot be too often stressed since it is so frequently misunderstood, especially by socialists, that technological knowledge tells us only which techniques are available, but not which is the most economical or efficient. Contrary to a widely held belief there is not such a thing as a purely technical optimum—a conception usually derived from the false idea that there is only one uniform factor, namely energy, which is really scarce. For this reason what is the most efficient technique of producing something in the USA may be exceedingly uneconomical in, say, India.

16 W. S. Jevons, *The Theory of Political Economy* (London, 1871), p. 159.

17 Much of the knowledge of the individuals which can be so useful in bringing about particular adaptations is not ready knowledge which they could possibly list and file in advance for the use of a central planning authority when the occasion arose; they will have little knowledge beforehand of what advantage they could derive from the fact that, say, magnesium has become much cheaper than aluminium, or nylon than hemp, or one kind of plastic than another; what they possess is a capacity of finding out what is required by a given situation, often an acquaintance with particular circumstances which beforehand they have no idea might become useful.

18 Ecclesiastes 9:11.

19 I suspect it was also this ignorance which Cicero had in mind when he argued that neither nature nor will but intellectual weakness was the mother of justice. See *De Republica*, 3, 13: 'iustitae non natura nec voluntas sed imbecillitas mater est.' This at least seems to be what he means when in many other places he speaks of 'humani generis imbecillitas'.

20 Cf. the passage by David Hume quoted earlier, above, chapter 7, note 12.

21 The distinction introduced by Wilhelm Röpke, *Die Gesellschaftskrise der Gegenwart* (fifth ed., Erlenbach-Zürich, 1948), p. 259, between acts of interference which 'conform' and those which do not 'conform' with the market order (or, as other German authors have expressed it, are or are not *systemgerecht*) aims at the same distinction, but I should prefer not to describe 'conform' measures as 'interference'.

22 Cf. L. von Mises, *Kritik des Interventionismus* (Jena, 1929), pp. 5ff.: 'Nicht unter den Begriff des Eingriffes fallen Handlungen der Obrigkeit, die mit den Mitteln des Marktes arbeiten, d.h.solche, die Nachfrage oder Angebot durch Veränderungen der Marktfaktoren zu beeinflussen suchen. . . . *Der Eingriff ist ein von einer gesellschaftlichen Gewalt ausgehender isolierter Befehl, der die Eigentümer der Produktionsmittel und die Unternehmer zwingt, die Produktionsmittel anders zu verwenden als sie es sonst tun würden.*'

23 The chances of any person picked out at random of earning a particular income would then be represented by a Gaussian hill, i.e. a three-dimensional surface one co-ordinate of which represented the probability of that person belonging to a class with a particular probability distribution of expectations of a certain income (arranged according to the value of the median) while the second co-ordinate represented the distribution of probabilities of the particular incomes for that class. It would show, e.g., that a person whose position gave him a better *chance* of earning a particular income than a certain other person might in fact earn much less than the latter.

24 The chance of all will be increased most if we act on principles which will result in raising the general level of incomes without paying attention to the consequent shifts of particular individuals or groups from one position on the scale to another. (The shifts will necessarily occur in the course of such a process, and must occur to make the rise of the average level possible.) It is not easy to illustrate this by the available statistics of the changes of income distribution during periods of rapid economic progress. But in the one country for which fairly adequate information of this kind is available, the USA, it would seem that a person who in 1940 belonged to the group whose individual incomes were greater than those of 50 per cent of the population but smaller than those of 40 per cent of the population, even if he had by 1960 descended to the 30–40 per cent group, would still have enjoyed a larger absolute income than he did in 1940.

25 It may help the reader if I illustrate the general contention stated in the text by an account of the personal experience which led me to see the problem in this manner. That a person in an established position inevitably takes an attitude different from that which ought to be taken in considering the general problem was vividly brought home to me as an inhabitant of London in the summer of 1940 when it

appeared quite probable that I and all the resources with which I might provide for my family would soon be destroyed by enemy bombing. It was at that time, when we were all prepared for much worse than eventually happened, that I received offers from several neutral countries to place my then small children with some unknown family with whom they would presumably remain if I did not survive the war. I had thus to consider the relative attractiveness of social orders as different as those of the USA, Argentine and Sweden, on the assumption that the conditions in which my children would grow up in that country would be determined more or less by chance. This led me, as abstract speculation perhaps never could have done, to realize that where my children were concerned, rational preferences should be guided by considerations somewhat different from those which would determine a similar choice for myself who occupied already an established position and believed (perhaps wrongly) that this would count for more in a European country than in the USA. Thus, while the choice for myself would have been influenced by the considerations of the relative chances for a man in his early forties with formed skills and tastes, a certain reputation and with affiliations with classes of particular inclinations, the choice for my children would have had to be made in consideration of the particular environment in which chance was likely to place them in one of those countries. For the sake of my children who still had to develop their personalities, then, I felt that the very absence in the USA of the sharp social distinctions which would favour me in the Old World should make me decide for them in favour of the former. (I should perhaps add that this was based on the tacit assumption that my children would there be placed with a white and not with a coloured family.)

CHAPTER ELEVEN   THE DISCIPLINE OF ABSTRACT RULES AND THE EMOTIONS OF THE TRIBAL SOCIETY

* José Ortega y Gasset, *The Revolt of the Masses* (London, 1932), p. 83.
1 This is surprisingly maintained by such an acute thinker as Michael Polanyi with regard to central planning in *The Logic of Liberty* (London, 1951), p. 111: 'How can central economic planning, if it is utterly incapable of achievement, be a danger to liberty as it is widely assumed to be?' It may well be impossible to achieve what the planners intend and yet the attempt to realize their intentions do much harm.
2 Cf. Peter Laslett, *The World we Have Lost* (London and New York, 1965).
3 See W. H. Whyte, *The Organization Man* (New York, 1957).
4 See Martin Bullinger, *Oeffentliches Recht und Privatrecht* (Stuttgart, 1968).

5 In the present connection we revert to the term 'abstract rule' in order to stress that the rules of just conduct do not refer to specific purposes and that the resulting order is what Sir Karl Popper has called an 'abstract society'.

6 Cf. Adam Smith, *Wealth of Nations*, ed. Cannan, vol. II, p. 43:

The natural effort of every individual to better his own condition, where suffered to exert itself with freedom and security, is so powerful a principle, that it is alone, and without any assistance, not only capable of carrying on the society to wealth and prosperity, but of surmounting a hundred impertinent obstructions with which the folly of human laws too often encumbers its operations; though the effect of these obstructions is always more or less either to encroach upon its freedom, or to diminish its security.

7 C. Perelman, *Justice* (New York, 1967), p. 20: 'A form of behavior or a human judgement can be termed just only if it can be subjected to rules or criteria.'

8 Since it is frequently ignored that this was both the aim and the achievement of classical liberalism, two statements from the middle of the last century deserve to be quoted. N. W. Senior (cited by L. C. Robbins, *The Theory of Economic Policy*, London, 1952, p. 140) wrote in 1848: 'To proclaim that no man, whatever his vices or even his crimes, shall die of hunger or cold, is a promise that in the state of civilization of England, or of France, can be performed not merely with safety but with advantage, because the gift of mere subsistence may be subjected to conditions which no one will voluntarily accept.' In the same year the German constitutional lawyer Moritz Mohl, as representative to the German Constitutional Assembly at Frankfurt, could maintain (*Stenographischer Bericht über die Verhandlungen der Deutschen konstituierenden Nationalversammlung zu Frankfurt a.M.*, ed., Franz Wigard, Leipzig, 1949, vol. 7, p. 5109) that 'es gibt in Deutschland, meines Wissens, nicht einen einzigen Staat, in welchem nicht positive, ganz bestimmte Gesetze beständen, welche verhindern, dass jemand verhungere. In allen deutschen Gesetzgebungen, die mir bekannt sind, ist die Gemeinde gehalten, den, der sich nicht selbst erhalten kann, zu erhalten.'

9 Cf. Franz Beyerle, 'Der andere Zugang zum Naturrecht', *Deutsche Rechtswissenschaft*, 1939, p. 20: 'Zeitlos und unbekümmert um die eigene Umwelt hat sie [die Pandektenlehre] keine einzige soziale Krise ihrer Zeit erkannt und geistig aufgefangen. Weder die rasch fortschreitende Entwurzelung des Bauerntums, die schon nach den napoleonischen Kriegen einsetzte, noch das Absinken der handwerklichen Existenzen nach der Jahrhundertmitte, noch endlich die Verelendung der Lohnarbeiterschaft.' From the number of times this statement by a distinguished teacher of private law has been quoted

in the current German literature it seems to express a widely held view.

10 J.-J. Rousseau has clearly seen that what in his sense of the 'general will' may be just for a particular group, may not be so for a more comprehensive society. Cf. *The Political Writings of J.-J. Rousseau*, ed. E. E. Vaughan (Cambridge, 1915), vol. 1, p. 243: 'Pour les membres de l'association, c'est une volonté générale; pour la grande société, c'est une volonté particulière, qui très souvent se trouve droite au premier égard, et vicieuse au second.' But to the positivist interpretation of justice which identifies it with the commands of some legitimate authority, it comes inevitably to be thought that, as e.g. E. Forsthoff, *Lehrbuch des Verwaltungsrechts* (eighth ed., Munich, 1961, vol. 1, p. 66) maintains, 'any question of a just order is a question of law'. But this 'orientation on the idea of justice', as this view has been curiously called, is certainly not sufficient to turn a command into a rule of just conduct unless by that phrase is meant, not merely that the rule satisfies somebody's claim for just treatment, but that the rule satisfies the Kantian test of universal applicability.

11 This is the main thesis of Carl Schmitt, *Der Begriff des Politischen* (Berlin, 1932). Cf. the comment on it by J. Huizinga quoted on p. 71 of vol. 1 of the present work.

12 See note 15 to chapter 9 above.

13 The constructivist prejudice which still makes so many socialists scoff at the 'miracle' that the unguided pursuit of their own interests by the individuals should produce a beneficial order is of course merely the reverse form of that dogmatism which opposed Darwin on the ground that the existence of order in organic nature was proof of intelligent design.

14 Cf. H. B. Acton, *The Morals of Markets* (London, 1971).

15 Cf. Bertrand de Jouvenel, *Sovereignty* (London and Chicago, 1957), p. 136: 'We are thus driven to three conclusions. The first is that the small society, the milieu in which man is first found, retains for him an infinite attraction; the next, that he undoubtedly goes to it to renew his strength; but, the last, that any attempt to graft the same features on a large society is utopian and leads to tyranny'; to which the author adds in a footnote: 'In this respect Rousseau (*Rousseau Juge de Jean-Jaques*, Third Dialogue) displayed a wisdom which his disciples missed: 'His object could not be to recall populous countries and large states to their primitive simplicity, but only to check, if possible, the progress of those whom smallness and situation had preserved from the same headlong rush to the perfection of society and the deterioration of the species.'

16 Cf. Richard Cornuelle, *Reclaiming the American Dream* (New York, 1965).

INDEX